About the author

Shirin M. Rai is a professor in the Department of Politics and International Studies, University of Warwick. Her research interests are in feminist politics, democratization, and development studies. She has written extensively on issues of gender, governance, and democratization. Her most recent publications are *Global Governance: Feminist Perspectives* (edited with Georgina Waylen 2008), *Gender and Political Economy of Development: From Nationalism to Globalisation* (2002), *Rethinking Empowerment: Gender and Development in a Global/Local World* (edited with Jane Parpart and Kathleen Staudt 2002) and *Mainstreaming Gender, Democratising the State? Institutional Mechanisms for the Advancement of Women* (2003). She is the co-editor of the Manchester University Press book series 'Perspectives on Democratic Practice'.

Shirin M. Rai

The gender politics of development
essays in hope and despair

Zubaan
NEW DELHI

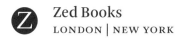

Zed Books
LONDON | NEW YORK

The gender politics of development: essays in hope and despair was first published in 2008

Published in South Asia by Zubaan (an imprint of Kali for Women), K-92, First Floor, Hauz Khas Enclave, New Delhi 110016, India
www.zubaanbooks.com

in the rest of the world by Zed Books Ltd, 7 Cynthia Street, London N1 9JF, UK and Room 400, 175 Fifth Avenue, New York, NY 10010, USA
www.zedbooks.co.uk

Cover designed by Andrew Corbett
Set in OurType Arnhem and Futura Bold by Ewan Smith, London
Index: ed.emery@thefreeuniversity.net
Printed and bound in the EU by Biddles Ltd, King's Lynn, Norfolk

Distributed in the USA exclusively by Palgrave Macmillan, a division of St Martin's Press, LLC, 175 Fifth Avenue, New York, NY 10010.

A catalogue record for this book is available from the British Library.
Library of Congress cataloging in publication data are available.

ISBN 978 1 84277 837 1 hb (Zed Books)
ISBN 978 1 84277 838 8 pb (Zed Books)
ISBN 978 81 89884 54 3 hb (Zubaan)

Contents

Acknowledgements | vi

Introduction: the gender politics of development 1

1 **Gender, nationalism and 'nation-building'** . . 10

2 **Women and the post-colonial state** 39

3 **Theorizing gender and democratization** . . . 59

4 **Mainstreaming gender, democratizing the state?** 71

5 **Quotas in context** 90

6 **Globalization, development and global governance** 113

7 **Knowledge and/as power** 137

8 **Networking across borders** 157

Conclusion: what hopes, why despair? . . . 175

Notes | 182 **Bibliography** | 190
Index | 209

Acknowledgements

I would like to take this opportunity to thank the publishers – Blackwells, Manchester University Press, Polity Press, Routledge, Sage, and Taylor and Francis – who have allowed me to use material first published through them in this book.

There are many people who have made this book possible and whose help I would like to acknowledge here. Ellen McKinlay's enthusiasm for this project, which took the form of encouragement, gentle insistence regarding deadlines and thoughtful comments on the balance of chapters, was critical for its completion.

Over the years, I have gained much through my conversations with friends, colleagues and students in the development of my ideas. With some, such as Georgina Waylen, Sharmistha Barwa, Bidyut Mohanty, Farzana Bari and Nazmunessa Mahtab, I have collaborated in writing and editing. Others, such as Shaheen Sardar Ali and Reena Patel, have been collaborators and fellow travellers in organizing the South Asian Network on Gender, Law and Governance. Many others have given me their time with generosity that has overwhelmed me. I have shared drafts with them and have received thoughtful comments, discussed ideas, agreed and disagreed on issues of style as well as substance. While they are too numerous for me to name all of them, I would like to thank here Molly Andrews, Cynthia Enloe, Niraja Gopal-Jayal, Catherine Hoskyns, L. H. M. Ling, V. Spike Peterson, Jindy Pettman, Jeremy Roche, Kathy Staudt and Georgina Waylen.

My family has been a source of immense support for me – always. My sons, Arjun and Sean Rai-Roche, my husband, Jeremy Roche, and my mother, Satya M. Rai, have provided me with the emotional strength and sustenance to complete this project.

I am also indebted to the many women and men who have shared with me their stories – of life and of struggle – which have found their way into my work. It is to these lives of struggle that I would like to dedicate this book.

Shirin M. Rai, Leamington Spa

Introduction: the gender politics of development

I have been writing in the broad field of gender politics of development for around twenty years. In this period, much has changed in the way in which we think about, speak of, are framed by and resist the dominant gendered social relations. Reflecting upon these changes, I am repeatedly struck by the gap between the improving political indicators of women's empowerment and their continuing social and economic marginalization. Women now have the right to vote and stand for elections at all levels of government in most countries. As early as 1985 90 per cent of countries had either established formal national machineries or policy agencies for the advancement of women or less formal governance systems to address gender in/equalities. Around forty countries operate some sort of quota for women in parliaments and around fifty in major political parties; from 1945 to 1995, women increased their presence in parliaments fourfold, and in 2007 just over 17 per cent of national members of parliaments were women. One hundred and eighty-five countries have signed the Convention for the Elimination of All Forms of Discrimination Against Women (CEDAW), though many with opt-out clauses, and are legally bound to put its provisions into practice. They are also committed to submitting national reports, at least every four years, on measures they have taken to comply with their treaty obligations. Despite these significant gains in institutional politics, the indicators of economic inequality pertaining to gender have continued to persist and even grow. The International Labour Organization estimates that GDP growth has not been reflected in decent employment – 'of the more than 2.8 billion workers in the world, 1.4 billion still did not earn enough to lift themselves and their families above the US$2 a day poverty line – just as many as 10 years ago'.[1] Women's employment continues to lag behind men's; the fact that women's work within the home is not counted as part of a nation's income underlines the gap between male and female employment. Gender segregation of work and wage differentials between men and women continue to haunt the labour market, even though women make up around 40 per cent of the global workforce. Despite the full participation of women in farming, especially among poor peasant households (it is estimated that women work two-thirds of the world's working hours, and produce half of the world's food), women, it is often claimed, own less than 5 per cent of land, represent only 2 per cent of registered farmers, earn only 10 per cent of the world's income, and own less than 1 per cent of the world's property. Oxfam has reported that 'Two-thirds of children denied primary education are girls, and 75 per cent of the world's 876 million illiterate adults are women.'[2] We also note that women's social position continues to be precarious – levels of violence against women (both individual and state) remain significant. Son preference continues to disadvantage girls within households and puts the lives of women in danger through abortions/fetocides; in many countries pressures of dowry place women in vulnerable positions. The right to choose is denied in both the selection of partners (often through practices of misnamed 'honour crimes') as well as in sexual orientation. The world at war continues to visit severe and sexualized violence on women. Of course, to separate out these three spheres – the political, the economic and the social – can only ever be a heuristic device, but in employing this device we can also begin to see a troubling pattern in terms of the winners and losers not only between men and women but also among women.

I have consistently reflected upon two aspects of inequalities, one so well addressed by Nancy Fraser in her work on inequalities of recognition and of redistribution. The question is often asked about the links between the descriptive representation of women in political institutions and the substantive representation of women's interests that might result from this. Other than insisting on issues of justice regarding the validity of women's descriptive representation and challenging the barriers to it, we also need to pause and examine why the translation of descriptive into substantive representation is taking so long. What differences are being privileged, what structural inequalities are proving to be most resistant to change, and why might this be the case? Why are certain accommodations regarding gender relations more feasible than others? What does this tell us about both the process of accommodation and consequently about the gap referred to above? The second issue that has informed my work has been addressed by, among others, Sonia Alvarez in her writing on the 'politicization of gender', which I would like to rephrase as the 'de-politicization of gender'. Women seeking equality that is both formal and informal have been aware that their struggles face both the danger of cooptation in governance regimes if they engage and work with the state to improve the conditions of women's lives and the risk of marginalization and therefore lack of policy influence if they don't. Questions about the nature of inequality allow us to reflect upon the nature of difference, its articulation within feminist theory and activism, and at the same time on the nature of privilege in our societies. The questions about political activism reveal a pattern of specific modes of inclusion of gender in public discourse and policy, which often stand in for/represent substantive equalities that continue to elude most women.

In their critique of mainstream development literature as well as practice, early feminist interventions were a plea for the inclusion of women in a 'man's world'. As feminist scholarship and activism became more self-confident, feminists noted that women were the constant 'other' who as a category were either marginal to development theory and practice or included in it in very particular ways. This 'othering' had many consequences, one of which was that women were always seen as victims – of men, of patriarchal social and political systems. Seeing women as agents has been an important development in feminist work. In order to do so, feminist scholars and activists have moved away from viewing women as victims in need of rescue. Rather, they have presented women as actors in struggles against their oppressions. In so doing, they have also moved away from 'adding on' women to male-dominated institutions, policies and frameworks of analyses, and have explored the underlying biases of socio-economic contexts and political institutions. This has allowed them to examine the various modes of struggle as well as of empowerment – within oneself (conscientization), with others (women's groups, movements and networks) and for change (transformative politics). This work has meant 'extracting' women from both policy and discursive 'frames' as objects and ensuring that women's subjectivity is placed centre stage. The literature on empowerment as development is an example of such extraction.

While women have been the constant 'other' within patriarchal societies, there have also been other 'otherings' going on as women have stepped out to challenge their subordinate position. These have been on grounds of class, race, disability, sexuality, religion and location – any number of categories that we have constructed in/through our stories of ourselves. These have posed important and difficult challenges for women by pointing to differences among them. The solidarity that formed the basis of much of the earliest organization and mobilization by women was shown to be assumed rather than 'owned'; some women were seen to speak for all women, and absence and silence were built into the growing presence of women in the public domain. The tensions between structure and agency then play out in complex ways and need nuanced analysis which I hope I provide in my various readings of multilevel politics.

Organization of the book

All these chapters address key themes that have emerged in politics in post-colonial states – the gendered language in which these have been articulated as well as the way in which state institutions and laws have given particular substance to these articulations in the light of the complex gendered political pressures. Women's movements have been at the forefront of these debates and have also mobilized public opinion to force the hand of successive governments to address key issues of concern for women. At the same time they have had to face difficult choices about the nature of their engagement with the state, issues of difference among women and their relationship with international feminisms as well as international institutions. The chapters in this book address these issues within the context of an engagement with feminist theory and politics.

The first five chapters broadly focus on the gendered politics of development in the context of post-colonial states. The argument that ties these chapters together is that the gendered nature of nation-state-building in post-colonial societies lays the foundations upon which a fractured modernity is constructed. This creates particular and deep fissures and pressures for social and political development. These are then reflected in the unfolding debates and policies on democratization of new and old institutions, as well as the ways in which globalization and its governance translate locally in post-colonial economies. I focus largely on the transformation of the post-colonial, developmental state by examining nationalism and its developmental framing of gender relations; the debates on the post-colonial state among feminists; policy agencies that have become the state's answer to women's struggles for political and economic inclusion; democratization of this state and the implications for the refashioning of gender as well as power relations; practical problem-solving through quotas for women in representative politics and the limits to such an approach to political equality. These chapters 'frame' the issues that women have faced in engaging in the politics of development.

Chapter 1 examines how nationalism and nationalist struggles have framed discourses and strategies of development. I argue that while nationalism provided new opportunities through the political mobilization of women, it also circumscribed development priorities in post-colonial contexts. A hierarchy of gender, class and ethnicity, among others, was reproduced, and some new spaces created during the nationalist struggles were closed off. The gendered political imagination of elites played a crucial part in setting the development agendas in post-colonial nations. I argue that in the process of nation-building, just as the 'economic man' was the critical player in the development discourse, so the 'political man' was the citizen. The citizen's interests that were articulated in a universalist language privileged some issues of socio-economic development and marginalized others. Some women and 'subaltern' men – of lower classes, castes, and weaker ethnic groups – were coopted into the new political elites. Thus, I conclude, many women, themselves part of the national elites, participated in the construction of nationalist imaginings and programmes, even though the process itself led to their simultaneous cooptation and/or exclusion from these constructions. Many local struggles waged by the majority were overlooked and sometimes even suppressed, resulting in social tensions that were to influence development trajectories in many post-colonial states.

Chapter 2 is a study of a struggle for recognition by some women street vendors in New Delhi. Through their struggle, these women sought to resist oppression by the police, as well as engaging with the judiciary in order to arrive at a negotiated position in defence of their position as street vendors. Their struggle showed how women in post-colonial states are often positioned in precarious and complex ways vis-à-vis the different fractions of the state and have to negotiate their way between/ through these if they are to realize their interests. I examine this struggle within the context of the debates on the state in the feminist literature. I argue that class as well as the gender positionings of women are critical to the ways in which they can/do interact with the post-colonial Indian state, and further that state structures are important in the lives of poor women, in particular in the ways in which they pose a threat to and need protection from other fractional state institutions. Targeting these through the struggles of women, then, is not just an option for women but a political imperative. I conclude by arguing for an understanding of post-colonial state formation informed by debates on the relative autonomy of the state on the one hand and state embeddedness on the other. Such an approach, derived from analysis of a particular struggle, also points to the potential for a strategy for struggle that is both 'in and against' the state.

In Chapter 3, I build on my discussion about the state to analyse institutional mechanisms for the advancement of women, also known as gender policy agencies. Institutionalizing women's interests in all areas and sectors of policy at all levels has been a concern of women's movements worldwide, as well as of international institutions such as the United Nations. Gender mainstreaming has emerged as a strategy for addressing this issue; it is relevant to all states and public institutions. National machineries for the advancement of women are regarded as appropriate institutional mechanisms for ensuring that gender main-streaming agendas are implemented and issues of gender equality remain in focus in public policy. Gender mainstreaming and national machin-eries have found added salience in international public policy through UN-led and national government-endorsed agreements on these issues, such as the Beijing Platform for Action (1995). Certain themes emerge in the analysis that follows. First, are national machineries as state institu-tions the most appropriate instruments for furthering women's interests? Two sets of debates inform this issue – the complex and plural nature of women's interests and the translation of these interests into women's engagements with the state. The second theme is the viability of national machineries as bodies promoting women's interests – do these institu-tions command the necessary resources to be able to promote women's interests? In this context I address issues of resources – economic and political – and the setting of goals and targets for national machineries, as well as the political environments in which these machineries are embedded. Here, the stability of governance institutions, the relative strength of civil society and the women's movements, and issues of accountability of the national machineries are important factors. The third theme focuses on the ways in which the hierarchical nature of state bureaucracies, and political parties, the presence or lack of audit-ing mechanisms within state machineries, leadership commitment (or not) to gender mainstreaming and, of course, increasing the presence of women within state bodies at all levels are key elements in the advance-ment of women's interests. I conclude that the democratization of the state becomes a key to mainstreaming gender effectively.

The developing discourse on democratizing the state led to important feminist engagements with the concept of democratization. In Chapter 4 three insights arising from the work of feminist scholars are presented, which extend our understanding of democratization at the theoretical level. These are: recognizing public and private spheres of political action, feminist methodologies, and patriarchy and democratic politics. I ex-amine the specific field of gender and democratization and the nature of women's participation in politics by assessing women's movements' contribution to struggles for democratization, the nature of women's political participation and women's participation in institutional politics. In the final section I reflect upon the wider socio-economic context in which men and women are engaged in democratic struggles. In particular, I argue that democratization and entitlements to citizenship must go hand in hand. I further explore how democratization of the state is being influenced by the pressures and possibilities of globalization. I conclude that democratization does not have the linearity that influential mainstream literature suggests, but rather is an untidy and unfolding process and feminist insights are crucial for its understanding.

In Chapter 5, after reviewing the historical and socio-economic context in which quotas have been introduced in South Asia and the evidence from the various studies on the implementation of quotas in local governance, my colleagues and I conclude that quotas form part of a long history of constructing post-colonial citizenship. They are part of contemporary state strategy for addressing a complex set of issues relating to, among other things, the status of the nation within the international community, a response to the growing strength of the women's movements and attempts by the state to 'manage' the demands for equality that continue to challenge social hierarchies within nations. The quotas in South Asia can thus be seen as an incremental as well as a 'fast track' (Dahlerup 2006) response to these equality demands in a historical context that is complex. We conclude that while quotas are important in addressing the exclusion of women from the public political sphere, they can form only one part of a multifaceted strategy for empowering women, which must, together with increased political participation, also involve a redistribution of socio-economic resources within societies.

As the post-colonial state becomes increasingly enmeshed in the global networks of economic and political power, feminist scholars and activists have had to deal with conceptual and political forces of globalization. Chapters 6 to 8 are more focused on the global politics of development, in particular the governance of the regimes of production, consumption and exchange that have transformed the political landscape in the last three decades. From the ways in which gendered processes of producing goods for a global market affect the lives of women and men to the ways in which women and men exchange information and make connections across space and time, our reflexivity as well as our corporeal selves are being globalized. Here Barwa and I focus on an analysis of the Trade Related Intellectual Property (TRIPS) regime and how governance of global regimes of production fundamentally affects the ways in which inequalities are being reproduced, between the North and the South, between men and women, and among women also. I examine gender networks that are creating new solidarities across borders of difference. Finally, I analyse global governance as a gendered regime in order to outline the modes of regulation within which we are functioning, as well as the challenges we can pose such regulation. While the chapters stand alone, there are clear linking themes that are also visible. Because of this, the reader can either access individual chapters or can trace these themes of gender politics of development sequentially.

Some definitional issues that are important to the debate on global governance are outlined and analysed in Chapter 6. The chapter assesses the competing mainstream definitions of global governance and addresses the implications of the non-gendered nature of these. It further assesses why the definitions that have emerged so far neglect the gendered nature of the global regimes, even as some have begun to acknowledge the consequences of such regimes on women in particular (and sometimes on men). The chapter examines how governance as a concept allows (or not) reflection on the imbricated nature of different levels of governance; how global governance can only be understood through examining it relationally to the state as well as the 'local', the grass roots. It argues that local, national, regional mapping of governance allows us to see the unfolding nature of global governance both theoretically and in terms of the building and working of institutions. The chapter outlines the importance of deconstructing existing definitions to show how engendering concepts can be part of the transformative impulse of feminist analysing. It does so by analysing four aspects of governance – markets, institutions, ideology and spectacle – as well as distinguishing between the concepts of governance of the polity and governance of the community. I conclude by suggesting that feminist conceptualization of the state and democracy has relevance for the way in which the regimes of global governance might be viewed.

Chapter 7 is an attempt to define a research agenda that explores the relationship between gender, knowledge, innovation and property rights against the backdrop of the processes of market liberalization and transformation of the relationship between states and the global economy. The chapter argues that women's contribution to creating knowledge and knowledge-based inventions is denied on counts of gender as well as of capitalist property relations. It suggests that TRIPS are institutionalizing the historically exclusionary bounded definitions of what counts as knowledge, and thus denying the role of millions of women across the world in the production of knowledge over time. The role of the World Trade Organization and specifically of TRIPS is examined to show how gendered capitalist governance regimes affect the production of knowledge as well as its exchange in the increasingly globalized markets. They also regulate what is counted as knowledge and what is marginalized as conventions, traditions or mores. The chapter concludes that this property regime challenges women to engage in the struggle over meanings of knowledge, invention and property.

Finally, in Chapter 8 I focus on a critical approach to women's organization and networks by examining the setting up of the South Asia Research Network (SARN) on Gender, Law and Governance, in which I, together with several other colleagues, was engaged. I reflect very briefly upon the construction of discourses about 'knowledge' and 'knowledge-makers' and issues of access that emerge as a result of these discourses and practice. By making a critical analysis of the subaltern epistemological perspective, I outline the ways in which it challenges the dominant modes of thinking about knowledge-making and activism. I argue that if 'knowledge' is a contested term, so is our understanding of political networks, which are increasingly becoming globalized. I do this by examining the founding and work of SARN in order to assess how women's networks address issues of change in the context of difference; how they address issues of recognition as well as of redistribution. I conclude by reflecting upon three aspects of a 'politics of networks' – the politics of process, by examining the concept of deliberative politics; the politics of outcomes, by distinguishing between integrative and transformative agendas; and the politics of framing, by focusing on cosmopolitan democracy. The analysis of SARN suggests that feminist networks need to be aware not just of national borders but also of borders of power.

These chapters thus traverse a changing political landscape, from nationalism to globalization, from concerns with equality and social justice to issues of identity, from the state to governance. In the conclusion to the book I outline the reasons for celebration and caution that are reflected in this book. I set out the achievements of women's movements as well as the anxieties that beset them – the importance of agency and the limits of structural power; the insistence on hope in the face of despair.

This book, then, is a contribution to the debates about the changing concerns of the gender politics of development.

1 | Gender, nationalism and 'nation-building'[1]

Development[2] has historically been a nationalist project. The edifice of eighteenth-century anti-colonial nationalism, which was a gendered ideology of resistance as well as power, included 'development' as progress and civilization sustained by religion, culture and tradition, as well as by science and technology, capital and markets. The creation of the nation-state, of 'its world of meanings' – in other words, nation-building – has been the starting point of what has been called the developmental state. In this chapter I examine how nationalism and nationalist struggles have framed discourses and strategies of development.[3] I argue that nationalism circumscribed development priorities in post-colonial contexts, gave them a hierarchy – of gender, class and ethnicity, among others – created some new spaces and closed off others. Ideology, religion and imaging of the nation-state played a crucial part in setting the development agendas in post-colonial nations.[4] In the process of nation-building, just as the 'economic man' was the critical player in the development discourse, so the 'political man' was the citizen. 'The citizen's' interests were articulated in a universalist language that allowed only certain issues of economic development to be addressed.[5] Both women and 'subaltern' men – of lower classes, castes and weaker ethnic groups – were coopted into the elite nationalist programme despite the local struggles waged by them in their own interests (see Guha 1982: 1–7). While nationalism provided new spaces for women to mobilize in – and even to use and endorse the universal construction of 'the citizen' in particular contexts – at the same time it framed those spaces, landscaped them through rhetoric and language in particular ways. Many women, however, themselves part of the national elites, participated in the construction of nationalist imaginings and programmes, even though the process itself led to their simultaneous cooptation and/or exclusion from these constructions (see Bereswill and Wagner 1998: 233). I argue, therefore, that the place of women within the discourse of development cannot be understood without reference to the struggles around economic and political agenda-setting by nationalist elites, and women's movements in their various forms.

Gender and nationalism

Feminist scholars have made an important contribution to the study of nationalism (Jayawardene 1987; Enloe 1989; Anthias and Yuval-Davis 1989; Sangari and Vaid 1990; Kandiyoti 1991; Hall 1992; McClintock 1993). They have suggested that women are central to the construction of nationalist discourses as biological reproducers of members of ethnic collectivities, as reproducers of the boundaries of ethnic/national groups, as central participants in the *ideological* reproduction of the collectivity and as transmitters of its culture.[6] They are also important to nationalism as signifiers of ethnic/national differences – as a focus and symbol in ideological discourses used in the construction, reproduction and transmission of ethnic/national categories, and finally as participants in national, economic, political and military struggles (see below). These different roles that women play mean that '[l]iving as a nationalist feminist is one of the most difficult political projects in today's world' (Enloe 1989: 46).

Gender relations are thus important as a frame for nationalist practices, and nationalism as an ideology is important for the configurations of gender relations within the national space. Biology and culture are key elements in the construction of new political spaces and of new discourses of empowerment. As Walby has commented, however, more work needs to be done on nationalism's *economic* consequences for women's lives such that the division of labour is not simply 'subsumed under biology or culture' but is made visible in the public domains of national development (1997: 182–3). Moving on from Walby, I argue that the gendered ideologies of nationalism framed the ways in which women's labour was configured, counted, assessed and rewarded. Masculine pride and humiliation in the context of colonialism had fashioned 'the (colonized) woman' as a victim to be rescued – first by the colonizers and then by the colonized male elites – and as the centre of the household to be protected and cherished. Thus, she served many purposes – to provide a node of self-awareness of a particular kind for men, and hence to be made visible in the public arenas in particular ways. As I will make clear below, in decolonized nation-states, policy-making acknowledged some of these complexities only by denying them.

Women's labour and women's citizenship are markers of this confusion that we see repeatedly in liberal nationalist discourses as well as in Marxist ones. Whether it is population policies, human rights, conditions of employment or endorsement of monogamous family structures, nation-states have used the discourses of both nationalism and development to circumscribe women's lives. And because of the history of colonialism, the pain of struggling against the idea of the community, culture and family, women have found it at times hard to oppose the boundaries being drawn around them, sometimes in their own names, by others – largely nationalist, masculine elites. In this way, the power of discourse was systematically used to frame women's role in development[7] – whether as reproducers of the nation and markers of its cultural boundaries, or as participants in its economic life.

Nationalism is a much theorized concept; as is development. While feminist scholarship provided a gendered critique of the concept of nationalism, interventions in the post-structuralist mode have opened up new spaces within development studies which allow us to examine the discursive power of nationalism in the economic agenda-setting of the nation-state (Escobar 1995; Crush 1995; Marchand and Parpart 1995; Sylvester 1999). Building on both these sets of literature, I illustrate the importance of the language of nationalism for the construction of the agenda of development, and suggest that women's particular positionings within the family and society were central to both these projects. I argue that nationalism allowed conversations to take place about development between colonial and nationalist male elites. Women were largely excluded from these conversations, which took place in very different contexts of power. I emphasize, however, that these conversations, while exclusionary, were by no means discrete; on the contrary, they were untidy, contradictory and allowed spaces for contestation that were utilized by women. The partiality of these conversations and exclusions was also reflected in the unfolding story of development in decolonized states. Nationalism and development then were 'Janus-faced' (Nairn 1981) creatures at once mobilizing and excluding women from the project of 'nation-building'. After examining the dominant yet unstable discourses of gender of the colonial and nationalist elites, I explore the contributions of women activists to national movements and the articulated projects of nation-building, the spaces that women were able to create both within the nationalist movement and within the nationalist discourse, and also the dilemmas that they faced in participating in nationalist movements and discourses of nation-building. I suggest that the trajectory of women's participation within different types of nationalist movements and different political systems had a profound impact on the kinds of citizenships that they were offered, and their ability to be active in the public sphere. Here, it is important to keep in mind the evolving nature of nationalism, of the nation, and of its development. The particularity of political and economic contexts led to 'rounds of restructuring' of the nation-state (Walby 1997: 190) and posed different issues of evolving social relations for women and men.

I conclude from this discussion that nationalism and nation-states born of nationalist struggles posed particular challenges for women. While remaining central to the project of 'nation-building', women were made 'invisible' through universalized discourses of citizenship and economic development. While the new citizenships allowed women to take their place within the political space of the nation as individuals, the ambivalence that surrounded the new citizenships meant that this individuation remained fragile; the social symbolism of 'woman' continued to threaten the civic rights of women. Nation-states as products of nationalist struggles remain fractured and fraught terrains for women. Upon this terrain development was crafted – as the means and goal of progressive society and economy, and as emblematic of legitimacy of the new nation-state. I argue that while women remained central to the continuing construction of national identity, they were peripheralized in the new discourse of development.

The discourses of nationalism did not disappear with the decolonization of the 1940s to the 1960s. They are again with us in complex and contemporaneous forms in the post-cold-war period – through the seeking of nationhood on the basis of race, ethnicity, religion and economy.[8] The processes of 'othering' communities, populations and groups continues to affect the drawing up of development agendas in eastern and central Europe, in parts of Africa, and Asia. Women have had to pay a high price for this new wave of nationalism, and have confronted issues that are very similar to those faced by women during anti-colonial struggles – rape, war, homelessness, insecurity, and being constructed without their consent as threats to, and symbols of, the new nations and national identities.

The chapter is divided into four sections. The first explores issues arising from the 'imaging of the nation' by political and economic elites. The second and third focus on the ways in which this imaging was employed in the service of colonialism and nationalism, and the final section explores how feminist and women's groups interacted with nationalism and with what results.

Imaging a nation

Remembering and forgetting 'All nationalisms are gendered, all are invented and all are dangerous ... in the sense of representing relations to political power and the technologies of violence' (McClintock 1993: 61; see also Hobsbawm 1990). This quotation raises several important issues. In a substantial amount of literature on nationalism the gendered nature of the concept is neither acknowledged nor analysed. So when Ernest Gellner wrote his now classic text on nationalism (1983) he constituted the nation as follows: 'Men are of the same nation if and only if they recognise each other as being from the same nation.' By using 'men' to mean 'men and women' he eliminates the possibility of discussing gender, since he is eliding the very difference (between women and men) that gender-based analysis studies. The gendered nation thus remains unacknowledged while at the same time important to the construction of nation. It is, for example, in the public space that men encounter each other and need recognizable markers for the nation to be imagined as home for them all (access to the public space is not automatic for women and this fact affects the nature of nationalism itself). It is also the public space in which they encounter men who are not recognizable, or are a threat to the recognizable self. This is because to the nation as an invention danger is an important motif – by naturalizing the nation as a recognizable togetherness, the threat to this togetherness can become central to the concept itself.

This threat can be either of physical violence against the national borders, or psychological violence represented by challenging the normative values recognized by the dominant male elites of the nation as important to all, or social and political violence against the institutions of the nation-state. The danger that lurks becomes the cement that binds men of a nation together in its defence. Danger is central also because it is often invented in order to raise national consciousness, which might be thought to be incipient and in need of mobilization. Political rhetoric becomes important in articulating this danger – to mores, customs, religion, which can find safety only within the political borders of a separate nation. Political rhetoric is at its most effective when it is able to harness the power of historical evidence. As the Greek historian Konstantinos Paparrigopoulos commented: 'History is not only a science. It is at once the Gospel of the present and the future of the fatherland' (Ben-Amos 1997: 129). As gospel, history provides as well as legitimizes accounts of 'the common possession of a rich legacy of memories' (Renan, in ibid.). Surendranath Banerjea, one of the founding members of the Indian National Congress in 1885, put it this way: 'The study of the history of our own country furnishes the strongest incentive to the loftiest patriotism ... For ours was a most glorious past' (Kedourie 1970: 235).

In this context, another history can become a threat to the unity of the nation; 'forgetting, and even historical error are essential for the creation of a nation' (Renan, in Ben-Amos 1997: 129). Memory and nationalism are thus intimately connected, and history is crucial to the documentation and erasure of collective memory, to the remembering and forgetting of recognizable commonalities. It is through the writing in or editing out of history that the invention of the nation takes place, and is placed under threat. In the need for creating a commonly (male) accepted history are also the roots of patriarchal compromise between different male elites in order to determine the spaces occupied by women (see below). Political self-determination thus becomes important to the articulation of the self. The growth of republicanism in Latin America, for example, saw struggles over the meanings of the image of 'the Indian' – excavated from the past to provide legitimacy to the political aspirations of the nationalists. Once this purpose was served, however, Earle suggests, by 1850 '"the heroic Indian ... had been converted into a wild beast lacking any capacity for civilization" ... virtually obliterating the brief period when all political factions had fought for the right to present the Indian as their own' (2001). This gendered nationalist self, in its remembering and forgetting, in the articulations of danger and of nationalisms, remains tied to the notions of purity and authenticity, which in turn are critically attached to the shadowy figure of the woman in the home. Nationalism in its psychological and political formulations thus posed significant problems for women.

Colonial, nationalist and feminist tropes There are three different discourses through which the figure of the national woman has been defined. The first was that of colonialism, the second of nationalism, and the third of feminism or the women's rights movement. In many ways these three were not discrete; they were overlaid with the intellectual baggage and historical knowledge of the others. The context of power within which they took shape and were played out meant, however, that the colonial discourse remained powerful even in the resistance to colonialism. This was because of the lack of confidence of nationalist elites in their own cultural histories, and their desire to find acceptance within the dominant structures of power and ideologies (Fanon 1967; Said 1979; Nandy 1983). The historical and the political economy contexts and international politics were important to the development of these discourses, in all of which I find a selective engagement with the 'other'. In the process of drawing new parameters, challenging existing

and emerging political forces and creating visions of future development, nationalism emerges as the dominant discourse in the period of
decolonization.

As Hoogvelt points out, 'Not only was the need for ... colonies argued in
economic terms [increased trade leading to jobs at home], it was indeed
often expressed as a vital national interest' (1997: 19). The competition
between European colonial powers was a competition among nations.[9]
Threat to national survival was seen as the consequence of losing the
conquest race, which would lead to the opening up and development of
colonies as estates that must become the markers of economic progress.
As in any process of state legitimization of huge economic investment,
the economic rationale was insufficient. The threat to the national integrity of Great Britain, for example, was made the basis for the ever-
expanding colonial boundaries by both political figures like Chamberlain
and colonialists like Rhodes: 'In their speeches and writings they argued
that half the population of Britain would starve if ... ever the British
Empire narrowed down to a "mere" United Kingdom dimension' (ibid.:
19). Another aspect of the colonial discourse was that of the threat posed
by the barbarity of the colonized. As Benjamin Kidd, a sociologist at
the turn of the eighteenth century, wrote: 'The task of governing from
a distance the inferior races of mankind will be one of great difficulty
... But it is one that must be faced and overcome if the civilised world
is not to abandon all hope of its continuing economic conquest of the
natural resources of the globe' (in ibid.: 20). Thus, the 'task of governing
from a distance' the barbarian nations, though an economic necessity,
was cast as 'the civilising mission' of the Christian nations – a cultural
trope of colonial expansion. So religion and nationalism came together
in legitimizing the economic interests of the colonial states.

The nation-states of the Third World emerged out of their encounter
with imperialism. This encounter encompassed struggles over the cultural, economic and political resources of the state and was extremely bit-
terly fought. Nationalism was the midwife of new nations. The imperialist
articulations of modernity[10] formed the bases of most successful nationalist movements. This was as much for reasons of political economy – the
insertion of new nations into the world economy required functioning
within the international capitalist or (after the Second World War) the
socialist planning framework – as of becoming modern, of growing out
of the chrysalis of 'traditional' culture to take their place in the modern
world. This was the first trope of nationalism. Nation-building needs to
be understood in this context: it was a consciously modernist political

term that was employed widely during the period of decolonization. The nation – imagined as well as imaged, remembered as well as forgotten, traditional as well as modern – was to be built through the efforts of mobilized 'masses' led by nationalist elites imbued with a vision of the reclaiming of a glorious if vanished past. This was the second trope of nationalism. Nation-building was thus a project that encompassed both the firming up of hegemonic cultural discourses through constitutional and legal arrangements and economic and militaristic infrastructures that allowed the knitting together of disparate populations into one stable political entity – the independent nation-state. This was the third nationalist trope.

The feminist discourses were caught between two impulses, and fractured further as the nationalist movements progressed. One impulse was universalist – the recognition of global patriarchy, which can be witnessed in the work of many Western feminists writing during colonial times, such as Mayo and Rathbone (see Liddle and Rai 1998; Ware 1992). Their particularistic, intimate narratives of the lives of women under traditional cultures were, however, often coopted by imperialist media to reinforce the message of 'the civilizing mission' that was the 'white man's burden'. Women within nationalist movements largely disassociated themselves from these 'imperial maternalist' discourses (see Liddle and Rai 1998). They too, however, were caught between the attraction of a universalist language of citizenship rights and the particular cultural and historical boundaries within which they knew women worked and lived (Agnihotri and Mazumdar 1995; Geiger 1997).

'Recasting history' (Sangari and Vaid 1990) thus became a potent means of aggression and contestation within each of the three discourses. On both colonial and nationalist sides, the question of legitimacy was tied to that of civilization and civility, which in turn depended upon powerful constructions of gender and gender relations.

Colonial ideologies and constructions of gender Colonial attacks upon the civilizations of the colonized countries took different forms to show how relations between men and women were symptomatic of the generalized degeneration of the societies themselves. Colonized men of Aryan races, such as Afghans and Sikhs, for example, were routinely categorized as either 'martial' or boorish and aggressive. This was quite different from the depiction of the African male as 'in a state of barbarism and savagery which is preventing him from being an integral part of civilization' (G. W. F. Hegel 1965, in Bayart 1993: 3). Others, especially Chinese or East Asian men, were 'feminized' by emphasizing their (small) size, and eugenically 'weak' constitutions (Ling 1997). 'Scientific' studies by colonial doctors abound in racialized descriptions of colonized men (Engels 1989). All sets of men, however, were presented as brutal towards women, and therefore uncivil. For example, in his *History of India*, J. S. Mill wrote, 'The condition of women is one of the most remarkable circumstances in the manner of nations. Among rude people the women are generally degraded, among civilised people they are exalted' (Kumar 1989). The colonial project then encompassed the rescue of women in the colonies from the men of their own communities by an external authority that had both the force of state power and the legitimizing power of a modernist discourse. Men's relationship to women was then used in colonial discourses as a 'means of mediating the West's relationship with the East' (Liddle and Rai 1998). Women were central to this social construction of the 'civilised people'. The boundaries that were drawn around women constituted the markers of civility. So colonized women play a central role in the legitimization of colonialism.

For the colonial powers, ideas of civility were rationalized through tying these to the frame of modernity. Enlightenment formed the backdrop of nationalism in Europe, where capitalist development fuelled by the enterprise of the rational man was valorized. Modern social relations were spoken of in the same breath as capitalist norms of individuation. Capitalism for its part became synonymous with progress as it followed a series of stages of human activity – from hunting to pastoral and settled agriculture. It was the historical mission of colonialism to pass on the tools of progress to the colonized countries. This 'sharing of progress' was brought about either through the recognition of ancient civilizations' indigenous mores, using these to craft new constitutions, as the orientalists demanded for India, or through completely new arrangements. As Bayart points out, 'There are some links between the reluctance to recognise African societies as historical and political entities in their own right and their subjugation by the west from the period of the slave trade to colonisation' (1993: 2). In the absence of recognition of pre-colonial civilization, for example in the Americas, it was emphasized that economic and social regeneration would be achieved only through the process of colonization itself (Cowen and Shenton 1996: 42–59; also Earle 2001). The crafting of modern economic relations thus had a profound impact upon not only the public relations of power between men at different levels but also the symbolic power relationship between the colonial and indigenous male elites. The dominant colonial male order was then able to humiliate the aspiring nationalist male elites in many different ways, perhaps one of the most potent being to recast the social relations among men and women of the colonies.

In the first stages of colonial conquest, humiliation was direct. As Stolcke writes in the context of Latin America, 'For the vast majority of indigenous women, the Conquest meant the loss of material, political and ritual privileges; exploitation of the labour, and sexual abuse by the invading soldiers and priests who crucified them in bed under the pretext of saving their souls' (1994: 8). In many countries and cultures, sexual abuse by the conquerors often meant the rejection of women by their male relatives in the name of 'honour' and 'purity' (Butalia 1998). This was one way of dealing with the humiliation experienced by colonized men.[11] These rejected women were often made part of the political economy of colonial war against their own countries, by becoming the 'servicers' of soldiers' sexual needs. Prostitution, necessary for survival, placed them in a grey zone of society – vulnerable, forgotten and constantly abused; the responsibility of none. As the colonial power settled into 'admin-istrative rationality', however, prostitutes became objects of regulation and confined exploitation, as can be witnessed in the drawing up and implementation of the Contagious Diseases Acts by the British colonial state in the late nineteenth century. While it is important to note that the prostitute women were also largely from the lower class/castes and therefore not necessarily of immediate concern to the nationalist male elites,[12] their concern about such women perhaps marks the process of formation of national sentiment.

The humiliation of the colonized male social order also took the form of selective refashioning of customary social and legal practices governing relations between men and women. These relations were both economic – regulation of property rights, delegitimization of certain forms of social organization of labour – as well as social – marriage and education. This refashioning emphasized the power relations between colonial and colonized male elites. As McClintock argues, 'All too often in male nationalisms *gender* difference between women and men serves to sym-bolically define the limits of *national* difference and power between *men*' (1993: 62). Gellner makes the same point, without the insight of feminist analysis, when he claims that it is the humiliation experienced by men of one national community in not being able to achieve communicative equality with men of the dominant national community which gives rise to nationalist passions (Gellner 1997).

It is important to note, however, that the colonial discourse on gender relations was not always challenged by nationalist movements. Some of it was also absorbed, rationalized and made the basis of the nationalist thinking on gender relations (see Metcalf 1995: xi; Parpart and Staudt 1999). Refashioned property and marital relations in particular were not disturbed in the post-colonial nation-states; indeed, in many countries such as India, as we shall see below, nationalist leaderships participated in this refashioning of gender relations. It was the markings of modernity which were recognized in the rationalizing of patriarchal relations in inheritance, and the quelling of 'uncivil' matrilineal marriage systems by both the colonial and the nationalist elites.

Under colonialism, modern capitalist relations required a 'rational' systematization of property relations; the inclusion of colonized states in the world economy needed recognizable property relations, which could not be achieved without the disturbing 'alien/uncivil' social relations. For example, in British India, the zamindar, the traditional landholder and tax-collector, was given property rights under the Permanent Settlement Act of 1793. Taking the model of the 'improving landlord' from the English context, the zamindar was given the same status and responsibilities. While this was a break with the earlier traditions of the zamindar's position as dependent upon the feudal nawabs, the English colonial administration insisted that the Act was 'restoring institutions of the country'. Though even the English establishment soon became disillusioned with the settlement, as the zamindars became the new *rentier* class uninterested in investing time and money in the improvement of land and continued to depend upon smallholders and their taxes, the idea was not repudiated by the colonial government. This was because it 'concealed a commitment to a European, and Whig, conception of the proper ordering of society. ... The ideas of property and "improvement" which defined it remained central to the Raj of the nineteenth century' (Metcalf 1995: 21). The resulting commercialization of Indian agriculture led to profound changes in rural social relations which resulted in the exclusion of women from the economic sphere. The sequestration of common lands meant women had little access to an important means of economic survival. Under the Permanent Settlement, as cash replaced kind in the payment of taxes, the production of cash crops necessitated changes in the patterns of agriculture production, and the division of family labour between the production of cash crops and the provision of food (see Sarkar 1983; Desai 1989; Shiva 1989; Mackenzie 1995). Women's labour became increasingly concentrated on provision of food for the family, invisible and unaccounted for within the new financial arrangements. The male contribution to the family income took on greater visibility.

In Africa, too, the expansion of merchant capital worked against women. In particular, colonial institutionalization of land tenure and usage systems left women tied to the land, unable to take advantage of rural–urban migration, but deprived of control over land resources (Chazan, in Parpart and Staudt 1999: 187). In Zambia '[c]olonial gender stereotypes, which identified men as farmers and women as wives and mothers, exacerbated this inequality by leading colonial officials to provide training and credit to male farmers' (Munachonga, in ibid.: 130).[13] Further, the position of male elders was reinforced through codification of customary marriage laws and therefore underlined the centrality of women for the reproduction of labour, and the need to maintain control over this resource (Lovett, in ibid.; Geiger 1997: 25). In terms of rural–urban migration, women were almost completely excluded. This, argues Geiger, was because of the colonial state's preoccupation with controlling African women's sexuality and their reproductive capacity. In Tanganyika, for example, the 'problem of women' was posed by colonial bureaucrats in terms of 'rights, needs, and responsibilities of men in relationship to their dependants' (ibid.: 23).

Modern capitalism also required the increased reach of the state in garnering resources, and expanding the narrow boundaries of market economies in the colonies. The first meant the exploitation of nature – terracing, logging and irrigating became widespread as colonialism became more confident. Mackenzie points out that 'For the European, political expediency in the promotion of a policy of land alienation demanded both the creation of a conceptualization of African agriculture as "backward" and "inefficient", and the privileging of environmental knowledge based on Western experience' (Mackenzie 1995: 102). Capitalist relations in agriculture led to an increased sense of 'improvement' of land through both changes in property relations and increased state intervention. State intervention often took the shape of conservation and infrastructural projects – the 'management of nature' through Western scientific knowledge to increase the productivity of land. Often these large infrastructural schemes were created and maintained through the forced labour of the men and women of the colonies. While resistance to such exploitation of labour was widespread, it was also gendered. In cases such as that of the Chipko movement in India, or the renegotiations around use of the traditional Matengo pit system of cultivation in Tanganyika, 'the boundaries of gendered knowledge altered ... in the context of changing relations of power' (ibid.: 105; also see Shiva 1989).

Such refashioning of property relations and land management altered the relations between the peasant and the landholder. It also altered the position of women within agrarian societies. These new social realities were then given a frame of law. Under the British, for example, the idea of the 'rule of law' as the central contribution of the English to the 'improvement' of the colonies was never abandoned. Through the codification of laws the colonial states, in particular the British colonial state, were able to combine the utilitarian principles of liberal philosophy sanctifying capitalist relations, and 'traditional' sacred texts to ensure that the disturbance brought about by the revolution of economic relations could be contained within recognizable social frameworks, through supporting traditional social hierarchies (see Parpart and Staudt 1999; Liddle and Joshi 1986; Mackenzie 1995: 108).

The nationalist response In his book *The Intimate Enemy*, Ashis Nandy, like Frantz Fanon before him, has argued that the reach of colonialism encompasses both the political economy of the colony and the mappings of its culture and its selfhood as expressed by its political elites: 'Colonialism is also a psychological state rooted in earlier forms of social consciousness in both the colonizers and the colonized. It represents a certain cultural continuity and carries certain cultural baggage' (Nandy 1983: 2). In political terms this translates, as Sartre so evocatively put it in his Preface to Fanon's *Wretched of the Earth*, in an attempt by the colonizers 'to fabricate an indigenous elite: they selected adolescents, branded them with the principles of western culture, stuffed their mouths with grandiose words which stick to the teeth ... Their living lies no longer had anything to say to their brothers' (1967: 6). However, 'all borrowings are also acts of reappropriation and reinvention' (Bayart 1993: 27). On the one hand, the violation of selfhood that the male elites experience through the process and administration of colonization leads to a '[p]articularly strong ... inner resistance to recognizing the ultimate violence which colonialism does to its victims, namely that it creates a culture in which the ruled are constantly tempted to fight their rulers within the psychological limits set by the latter' (Nandy 1983: 3). The penalty of crossing these limits is often marginalization within the nationalist political process. On the other hand, colonial constructions of dominant modes of civility posed difficult issues for nationalist elites and movements. (Chatterjee has called nationalism of these elites 'a project of mediation' (1993: 72).) This involved, as we shall see below, the appropriation of the popular – the innocent and the wise 'common man' rooted in the 'timeless truth of the national culture'; the 'classicization of tradition', which started with colonial disturbance and then the fixing of culture as law; and finally, the 'structure of the hegemonic domain of nationalism ... where it sought to overcome the subordination of the colonized middle class' (ibid.: 72–5).

Nationalism and 'social reform' was a particularly thorny issue for elites in colonial countries; no unified response was available (Oberoi 1996; Parpart and Staudt 1999). These elites, who were to significantly influence the trajectory of post-colonial development, were divided on the question of social reform. To one section the need for social reform tied in with their modernist conviction that the country needed to look 'forward' – westward – to regain its independence and its place in the world; that ancient customs needed modification, and sometimes to be rejected, if a modern nation-state was to take shape. The liberal modernists found much in common with the Marxists during the early phases of nationalist movements, which secured in many colonial countries the dominance of a linear, structuralist perspective. The alliance between the two was particularly visible during the early twentieth century when the Leninist intervention in Marxist theory gave legitimacy to nationalist struggles through the trope of 'self-determination'. As Hobsbawm points out, 'Nationalism thus acquired a strong association with the left during the anti-fascist period, an association which was subsequently reinforced by the experience of anti-imperialist struggles in colonial countries' (1990: 148; see also Sarkar 1983; Bianco 1971) To the other nationalist section, social reform was part of the discourse of colonialism – an attack upon ancient tradition on the one hand, and a reminder that the peoples of the country were not free to refashion their own social and political system. In the hierarchy of issues, independence came before the need to re-examine social mores; social reform should be undertaken in the privacy of the home/national space and not in the glare of colonial dominance and internal discord (Kandiyoti 1991).

While there was no unity among the male nationalist elites in responding to the colonialist attacks upon 'rude cultures', for all sections the nation took shape through nationalism. Nationalism was an essentialist discourse – of empowerment, of inclusion, but also of exclusion. The demarcation of the 'self' and 'other' that had been at the heart of the colonial encounter needed to be carried on for the nation to be secure in its borders. Nira Yuval-Davis has emphasized the need to distinguish between different types of nationalisms – cultural, ethnic and civic – because '[d]ifferent aspects of gender relations play an important role in each of these dimensions of nationalist projects and are crucial for any valid theorization of them ...' (1997: 21). While agreeing that these distinctions were critical to the political projects of nationalist elites, I would argue that whichever form nationalism took, the processes of 'othering' remained central to it (Giddens 1987: 117). The creation of the nationalist 'self' required a universalist language of self-determination and equality which allowed nationalist elites to stake a claim to freedom. Nationalism could, thus, provide an ideal for anti-colonial elites which was based upon a complex recognition of glories past and contemporary degradation, but also the promise of resurgence and self-determination (Said 1979).

The language of idealism was very often used to describe the nation in the making, and very often this description was imbued with notions of sanctity and sacredness. As the Turkish nationalist Ziya Gokalp asserted, 'This sacredness, even before it has reached consciousness, exists in an unconscious state in the psychological unity of the social group. So far it has remained a hidden treasure ... [but] with all its halo of sanctity ... [t]he emergence of an ideal means its rise from the subconscious to the conscious level' (Kedourie 1970: 199). Gokalp speaks of 'hidden treasures' which invest the past with legitimacy, while at the same time ensuring that the process of recovery is allowed through the mobilization of nationalists imbued with idealist visions of a sacred homeland. The nation itself became symbolic of familial relations by being called either 'fatherland' or, more generally, 'motherland', 'for whose sake people shed their blood. Why is it that all other lands are not sacred, but only that which is called fatherland?' asked Gokalp. By familializing the nation, the home becomes critical in the discourse of nationalism. Nothing is more imagined than this community of people subscribing to a singular idea of the home. '[C]ertain ideals of womanhood are propagated as indispensable to the attainment of an ideal society. These ideals apply to women's personal behaviour, dress, sexual activity, choice of partner, and the reproductive options ... women [are] the "carriers of tradition" or "the centre of the family" especially during periods of rapid social change' (Papanek 1994: 46–7). What is also demanded at this time of crisis, however, is that women's 'actions and appearance should alter less quickly than that of men, or should not be seen to change at all ... [and that they should] conform to prescriptive norms of a *collective* identity that is seen as advancing the goals of the group' as a whole (ibid.: 47).

In this context, the ideals of society get attached to notions of appropriate behaviour of women, and the restoration of social order becomes a process of imposition of stringent controls over women rather than addressing the structural issues leading to and arising from conflict. As Liddle and Joshi (1985) have shown in the context of India, this concept of the ideal home and the ideal woman within the home was very much an upper-caste/class idea of familial space and relations. Systems of social interaction that underpinned the upper classes were made the basis of a 'national' understanding of social relations through both colonial acceptance and their use by the dominant nationalist elites. So what was a limited and contested terrain of social relations was then translated into the norm through the systems of laws and constitutions. Moghadam argues that this move became possible when, in line with Anderson's analysis, nationalism came to be viewed not simply as an ideology but as akin to kinship and religion (1994: 4). According to Anderson, nationalism allowed the secular transformation of fatality into continuity – something that only religious discourses had articulated before the rationalizing thrust of the Enlightenment (1991: 10–11). As continuity demanded reproduction of future national generations, of national/cultural values, and stability of social forms, as well as the reproduction of the national populations, the family became critical to this new secular articulation of the nation, and the idea of the nation came to be symbolized in the family.

This imagined home/nation symbolized many things – security, familiarity, tradition. It was a space that remained open to the male elites as their domain, untouched in most part by the colonizer who structured the public life so ruthlessly. Indeed, the autonomy of the patriarch within the home was allowed by the colonial state in the hope of undermining anticolonial resistance. In Northern Rhodesia/Zambia and Nyasaland/Malawi, for example, the male elders allied themselves with colonial rulers to re-establish control over women through a contrived 'Customary Law' (Chanock, in Lovett 1990: 29; also Mackenzie 1995). Some of the bitterest opposition to British rule in India came from nationalists such as Tilak, when the colonial state sought to refashion dominant familial relations through legislation on age of consent, or *sati*. The modernist nationalists, on the other hand, supported these interventions as they became part of the story of the contemporary degeneration of the Indian society and its need for regeneration through secular nationalist revolution (Sarkar 1983; Oberoi 1996). The relations within the home, then, were very much part of the nationalist discourse; the home/nation was the authentic space but was under threat. This threat came not only from without – the colonial state – but also from within – the traditionalists who opposed change and thereby endangered the future, or the modernists who argued for a refashioned space without regard to the resultant pollution of authentic culture. And this authenticity was firmly attached to the body of the woman within the home/nation (Mani 1993; Kandiyoti 1991).

The contours of the woman within the home were very particular; 'only the women of the nation are the beautiful ones. Other men's/nations'/states' women ... are not beautiful like the home/national woman is' (Pettman 1996: 51). National identity was bound up with notions of boundary, purity and chastity; threat to this identity came if women's role within the boundary of the home/nation was compromised. The woman created the future generations and she ensured continuity of cultural traditions through her own appropriate social conduct and through the religious and cultural education of her children. The woman was thus seen as the stable entity in periods of change. While male elites argued about the need for change to the outer garb of the woman, her inner core was conceded by all nationalist sections to be chaste and immutable, as was the idea of the nation. This double move in imagining the female figure allowed the discourse of modernity to encompass the woman, but at the same time leave enough untouched within the parameters of the home. In this way the nationalist Janus resolved the 'woman question'. The tension between identity/culture and modernity was harmonized by making and endorsing the classical distinction between the scientific/technological and culture/tradition. The Chinese modernizers of the eighteenth century, for example, formulated this tension by distinguishing between *it* and *yong* – the thinking and doing, the philosophical and mechanical (Grieder).[14] And in the African context Senghor wrote: 'Negro-African reason is traditionally dialectical, transcending the principles of identity, noncontradiction, and the "excluded middle". Let us ... be careful not to be led astray by the narrow determinism of Marxism, by abstraction' (in Dahbour and Ishay 1995: 269). Whereas Western science was needed for the economic sphere, the traditional national values were central to maintaining the authentic 'self' so important to the stability of the new nation. As Judith Stacey has so powerfully argued in her critique of the Chinese communist movement (1983), this distinction allowed a compromise between the communist and the peasant elites on the 'woman question'. It resulted in the communists pursuing the project of nation-building with the support of the peasantry, and allowed patriarchal social relations to remain stable in a reconfigured space under the communist regime. Thus, the modernist discourse was constantly being disturbed from within nationalist movements.

The debates about the characteristics of the new nation and the re-fashioning of gender relations within its boundaries became accessible to increased numbers of people in the colonies through the growth of print capitalism, and the consequent undermining of the earlier administrative languages of the elites with the growth of the vernacular press (Hobsbawm 1990: 141; Anderson 1991: 44). The vernacular presses carried the nationalist message across the colonial territories and 'created unified fields of exchange and communication' (Anderson 1991: 44). One of the important currencies of this communicative exchange was the delineation of the woman. Modern or traditional, home-bound or participative in the nationalist struggles, bearer of authentic values or challenging both inherited and imported boundaries and positionings – the vernacular presses of nationalist movements are full of struggles of meaning around the body of the woman. Vernacular journals also, for the first time, carried the voices of women themselves, and became the vehicles of the first feminist articulations that challenged both the colonial and the nationalist/patriarchal delineations of women's positions in society (Talwar 1993; Geiger 1997). How important this feminist challenge was to the nationalist elites' views of the national community and women's position within it varied enormously from country to country. It would, however, be fair to say that in no context did feminist voices gain equality with male agendas within the discourse of nationalism. One of the reasons for this might be that feminist voices needed to keep hold of 'the woman' as a recognizable and stable entity as much as did the nationalist elites. Recognition of diversity was not part of the challenge at this stage. The struggles centred around the constructed woman and the space she occupied. The struggle over the space within was then very much a struggle over the contours of social relations, with the figure of the woman central to it. Print capitalism did, however, allow the voice of women to be heard, and in many cases to be mobilized in the nationalist cause. This mobilization, whatever its premises, became the basis of the first demands that women made in their own articulated interests.

The struggles over meanings within the nationalist movements regarding the place and role of women are important for understanding the alternative visions of post-colonial development that the nationalist elites put forward. These debates also indicate an acceptance by these elites of the powerful rhetoric of modernity that the colonialist powers had thus far monopolized. This acceptance of modernity and fashioning of alternative modern visions for new nations were also the basis upon which a new legitimacy was constructed by nationalist elites. It was by accepting norms of modernity that the nationalist elites asked first for the return of sovereign power to the national elites from the colonial centres, and then for the trust of the people of the country and for a recognition of the centrality of political elites to the process of development.[15]

In the twentieth century, in most countries, bourgeois liberal nationalist elites became dominant in nationalist struggles.[16] As a consequence their imaginings of 'the woman's' place in the new nation-state became dominant; as Jayawardene notes, upon this view 'the women of the peasantry were ... proletarianised, those of the bourgeoisie were trained to accept new social roles in conformity with the emerging bourgeois ideology of the period' (1987: 9). The constitutional reforms that were put forward in the post-colonial period remained largely political: equality for women within the legal processes, rescinding of obviously discriminatory practices, the right to vote, to education and in most cases to property, and laws against violence against women.[17] As the following example illustrates, both class and gender disturbed the stability of the new social relations that were normalized through nationalist political discourses and later through post-colonial constitutional and legal mechanisms.

In 1938, years before India gained independence, the National Congress set up a National Planning Committee. It was chaired by Jawaharlal Nehru and sought to draw the developmental map of the new India. One of the nine subcommittees established by the NPC focused on 'Woman's Role in the Planned Economy' (Chaudhari 1996: 211). The subcommittee was to deal particularly with issues of equal opportunities and rights for women and access to the world of economic production, which was identified as key to resolving the unequal status of women (ibid.: 213). The individual (woman) was the central figure for the committee, while the 'social' largely represented the hindrances in the form of custom in the way of the individual participating as a 'useful citizen' in the life of the new nation (ibid.: 219). The nation was the only social unit that was liberating for the Indian woman, and the liberation of the Indian woman was important to the functioning of the modern nation within the global order (ibid.: 223). From the beginning, however, there was a tension evident in the discussions of the committee. While the 'social' as custom was suspect, the committee was also concerned with maintaining customs and 'traditions': 'It is not our desire to belittle in any way these traditions, which have in the past contributed to the happiness and progress of the individual and have been the means of raising the dignity and beauty of Indian womanhood and conserving the *spiritual attributes of the Indian Nation*' (WRPE 1947: 32–3, emphasis in the original). The converging lines of womanhood and spirituality of the Indian nation within this document reveal the fraught nature of the enterprise upon which the Indian modernizing elites were embarked. 'There was a constant redrawing of the social and historical map around the body of the woman to keep hold of the convergence that had been created'; this was a project which could not reconcile the tensions with the affirmations of culture.[18] Thus, we see nationalism's 'capacity to appropriate, with varying degrees of risk and varying degrees of success, dissenting and marginal voices' (Chatterjee 1993: 156). We find, therefore, that the report of the committee is scarcely mentioned after the formal citizenship rights are granted to women in the Indian constitution in 1950.

Nationalism as development The successful post-colonial nationalist elites saw themselves as participants in the regeneration of their countries through gaining independence from the colonial rulers and envisioning a 'progressive', 'modern', 'industrialized' state. Indeed, the role of the state, of planning, of regulation and of rationality, was constantly emphasized in the nationalist rhetoric (see Nehru 1990; Nyerere 1973).[19] This was evident in liberal, socialist and Marxist states (Mao Zedong 1941). Such visions of modernity had direct consequences for structuring gender relations in post-colonial states. The emphasis on industrialization, for example, meant that the focus remained on male employment; the acceptance of commercialization and mechanization of agriculture meant the marginalization of women's work in rural societies, and the 'taming of nature' by the construction of dams across rivers – Nehru called these the 'temples of modern India' – for the production of electricity meant the displacement of populations, resulting in particular vulnerabilities for women. The equation of 'modernization' with the preferred political system was at times crude and explicit – 'fertilizers would enable increased agricultural output. [This] in turn, means socialism' (Nyerere 1973: 46) – and narrowed the spaces from within which women could challenge their marginalization. Indeed, as Heng points out in the context of China, 'the "modern" and the "Western" [were] conflated [which] ... meant that a nationalist accusation of modern and/or foreign – that is to say, Western – provenance or influence, when directed at a social movement, [was] sufficient for the movement's delegitimisation' (1997: 32). Other than in the Marxist nationalist states, private property was taken as given. In terms of agrarian gender relations it meant that non-Muslim[20] women could rarely inherit under recognized or accepted 'cultural' regimes, and this further supported the 'traditional' or modified colonial legal arrangements.

To recapitulate my argument thus far: to the colonized male elites the nation came into view through the lens of anti-colonial struggles. Through these struggles the colonized peoples and elites experienced nationalism. The nationalist elites were able to convey to the colonized peoples the image of the nation (Anderson 1991) in freedom together; they were able to visualize the possibility of articulating their own norms and rules of governance rather than being humiliated by working to the rules, hated and imperfectly understood, of the colonial state (Gellner 1983). While all these images of the nation were deeply gendered, there was little acknowledgement of this. If there was a recognition of women's interests as different from the constructed nationalist interests, it was considered essentially divisive. In the political hierarchy of issues nationalism secured primacy, while 'the woman' continued to have a shadowy existence on the periphery of nationalist consciousness – mobilized in its cause but confined within the home, which was also the nation. Through gaining independence a separate identity and a new home/nation would be created upon the foundations of the old, recovered one, claimed the nationalist message. Within the boundaries of the new nation both men and women would move to a civic nationalism symbolized as much by a new universal citizenship as by a new economy.

Nationalist movements and the 'self-determination' of women

Jayawardene (1987) has shown convincingly the importance of the link between nationalist and feminist struggles. She emphasizes the link between 'women's participation in feminist movements for emancipation and their simultaneous involvement in struggles for national liberation and social change' (ibid.: 23). She seeks to discover the roots of Third World feminism in the participation of women in nationalist struggles. She argues that the economic and political challenges thrown up by the anti-colonial struggles allowed women to be constituted by, and to make demands upon, the nationalist agendas. The development of capitalism in the Third World brought the women into the labour markets; the restructuring of agriculture fundamentally altered their position within the village community and the local economy; the administrative changes that created new political stabilities under colonial rule brought forth questions of local versus national identity for women, especially in the context of increased mobility and migration to urban conurbations. Vernacular newspapers circulated information, and became a vehicle for articulations of discontent, and the proposing of alternative visions by women. The nationalist response to the challenges posed by colonialism opened up the debates on women's social status, and created new spaces that women could occupy and use. Nationalism also posed significant challenges to nationalist women, however.

The biggest challenge posed by nationalism to women's consciousness was that of unity – the fight against imperialism demanded discipline and sacrifice. The nationalist movements – liberal as well as Marxist – spoke in the name not of particularistic groups but of pan-national interests. 'Particular interests' were regarded as threats that would only disturb and dislocate the coalescing of national agendas. As Helie-Lucas has commented, 'This is the real harm which comes with liberation struggles. People mobilise against such a strong, powerful and destructive enemy that there is no room for practical action in mobilising women at the same time. But worse, liberation struggles erase from our mind the very idea of doing so, which is seen as anti-revolutionary and anti-nationalist' (Wallace and March 1991: 58).[21] Second, unity meant keeping all sections of nationalist opposition on board. Here the element of sacrifice became paramount – if in the interests of unity certain rights of particular groups were compromised, this was not expediency but strategic bargaining. Recognizable social relations were the cement for political unity, and what could be more immediately recognizable than the figure of the woman within the home? For women's groups these issues of unity and sacrifice posed serious difficulties. On the one hand most groups accepted that the urgency of the nationalist struggle must give it primacy; on the other hand they were also aware of the particular constructions of the nationalist agendas that marginalized their interests. On the one hand the goal of non-gendered citizenship beckoned; on the other was the reality of differentiated experiences of the public and private lives of men and women. Women being cast as victims of their own society, women's groups rebelled against such delineations and asserted their cultural identities; being recast as 'new women' of a new nation-state, they were aware of the gaps between the political rhetoric and social reality. While self-imposed and self-regulated codes of silence (Crenshaw 1993; Papanek 1994) protected their communities from the attacks of the imperialist Western powers, women's groups also remained uncomfortable with the nationalist leaderships' articulations of women's place within the national movements. In the demands for unity lay the key to future agenda-setting, but often women's groups were unable to intervene in time because of the ways in which the burden of solidarity was placed upon them. '[A] power structure was being built on our mental confusion: a power structure which used the control of ... women as a means to get access to and maintain itself in power. ... During this crucial period, women had been assigned a place in society which could not be challenged without questioning both the past and the future ...' (Helie-Lucas 1991: 58).

If the demands for unity posed a dilemma to women's movements, this was compounded by divisions within women's groups on two issues. The first was modernism versus culture; the second that of differences among women. Most women whose voices were heard in nationalist movements were bourgeois women – educated and well connected, promoted by their politicized families, symbolic of a new modernity, even sharing more intimate aspects of their life experiences. As Geiger comments on the lives of Tanzanian women activists: 'At the time of mobilization, the TANU activists were ... divorced ... "middle-aged" by Tanganyikan cultural norms ... were freer than young women ... had very few children. Many had only one. Several had none ...' (1997: 68).[22] And yet the tension between modernity and tradition formed the backdrop to their activism as much as it did to that of the men's. This was because of the need felt by women to rescue cultural practices that could be owned by them, which would be self-representational as well as empowering in the context of colonialism and nationalist struggles. To be defined outside the cultural trope would risk marginalization and delegitimization. Motherhood in this context occupied an important contested place. As Malathi de Alwis has argued within the Sri Lankan context, '"Motherhood" ... can be defined as not only incorporating the act of reproduction ... but also the nursing, feeding and looking after of babies, adolescents, the sick, the old and even grown women and men, including one's husband' (in Maunaguru 1995: 160). In this role, women were able to occupy particular public spaces; the acceptance of the place of women within the 'natural' order of family allowed them access to oppositional politics against the colonial state and its perpetration of violence on their homes and children. In consequence, however, the constructed motherhood of the nationalist discourse was allowed a homogenizing and essentializing power; motherhood was contained within the boundaries of recognizable family forms which were validated by the nationalist elites. Issues of class, ethnic diversity and religion then became blurred and later emerged as real divisive issues for women's movements.

The anti-imperialist mobilizations led to what Kandiyoti has called 'the era of patriotic feminism' (1991: 28). In Turkey, Kandiyoti points out, 'no less than a dozen women's associations [were] founded between 1908 and 1916, ranging from primarily philanthropic organizations to those more explicitly committed to struggle for women's rights' (ibid.: 29). The same phenomenon could be seen in other countries engaged in nationalist transformations. In many cases, however, women's organizations were established by and with the support of male nationalist elites; in others already existing women's groups were coopted into dominant nationalist parties. The dilemmas that were posed by these cooptions can be illustrated by the example of Turkey under Mustafa Kemal's regime in the 1920s. On the one hand, the 'new woman' of the Kemalist era became symbolic of a break with the past; on the other the paternalist benevolence of the Kemalist regime hindered women's autonomous political initiatives. Kemal refused, for example, to authorize the founding of the Women's People's Party in 1923. Instead he advised women's groups to establish a Turkish Women's Federation – an association rather than a party. Even this was disbanded in 1935, a fortnight after it had hosted the 12th Congress of the International Federation of Women. The official reason given by the president of the Federation was that Turkish women had achieved complete equality and full constitutional rights, and that, the goals of the Federation having been achieved, its continued existence could not be justified. What was also clear, however, was that the Kemalist regime felt compromised by the pacifist speeches made by the British, American and French delegates to the conference; at a time when the Turkish army was gearing up for conflict, Turkish feminists' stand on disarmament was seen as a grave embarrassment (ibid.: 40–41). Thus, Kandiyoti concludes, 'the republican regime opened up an arena for state-sponsored "feminism" but at one and the same time circumscribed and defined its parameters' (ibid.: 42).

The Turkish example poses questions about the relationship between nationalism and feminism in two different ways. The first is about the primacy of the dominant nationalist agendas in contrast to the concerns of the women's movements. The second is about the difficult relationship between different feminisms – national, local and international.[23] As Kandiyoti notes, 'Turkish nationalism could be perceived as divisive in a situation where other ethnic minorities were restive ... the notion of a Turkish nation constituted a threat to the Islamic *umma*' (ibid.: 33). Similarly, the dominant Brahmanical codes of social interaction were naturalized as Indian social codes by the British in India, thus erasing the different regional and caste-based norms (Liddle and Joshi 1986). Women who subscribed to the secularization of social and public life often supported such hegemonic positions, becoming vulnerable to the charges of cultural ignorance, insensitivity, class bias and a slavish mentality in accepting Western ideas on religion and secularism. The support of women's groups for one articulation of nationalism could be presented as denying other identities, which made the identification of feminisms with Western ideologies easier within the context of the home/nation.

Further, feminist interventions from the outside, especially from Western feminists, created difficulties for local and national feminisms. Ramusack identifies the approach of most Western feminists of the time as that of 'maternal imperialists' (1990). They saw themselves as the agents of civilization and progress; they 'sought power for themselves in the imperial project, and used the opportunities and privileges of empire as a means of resisting patriarchal constraints and creating their own independence' (Liddle and Rai 1998). While most nationalist feminists rejected such delineations of women in their own countries, their acceptance of the liberal values that Western feminists espoused made them easy targets for traditionalists' attempts to delegitimize their struggles for women's rights. Also, their anger at maternal imperialists' complicity with imperialist discourses of orientalism meant that fruitful transnational alliances of solidarity were not possible; the solidarity of Western feminisms came at a price unacceptable to nationalist feminists. The national boundaries thus continued to delimit the space within which nationalist women's groups could organize, mobilize and negotiate. And the tensions within nationalisms and discourses of culture continued to pose significant challenges for women.

Codifying nationalism

These challenges were, however, least visible at the very moment when a nationalist movement made the transition from being an oppositional movement into being the dominant political force in an independent nation-state. At the cusp of historical change, most women's groups remained convinced of the nationalist transformative agendas and were reluctant to seek 'special' political dispensations from the state. In India, for example, three women's organizations (the All India Women's Committee, the Women's Indian Association and the Central Committee of the National Council of Women in India) wrote to the chair of the Minorities Committee on the status of women in the proposed new Government of India Act, 1935, demanding equal political rights with men. They also insisted that they would resist 'any plea that may be advanced by small individual groups of people for any kind of temporary concessions ... [for] securing the adequate representation of women in the legislatures ... To seek any form of preferential treatment would be to violate the integrity of the universal demand of Indian women for absolute equality of political status.' Women's groups within most nationalist movements saw themselves as freedom fighters, and as citizens of a free country. Liberal ideas of individual freedom were very attractive to women who participated in the nationalist struggles, even though they were mediated through the ideologies of nationalism. However culturally bounded, the freedom of the individual found its political form in the figure of the citizen.

The early conversations about nationalism helped demarcate the boundaries within which citizenship was operationalized. This concept was translated in very particular ways in order to stabilize new polities. Different visions of the future of the nation-state, and of its citizens, determined where women were positioned within this discourse in different political systems. In liberal political systems, a civic nationalism became the hegemonic political rhetoric. A pan-nationalist discourse of a citizenship tolerant of differences was developed to tie in the various groups, ethnicities and religious communities that formed the new nations. This was important for political stability, which in turn was essential for economic development. In this context, women continued to be regarded as markers of non-secular group identities, and at the same time became individualized as citizens of the new nation. The Indian case[24] is a good one to reflect upon here. As citizens, Indian women were equal to men. As women, however, they were deemed to be markers of identity first, and individuals later. Thus, in the interests of political stability after the trauma of the partition of the country at the time of independence, Muslim women were denied many of the rights granted to Hindu and Christian women. So the 'traditions' of Islamic family law were accepted, maintained and endorsed through the Indian constitution whereby Muslim men could marry more than one woman, and divorce proceedings, claims of custody of children, maintenance of the divorced wife and division of property and inheritance were decided according to Islamic rather than 'Indian' constitutional law.[25] As most successful nationalist movements were led by urban male liberal elites, the equality legislation fulfilled their commitment to democratizing gender relations. The process of reconciling the two impulses of social and political order and ideology and cultural traditions has, for example, resulted in very painful consequences for women in Algeria. The revolutionary state tried to maintain both a 'socialist' and an 'Islamist' identity but was unable to placate the fundamentalists and to deliver economic goods to the people, and the political situation careered out of control, with tragic consequences for the country and for Algerian women (see Rai 1996; Bouatta and Cherifati-Merabtine 1994).

In non-democratic political systems, such as Nigeria, for example, we find a 'strategy of exclusion rather than of unequal incorporation. Until recently ... military rulers (much like colonial administrators) pursued a policy of purposeful female neglect' (Chazan 1999: 190). The near-total masculine membership of the military and the army-led public bodies left women marginalized within the formal power structures. Further, owing to the unavailability of these formal institutions to women, they were also largely excluded from the patron–client relationships that took the place of more visible political participation (ibid., and Mba, in Parpart and Staudt 1999).

In Marxist states the concept of citizenship became subsumed under the categories of class while cultural nationalism was aligned to the modification of ideology – the state and nation became blurred, with seepage of some of the dominant cultural norms into state policies, and the suppression of others through state power. Evans notes that 'the subordination of gender to the supposedly more substantial matters of economic development and political power has been a recurring feature of the party-state's approach to woman-work since the early days of community control' (1997: 31). Construction of socialism in the 1950s in China required producing children for the development of society and, as a political commentator suggested in 1953, 'having children was a social duty, failure to observe which "should be severely criticized by the party"' (ibid.: 44). As Stacey has observed in the context of China, however, the 'new democratic morality linked sexuality not with procreation, but with felicitous marital relations, and, thereby, with the construction of socialism' and the maintenance of a social order where concerns about women's appropriate behaviour within the family were implicitly accepted and given succour through policy-making and implementation (1983: 188). In all three political contexts, the articulations of nationalist aspirations remained crucial to the setting of political and economic development agendas. In the moment of victory, whatever the ideological framework of decolonized nation-states, women seemed to be shut out of institutional design.

It is in this context that the ideological framing of women's aspirations – as patriots, nationalists and citizens – becomes important for an understanding of the places they occupied in development agendas. First, while social reform was considered a priority by all post-colonial elites, it was also emphasized that the 'essential distinction between the social roles of men and women in terms of material and spiritual virtues must at all times be maintained. There would have to be a marked *difference* in the degree and manner of westernisation of women, as distinct from men, in the modern world of the nation' (Chatterjee 1989: 243). Second, the above distinction was made but not acknowledged. This non-acknowledgement took different forms, but the assumptions about the social placing of men and women were built into the constructions of these concepts, and then naturalized through law and state policy. As Carol Smart has argued, 'we can begin to analyse law as a process of producing fixed gender identities rather than simply as the application of law to previously gendered subjects ... Woman is a gendered subject position which legal discourse brings into being' (1991: 9). The language of equality was used in most post-colonial states to firm up the contours of citizenship, while citizenship remained differentially constructed for men and women. The legitimacy of the state rested upon social and political reform, and upon the assembling of the values of citizenship in constitutional design. The hegemonic language of nationalism made it difficult for minorities and other marginalized groups to challenge this location of citizenship values in a universalized 'citizen' – bourgeois or socialist. Nationalist elites took this universalized (male) citizen as both the agent and target of policies of development agendas, while women remained very much targets and not agents. As we shall see in the next chapter, the combination of the particularities of the post-colonial nation-states and this universalized ideological framing of women was a powerful one in the marginalization of women in development.

Conclusion

It is perhaps for this reason that increasingly women and feminist scholars have become convinced that the nationalist project is incompatible with feminism (Moghadam 1994).[26] This growing distance, however, did not, and does not, address the painful issue of women's political participation. Disengagement from nationalist movements also has costs. The struggles to shift the meanings of the nation and nationalism have been only partially successful – as much because of the struggles over these meanings within and outside the women's movements themselves as the contexts in which questions about the form of nationalism are raised. In no contemporary nationalist movements for sovereignty do we find the 'mainstream' programme of national development being systematically gendered in its programme. The story of nationalism is thus not an entirely happy one for women. In the first phase of nationalist struggles against colonialism, however, women did find a place in the public arena, which, in its popular imagery as well as its wide participation, was unique. And access to this space allowed the further development of feminism which has ironically challenged nationalism and perhaps made it more incompatible with women's concerns for equality.

2 | Women and the post-colonial state[1]

In 1991/92 forty women in New Delhi engaged in a dispute with the metropolitan authorities about their right to trade from a pavement from which they had been working for the last five years. As the dispute progressed, these women came into contact with different agencies of the state and law. This chapter analyses the struggle and negotiations of these women and poses questions about the relationship of Indian women to post-colonial state formations. The examination of the struggle of these women focuses on several different agents/actors, and the space(s) that they occupy within the Indian political context – the individual women, and the group identity that they form during their struggle, the municipal corporation of Delhi, the Supreme Court and the judicial committee instituted by it to deal with the question of the women's occupancy and trading rights, and the individual 'outsiders' who impact upon this struggle and its outcome. It argues that the relationship between these women and the Indian state is a fraught and particular one. The forms of oppression and the opportunities for struggle that women have endured and availed themselves of are linked to the processes of state formation that the country has gone and is going through. These processes have been complex, multilayered and untidy, as have been the evolving discourses and struggles of Indian women.

The claim that I make for this study is that the case of these Gujarati women street traders demonstrates not only the particular fractured complexity of a post-colonial state formation such as India's, but also the multiplicity of the strategies of struggle needed by women to confront and/or use state fractions in their own interests. I argue that the class as well as the gender positioning of these women means that they operate, economically and politically, in the interstices of the system, only occasionally moving on to the ground of legal arrangements. Further, as we follow the course of this particular struggle we are faced by the importance of state structures and the targeting of these through struggle in the lives of these women, while at the same time becoming aware of the limitations of strategies directed only at state organizations. I conclude by arguing for an understanding of the Indian state formation informed by issues of a relative autonomy of state fractions from the existing social relations and infrastructural capacity of the state on the one hand, and the state's embeddedness in social relations and the consequences of such embeddedness for women on the other. Such an approach, derived from analysis of a particular struggle, also points to the potential for a strategy for struggle that is both 'in and against' the state. The chapter is divided into two sections. The first is an analysis of the struggle of the Gujarati women street traders in New Delhi. The second is an analysis of the struggle in the context of the role of legal institutions, in particular the Supreme Court of India and its philosophy of 'soft legalism'.

Women in struggle

Exoticism and profit Perhaps the most well-known handicrafts from India come from the north-western state of Gujarat. Mirror work, *bandini* (tie-and-dye) and hand-block prints are today available in most parts of the world. The colours are striking and the hand-done embroidery exquisite. These materials have earned the Indian state millions in much-needed hard currency, and have in themselves become tourist attractions, whether displayed in handicrafts museums or in shops and emporia. One of the most accessible displays of these handicrafts in New Delhi is on Janpath Lane. Janpath is one of the premier shopping areas in Delhi, and is particularly well known for handicrafts from all parts of India. Janpath Lane runs off this road. It has no public lighting, and was not used very much at all until about forty Gujarati women were relocated there by the New Delhi Municipal Corporation (NDMC) five years ago. 'We have kept the ethnic trade going in Delhi,' said Ratan, one of the women traders on Janpath Lane. 'The foreigners spend so much money here. The government has benefited from our trade, but has given us nothing in return. We want the government to at least let us put up some sort of shelter. Our wares get wet in the rain. But they are not bothered.'

These women come from the *banjara* (gypsy) community of Gujarat. There are more than 1,800,000 *banjaras* in India. They are low caste and are not integrated into the Hindu communities in their villages. 'They are so low in caste that they are not even registered as having any caste; they can't even draw water from the village wells,' said Livleen Sharma, a social worker who worked with the Gujarati women on Janpath Lane. Traditionally the *banjaras* travelled from one part of the state to another, grazing their animals, working as ironsmiths, and undertaking petty trading to survive. Regarded with suspicion whereever they went, these people have remained marginalized in the Indian society and economy, despite the changing nature of their economic activities over a period of time. They are not considered politically relevant because they do not form a settled community to be wooed by politicians for votes. The *banjaras*, therefore, cannot be easily characterized in terms of class, caste or even religion. The best description that we can give them is a situational one – they are the subaltern (Guha 1982–87).

In the last two decades there has been a gradual exoticization of these peoples in order to create an image of/for India as the home of beautiful handicrafts. In all international and national exhibitions their crafts are prominently displayed. At all government-sponsored cultural functions the *banjara* men and women are asked to perform their traditional dances. Their colourful clothes and beautiful jewellery lend themselves easily to creating an exotic appeal. This exoticization has been a deliberate policy which has reaped rich rewards for the Indian state. Handicrafts earn the Indian government more in exports than any other commodity, and the growth of this sector since 1970 has been remarkable. (Handicrafts as an export category include pearls and jewellery, which are the major earners, but more traditional crafts like embroidery or patchwork form a considerable proportion of India's export earnings.) 'During 1989–90, handicrafts exported were of the order of Rupees 6,285 crores [£1,256 million] ...' (Dutt and Sundaram 1991: 627).

Hawking in the city Street trading (or hawking as it is called in India) has been a tradition among the *banjaras*. What is distinctive among the *banjara* traders is that it is the women who do the actual selling of goods on the street, while the men act as suppliers, travelling to their villages to collect materials for sale. As a result the women are extremely articulate and self-confident. 'These are ambitious women. They come from women oriented clans that believe in Durga and Kali.[2] They are very aggressive saleswomen which is why they posed a threat to other traders in the area,' said Sharma. Most have grown up on the streets of Delhi helping their mothers in the trade. They know the market, the constraints and the areas of opportunity in the city – 'We have been doing this work for the last twenty years,' said Ratan, 'and we want to continue this way.' Because of their success, these are not poor women. They have been able to build a significant clientele for themselves among both local and foreign buyers. This is not to say that all *banjara* women in India, even in big cities, are in such a happy economic position. The vast majority lead a precarious existence; for most there is no hope of earning more than the minimum to support themselves and their families. Within Delhi's parameters, Janpath Lane is unique in its concentration of *banjara* women and their crafts. This allows these women not only to sell their own goods, but to sell the goods of other women of this community who have not been able to secure a settled area to sell from. The importance of the right to trade from this particular place is therefore very great for these women.

Forty women were involved in the court case that is the subject of this study. Before they were 'relocated' on Janpath Lane they used to sit on the pavement outside the Imperial Hotel on Janpath itself. They had traded from there for more than ten years, until the hotel administration put enough pressure on the NDMC to get them removed. The women are convinced that this was because they were competition for the hotel's very expensive shops. In 1989 these forty-odd women were 'given notice to quit' from their place outside the hotel and moved ('dumped', said one) to Janpath Lane. 'There was no lighting here (there still isn't, as you can see) and it was absolutely *sunsan* [quiet] on this road. This is not a main road, but it soon began to prosper once we started trading from here,' said Radha. Very soon the lane came to be known as a centre for Gujarati handicrafts that were authentic and affordable. Foreign tourists began to arrive, and trade prospered. The Gujarati women's aggressive but engaging style of selling goods – many speak enough English, German and French to be able to negotiate a price with foreign customers – meant more profit for them, but also brought them into conflict with other traders on Janpath.

These traders have regular (*pucca*) shops from where to trade, and more capital to invest than their competitors on Janpath Lane. As they began to feel the pinch of losing their customers to the women on the Janpath Lane pavement, they began to put pressure on the NDMC officials to 'do something about this situation'. In 1991 matters came to a head, and the Gujarati women were served notice to quit yet again. The NDMC decided it was going to build a public lavatory on the pavement. The women decided that they had no other option left to them but to fight for their right to sell from the pavement of Janpath Lane.

A case of rights The Gujarati women trading from Janpath Lane decided to approach the Thareja Committee, which had been set up in 1989 by the Supreme Court of India to look into claims of trading rights by large numbers of pavement hawkers. In a landmark case, *Sodan Singh and others* vs. *NDMC and others*, it was argued by the petitioners that their fundamental rights under Articles 14, 19(1)(g) and/or 21 of the Indian constitution to equal protection (with other traders), freedom to practise any profession or to carry on any occupation, trade or business, and protection of life and personal liberty had been violated by the NDMC in not allowing them to trade from the pavements within its jurisdiction. The NDMC contended, on the other hand, that the 'grant of exclusive right to occupy any part of the road amounts to the negation of the Common Law theory of dedication of a road for public use' (Supreme Court of India 1989). In its judgment the Supreme Court concluded that 'The petitioners do have the fundamental right to carry on a trade or business of their choice, but not to do so on a particular place' (ibid.: 18). It rejected the right-to-life plea of the petitioners. The court recommended that 'detailed necessary provisions, dealing with all relevant aspects, and capable of solving the problems arising in the situation in a fair and equitable manner should be made' (ibid.: 22). The NDMC was instructed to draw up clear guidelines and procedures according to which pavement traders could be dealt with. This was done via Resolution 28 of the NDMC. A one-person committee headed by Additional District Judge G. P. Thareja was appointed by the Supreme Court to 'examine the claims made by the squatters [pavement traders] in the light of the said scheme and the decision [of the Supreme Court], and identify street pavements in different areas where street hawking could be regulated without being a hindrance to other users' (Supreme Court of India 1992: 10).

The key features of NDMC Resolution 28 affecting the *banjara* women of Janpath Lane directly were:

1 'The squatters squatting since between 1981 to 1987 shall be considered for allotment for a *tehbazari* [rent for business premises] site subject to availability of vacant space.' This meant that the principle of seniority was introduced: given the scarcity of sites, the longer a trader had traded the greater her priority.
2 'The eligibility of a squatter shall be determined by documents such as receipts issued by the NDMC, *challans* [receipts for fines paid] by Police etc.' This caused particular problems for the women. Not all had the requisite documentation.
3 'Not more than one member of the family, as defined by the NDMC, will be eligible for benefit under the Scheme' (ibid.: 10, 11).

Examining the claims of the hundreds of squatters was a time-consuming process. The committee therefore issued directions on 23 February 1990 to the effect that until the cases were decided the petitioners should be 'permitted to hawk in the area where they claim to be carrying on the operation without a right to either sit down with or without their merchandise to be sold on the pavements in front of licensed shops or on the pavements as such but as soon as the shops close down in the evening it shall be open to them to settle down with their goods and squat on the pavements ...' (ibid.: 12).

While all these legal and procedural issues were being aired, the *banjara* women on Janpath Lane continued to trade. They were harassed regularly by the NDMC officials and the local police, *challan*ed (fined), but allowed to work. Corruption is part of the network of administration, and petty corruption is endemic. Police routinely take what is called *hafta* (literally 'week', i.e. a weekly payment/bribe) from traders of all descriptions and in turn allow them to operate illegally. Though the women on Janpath Lane did not admit to giving any bribes to the police, both Livleen Sharma and Judge Thareja said that they did. Indeed, the Supreme Court in its judgment quoted above made reference to the fact that 'corruption at a large scale was rampant and huge amounts of money were being realised illegally by some of the servants of the Municipalities from the poor hawkers' (Supreme Court of India 1989: 22).

In November 1991, however, things came to a head when the demands of the NDMC officials became too great for the women to meet. They were in no position to compete with the shop owners on Janpath, who could afford to pay far greater amounts to officials and police. Diwali is one of the most important Hindu festivals in India, and a time when trade is generally brisk. Just before Diwali in November 1991 the Gujarati women were ordered to cease trading. But these women decided not to give up. A rather unusual protest 'strike' followed.

The strike 'We decided we will not move from here,' Ratan said. 'It is the NDMC who put us there so why should we move? They never gave us anything in writing, but always ask for written proof from us. We have been paying *challans* of Rs200–250 every time they decided to trouble us, two or three times a week, and every time they also take away one or two "pieces" of work that we sell. That's another Rs100–200 gone.' The women knew that if they vacated the pavement on Janpath Lane they would never return to trade from there. Others, who could afford to pay more, would be granted the right to sell from there. They also knew that shopkeepers from Janpath wanted to expand their shops on to Janpath Lane. 'For four months we didn't move from this pavement.' Amma takes up the story. 'We could not trade, but we didn't move. We slept here, cooked here, our men also used to come and stay here with us.' They suffered not only the bitter cold of November nights in Delhi, but also the increasing impatience of their families. 'For twenty to twenty-five days we [the women] slept here,' said Krishna. 'After that our men started getting irritated with us. They found it difficult to look after children. The children missed us too. So our men took over from us for the night. We used to go back, feed the children, cook for ourselves for the next day, and be back on the pavement at eight in the morning after sending the children off to school.' During the day they kept vigil on the pavement. But as the strike wore on, together with the harassment, they decided to approach the politicians and to raise the profile of their struggle.

'First we went to the NDMC chief Ramesh Chandra, but he refused to listen to us,' said Ratan. Indeed, even after Judge Thareja decided in favour of the Gujarati women, Ramesh Chandra said, 'I will knock [at] the door of the Supreme Court if they are permitted to legally occupy the pavement' (*The Pioneer*, 2 October 1992: 2). The women's defiance in the face of NDMC harassment made them particularly vulnerable to the anger of the local bureaucrats. 'When we got no *sunwai* [hearing] from Chandra, we decided that we must approach the national politicians. We went to prominent Delhi MPs – Saajan Kuman, Gulam Navi Azad, Jagdish Tytler, and the Governor General of Delhi, M. M. Jacob, and many others whose names we don't remember. We are not educated, you see,' Krishna adds. 'We decided the night before where we would go. We used to gather here at eight a.m., hire a "tempo" [small truck], and start off. We never made an appointment; just reached the home or the office of the MP we had decided upon for the day, and waited for them to see us. Some did, others didn't. Some even signed a petition for us,' Krishna concludes. 'Our case was raised in the parliament after we spoke to an MP from Gujarat,' says Amma. 'We didn't go to any women MPs', adds Ratan, 'because we didn't know of any. We weren't very systematic about meeting politicians.' During this period no social or political organization helped these women out. The only other person who helped the women was Livleen Sharma, an influential person in Delhi, but in her individual capacity. 'Livleen Sharma used to buy fabrics from us. That is how we got to know her. When we started our struggle she got involved ... she came to us, we didn't go to her ... she came to ask after us,' says Ratan.

The flashpoint came in March 1992 when 'the NDMC ... swooped down on them and dug up the entire pavement as part of the anti-encroachment drive. A railing was put up, an NDMC van put on vigil and the women denied permission to sell their handicrafts ... ' (*The Pioneer*, 2 October 1992: 2). This was obviously in contravention of the order made by the Thareja Committee in February 1990. A contingent of policewomen was sent to enforce the order. 'Lady police came here. They beat us, and locked us up. We were locked up in the police station at ten a.m. and released only at midnight. We came straight back here,' said Krishna. By this time, however, the story of the struggle of these women was in the national newspapers. 'Usha Rai of the *Indian Express* came to talk to us and wrote very good articles about our plight. People began to take an interest in our case.' Soon after this the women were allowed to return to the pavement by the NDMC and were selling their goods again. This was not just because of the high profile that the women had been able to generate for their case; there were also other, more cynical reasons for the NDMC allowing them back. In June there was to be a by-election in Delhi, and continuing agitation by these women, who were now gaining support from the media, would not go down well with the local people (*The Pioneer*, 2 October 1992). One phase of the struggle was over, but the legal decision about their standing on Janpath Lane itself still had to be taken by the Thareja Committee.

For this, in accordance with Resolution 28 of the NDMC and the Supreme Court directive discussed above, the women from Janpath Lane had to prove that they had been trading from there since 1985. The judge also made surprise visits to the site in order to establish that the petitioners were none other that the traders present at the site in question. As a report of the Supreme Court on the work of the committee pointed out, the petitioners felt that the burden of proof they were asked to carry was 'too strict and resulted in injustice even to genuine claimants'. The committee overlooked the fact that 'most of the pavement-hawkers were poor and illiterate persons who could not be expected to have maintained proper records of receipts, *challans*, etc. issued by the police or other local authorities to support their claims' (Supreme Court of India 1992: 13). This was important because of the high levels of corruption operating with respect to street trading. For example, seventeen traders contended that they could not provide any written proof to the Thareja Committee because they had never been *challan*ed. They 'were under the patronage of one Arjan Das, a local politician, and hence they were never disturbed by the police or by any other authority' (ibid.: 16). The Gujarati women on Janpath Lane did not have such powerful patrons.

The view from the judges' bench was different. The Thareja Committee's view was that 'minimum proof as would enable the Committee to weed out bogus claims from genuine ones had to be insisted upon to maintain credibility in regard to the scrutiny' (ibid.: 15). The strictness with which the committee was enforcing the minimum-proof principle can be seen from the fact that out of the 440 claims initially scrutinized by the committee it cleared only 224. This prompted the Supreme Court to observe that 'we are dealing with the question of livelihood and sur-vival of a large number of families', and 'we do not think we would not be justified if we adopt a compassionate approach so as to ensure that genuine squatters/hawkers are not denied their daily bread at the altar of technicalities while at the same time ensuring that those who are out to ... abuse the process of law do not succeed' (ibid.: 18–19). The court therefore ordered the Thareja Committee to 'review the cases of those claimants whose claims have been rejected for non-compliance of [*sic*] the standard of proof laid down by Resolution 28 ...' (ibid.: 19). The women on Janpath Lane also benefited from this order. In September 1992 twenty-two women were given *tehbazari* rights, thus regularizing their position on the pavement. It was only in March 1993 that another twelve women were granted a place.

Out of the forty women involved, only six have failed to secure *teh-bazari* rights because they were unable to provide the required receipts. 'We don't know why we kept these receipts. People told us to. I have receipts since 1976,' said Amma. 'I keep everything that is written; all receipts. All bills, children's school receipts, *challan*s, prescriptions. It might come in handy. I have a huge pile of *parchis* [notepaper]. It took me a long time to get the *challan* receipts sorted, but I got them all in the end.' Not everyone was so aware of the power of the written word when confronting bureaucracies. The six who have been excluded from trading from Janpath Lane are among those who did not keep their receipts. They were bitter about the Thareja Committee. 'Just because we haven't got all the receipts why should we not be allowed to trade from here? All the other women here can vouch for us. Why doesn't Thareja accept their *gawahi* [evidence]?' said Paro. There was also the question of seniority. Many felt that they had lost an opportunity to be eligible for a kiosk under Resolution 28 of the NDMC because of missing receipts. 'We trade here every year, in all seasons. Sometimes we have to go back to our villages to deliver babies, or if the children or our elders are sick. Many have lost their seniority this way. Many who have been working for the last twenty years were counted only since 1986 since when they could produce regular receipts,' said Krishna.

Supporters and supports The struggle of the Janpath Lane women was an important one in their lives, and for their survival. It was important that they struggled and that they won. As their testimony makes clear, they did not seek to establish links outside their own group. Nor, it seems, did groups like SEWA (Self-Employed Women's Association) that are very active in mobilizing self-employed women across India offer any help or support to these women. The fact that these women were traders and not engaged in any production of goods, and could be seen as exploiting other women from whom they bought the handicrafts they sold, could be one reason why women's organizations kept away from the Gujarati trader women on Janpath. As a result, their strategies were ad hoc, and their decisions taken by consultation among themselves. The only outsiders who touched upon their struggle in any significant way were Livleen Sharma and Judge Thareja. The inclusion of both these actors in this narrative is important, for different reasons. Both Sharma and Thareja represent different and powerful elites in Indian society. Their support for the Janpath Lane women had different sources and forms, but was important for the final outcome of the struggle of the forty Gujarati women. This, of course, does not take away from the struggle itself, but points to the variables that can affect the lives of the less privileged; variables that are not linked to organizations or institutions, which are often random though critical. Their inclusion in the story of the struggle of the Gujarati women underscores the systemic frailty of the Indian politico-legal system, where random interventions by exceptional individuals rather than an effective machinery of implementation of state policies become critical to the outcome of the struggle (a point I develop further in the discussion in the next section).

Livleen Sharma is a very articulate and charismatic person. 'I do not know where I was born ... since I was a child I roamed from place to place in Rajasthan and Gujarat. I have no memory of my parents. I only remember that I wanted to better myself,' she recalled. Sharma considers herself therefore as a *banjara* and identifies with the *banjara* people. Her rather chequered life has included a stint as a fashion model in France, marriage to a French count, a divorce, and remarriage to an upper-caste and wealthy Brahmin. 'But my roots were calling me. I knew something was missing in my life. I had to come back,' she said. After a dramatic encounter with a *banjara* woman on the road to Jaipur in Rajasthan, Sharma decided that she would dedicate her life to improving the lot of these, 'her' people. 'Everything that I am wearing is given to me by them,' she said, pointing to the very traditional *banjara* jewellery and clothes in which she always dresses. 'I promised never to leave my home without wearing these.' Sharma is influential in her individual capacity. 'I am against organizations. I think they exploit those they purport to represent. I want my people to organize themselves.' She has the support of her wealthy husband. 'Sonny has supported me in everything I do' – which is very important if she is to use and build upon the influence that her marriage ties can give her. 'If I was not what I am I would have been treated very badly. The law is blind towards the poor.' Once she decided to support the women in Janpath, they had won a powerful ally.

'I have to meet my Maker soon. How can I show him my face if I cannot do my duty by the poor of this country?' Judge Thareja is a deeply religious man. His language is steeped in religious metaphor. He speaks as much of law and legality as of morals and morality. There is a sense of personal sympathy for the poor which allows him to take decisions that might seem rather eccentric to another lawyer. He was quite aware of the NDMC harassment of the women on Janpath Lane, and of the bribes that its officials took. He knew that top NDMC officials were asking bribes of five to six lakh rupees (£12,000) for granting trading rights on Janpath Lane, and that the women there could not possibly afford this while the shopkeepers on Janpath could. He also said that these women themselves would sell off their *tehbazari* rights to others as soon as they could. 'But I feel that it is better for them to get one or two lakh rupees [£2,000–4,000] than corrupt officials pocketing five to six lakhs.' A sense of moral justice compelled him, he said, to favour those who have actually developed the commercial potential of Janpath Lane rather than speculators who have risked nothing and would simply cash in on the labour and enterprise of others. He was also convinced that fate had favoured the women on Janpath Lane in his appointment to the Supreme Court-established judicial committee to look into the question of street trading in Delhi. 'It was their good fate that I was appointed. They must have done good *karma* [deeds] in their previous lives.' Without his faith he could not have withstood the financial and political pressures that are part of the legal and political system. If he had not been occupying a chair on the committee, he suggested, the women would not have had a sympathetic and honest hearing.

The story of the struggle of the Janpath trader women can be an instructive one in understanding the relations between women and state institutions in India. In the next section I want to examine the role that the Supreme Court played in this case, how it positioned itself vis-à-vis the other fractions of the state, and whether its philosophy of 'soft legalism' allows it to be more responsive to certain struggles, on what basis and to what extent.

Negotiating boundaries

What becomes evident when we read the narratives of the Gujarati women is that they are highly articulate, and to a great extent aware of the context in which they live and earn their livelihoods. They are not reactive or passive, but always conscious of the huge power of the state, as exercised in their lives by the petty officials of the NDMC. That power is backed by laws, by the enforcers of laws, and by violence. They have experienced the various faces of state and survived, and continue to struggle to guard their existing gains and repair their losses. The Indian state is for them a crucial network of power relations, which translate into different levels of organization, and they can ill afford to ignore the boundaries that it draws around them. Transgression of these boundaries is a different question, however. Transgression involves knowing the boundaries that are to be pushed. The knowledge of these boundaries comes in different ways to people of different classes, races and cultures. At times boundaries become visible only in the process of transgressing them, whether the transgressor saw their actions as a transgression or as not forming a critical part of the story. Transgression of boundaries also involves countering strategies that are multilayered. Acquiescence and opposition, anger and conciliation, idealism and pragmatism are all interwoven in a complex pattern of interaction with the state. In the story of the Janpath Lane women we see all these strategies played out.

One of the most significant contributions of post-structuralist argument to the theorizing of the state has been its insistence that there is no unity that we can point to as the state. What we have been used to calling the state can be regarded only as a network of power relations existing in cooperation and also in tension. The study of the functioning of the various agencies of power in operation in the case that we discussed above illustrates the validity of the post-structuralist approach to the state. Precisely because of this fluidity and dispersal of power, however, we cannot regard the 'touch' of the state as universally suspect and instrumental in structuring women's lives. We cannot simply argue, as many radical feminists have done, for example, that an appeal to the state for protection 'involves seeking protection against men from masculinist institutions ...' (Brown 1992: 9; see also Kapur and Cossman 1993). This is not only because one of the implications of the post-structuralist arguments about the dispersal of power is the acknowledgement of the varied forms that power takes and the uses to which it is and can be put. If we add to this reading of power relations our understanding of the complexity of the civil society, taking simply an 'against the state' position becomes positively dangerous. The civil society is as deeply masculinist as the infrastructure of state relations. Women cannot look to one to oppose the other. Both spaces – of informal and formalized networks of power – are imbued with masculinist discourses (see Pateman 1989); neither is 'uncoerced', however different the forms and mechanisms of coercion.

Political rhetoric and legitimacy Through our study of the Gujarati women we can witness the unfolding character of the state. In their dealings with people ranging from the officials of the NDMC to the judges of the Supreme Court of India, these women slowly became aware of the power of the state in its different forms as they carried on their struggle. The different roles played by the Supreme Court and the NDMC, the police and the Thareja Committee in this case indicate both the various organizational forms and the discourses of the state. The importance of the rhetoric of 'socialism' and the welfare state in India, for example (embodied in its constitution in the Preamble, the Directive Principles of State Policy and the First Five Year Plan), allows the Supreme Court to take positions on this case that it might otherwise not have taken. In his classic study of the Indian state, Anupam Sen has argued that a feature of the Indian state that indicated its relative autonomy from social classes was its ability to promote and develop a cultural environment hostile to private capital and conducive to state capital (1982: 160). Sen's analysis, however, falls short of acknowledging the relative autonomy of the political. The rhetoric of socialism is cast as a legitimizing instrument in the hands of the state. Its potential to be used by oppositional groups as a means of holding the state organizations accountable, and of delegitimizing state fractions, is not analysed. The importance of this rhetoric has been seen by us in the approach that the Supreme Court took towards the hawkers. In the 1989 judgment the Supreme Court noted: 'We as a Court in a welfare state do realise the hardship to which many of the petitioners may be exposed if they are prevented from carrying on their business ... We hope and trust that in administering the laws in force the authorities will keep in view humane considerations' (Supreme Court of India 1989: 25). The belief that 'social justice must inform a welfare state' is thus regarded seriously by many senior legal professionals in India, as is the characterization of the Indian state as a welfare state despite the lack of resources that severely constraints its welfare functions.

Taking the relative autonomy of the political seriously would also allow an examination of the democratic processes and functioning in the country for the last forty-seven years. To dismiss this feature of the Indian political system as a 'charade', as Alavi did (1972: 63), and many others subscribing to the post-colonial state analysis continue to do, is to fail to see how important this very uneven, pitted and sometimes dangerous political terrain is for mobilization of opposition by various groups, including women. The fact that an important parliamentary by-election in Delhi was approaching at the time that the women traders went on strike was significant. Public interest in state functioning was high at the time, and allowed the women to make their campaign more visible than they otherwise might have. In the context of a non-democratic state formation, the struggle might not have had access to the media and local politicians at all.

Soft legalism and legal intervention In asking the Thareja Committee to reconsider rejected cases compassionately, to take into account the economic and social position of the petitioners, the court moved beyond a purely 'legal' position. This softening of legal interpretation by taking into account the socio-economic positionings of the litigants on the one hand, and the role of a welfare state on the other, is what I would call 'soft legalism' (see also Anthony 1993). Indeed, since the 1980s the Supreme Court in India has often taken a social interventionist position in its judgments. The court has increasingly taken the view that 'in a developing society judicial activism is essential for participative justice. Justices are the constitutional invigilators and reformers [who] bring the rule of law closer to the rule of life' (P. N. Singh, 1981/82, in Cooper 1993: 6). In this spirit the Indian Supreme Court, through a group of radical judges, has stated that 'constitutional interpretation fundamentally differs, almost mystically, from statutory interpretation' (ibid.: 8). In a landmark case *People's Union for Democratic Rights* vs. *Union of India*, 1978, the Supreme Court allowed the petitioners to charge the government of India for failing to uphold the fundamental rights of its citizens. The judgment established the precedent of interpreting the fundamental rights of Indian citizens in a more flexible way. A leading exponent of this 'soft legalism', called Public Interest Litigation in India, Justice Bhagwati, urged that the constitution 'must be interpreted creatively and imaginatively with a view to advancing the constitutional values and spelling out and strengthening the basic human rights of the large masses of people in the country ...' (ibid.). 'Soft legalism' also indicates a certain autonomy for various state fractions from 'peak interest groups' in Indian society. It is clear from the judgment in the *Sodan Singh* case that the street traders in Delhi, and therefore also the women on Janpath Lane, benefited enormously from this approach of the Supreme Court to the constitution and the rights of Indian citizens.

The gendered nature of this 'soft legalism', however, cannot be disregarded. Indeed, it has been argued that where women are concerned, 'with some notable exceptions, the judicial approach to the equality guarantees of the Constitution [of India] is informed by a problematic approach to both equality, and gender difference' (Kapur and Cossman 1993: 1). This gendering of the Supreme Court's 'soft legalism' can be explained by what Johnson, and before him Karl Polanyi, called the embeddedness of the state. The state capacity literature (Johnson 1982) regards 'embeddedness' as a characteristic of 'strong' states as it is able to harness 'peak interest groups' in society to the purposes of economic development; it does not reflect on the consequences of this embeddedness on marginal, less powerful or weak social groups. If state fractions are embedded in interest groups, they are also vulnerable to infiltration by these groups and by the discourses of dominant interests in society (see below, and Kandiyoti 1991). Further, this 'embeddedness' is not a neat fit – the levels of embeddedness may vary for differing state fractions functioning in varied social and political contexts. I would argue that, though gendered in its interpretation of the laws of the country, the Supreme Court's 'soft legalism' approach makes a difference in particular cases to women's lives, and also sets precedents for future judgments.

Infrastructural power and political capacity While 'soft legalism' focuses on legal interpretation and decisions, however, it tells us little about the capacity of the state to implement these decisions. Michael Mann has made the distinction between the 'despotic and infrastructural power' of the state. The former denotes the power of state elites with little 'institutionalised negotiation with civil society groups', while 'infrastructural power' presumes the ability of the state to 'penetrate and centrally co-ordinate the activities of civil society through its own infrastructure' (Mann 1984: 190, 188). This distinction is important, to emphasize that there exists no direct, linear correlation between 'state autonomy' and 'state capacity' (Onis 1991: 123). The first will not automatically lead to the other. The 'soft legalism' of the Indian Supreme Court, therefore, faces considerable constraints from the lack of political and economic resources that go into building a stable infrastructural power. This undermines its capacity to ensure the implementation of its decisions, posing a threat to its legitimacy.

In the case of the Gujarati women both the welfare state rhetoric of judicial authorities and the coercive and arbitrary power of the local police and administration were evident, pointing to the tensions within/ between state fractions. The ability of state organizations to enforce their laws and regulations in this case (as in others) was crucial. As we saw in our discussion of state capacity above, where the 'infrastructural power' of the state organizations is weak, the implementation of directives can become hostage to random factors. As we have seen in the Janpath Lane case, the implementation of Supreme Court directives could be read to be contingent upon the personal attributes of enforcers rather than the capacity of state institutions to ensure the implementation of legal judgments. Judge Thareja quite clearly believes that his occupation of the chair of the judicial committee set up by the Supreme Court was crucial to both the procedure that followed and the decision arrived at in the case of the Janpath Lane women.

The Indian state organizations are also largely unchecked at local levels in terms of the scale of the violence they operate against the people. The women's movement in India, for example, is rooted in women's opposition to police brutality (Spivak 1987) in the 1970s. Rape, murder and beatings in police custody continue to be a common feature of state operation, especially in rural areas. At the present time, depending upon their race, class and caste situation, most Third World women have fewer resources to withstand the violations of state fractions. The lack of education, economic vulnerability, weak infrastructural social support and the unavailability of information leave women in these countries more dependent upon their own resources, which in themselves are meagre. These also determine to a large extent the options that women have, and think they have, available to them in their dealings with state organizations.

Further, 'weak' state capacity does not allow the state organizations to effectively regulate themselves internally, adversely affecting not only implementation of policies, but also the relationship between citizens and state fractions. We have already spoken of the high level of corruption among the Delhi metropolitan bureaucracy. Like that of many other 'weak' states, the Indian administrative bureaucracy is generally too 'flabby' to be effective and too huge to be controlled. As a result corruption becomes an independent variable in the functioning of the Indian state organizations, further subverting the implementation of policy. This can be partly explained by institutional factors such as the size of the bureaucracy, or the effectiveness of controls put in place by the political executive, and partly by the particularity of the state organizations' 'embeddedness' in civil society (Lie 1991: 220). While linked to the question of resources and state capacity, corruption as a feature of state functioning in India is often taken for granted or overlooked as an independent factor in the state–citizen relationship, and as a mobilizing feature for oppositional groups. Women, of course, are affected in different ways to men; the 'favours' asked for are not just financial, but can also be sexual. The fact that the Janpath Lane women could not afford to pay the officials of the NDMC bribes that were being offered them by the shopkeepers of Janpath adversely affected their bargaining position. It is on this question of police corruption and violence, however, that the 'soft legalism' of the Supreme Court has been much in evidence through the late 1980s, with the recent judgment imprisoning two police officers for the beating of prisoners the latest in a series of cases of police brutality that the Supreme Court has dealt with. We can see here the relative autonomy of various state fractions and discover how these might emphasize different aspects of political rhetoric and administrative functioning, at times creating severe tensions within the system which can potentially be taken advantage of by those struggling against aspects of state policy.

Looking to the state enforcement agencies to implement the decision of the Supreme Court could not therefore be the only way open to the women. The tension between the metropolitan authorities and the police on the one hand, and the Thareja Committee and the Supreme Court on the other, on the substantive issues at stake in this case was evident (see above). Protest had to be organized in tandem with petitioning the courts, and as their strike showed, support had to be mobilized outside the institutions and corridors of state power.

Visibility as strategy This they did by first making themselves visible in the public political arena by refusing to leave the pavement from which they traded. In doing so they forced the coercive arm of the state – the police – to become visible too, thus exposing it to public scrutiny. When the women were lathi-charged (baton-charged) and arrested, the media took up the story. The support offered the Janpath Lane women by a socially prominent person like Livleen Sharma, itself in part the result of increasing public interest in their plight, also strengthened their case outside the courtroom of Judge Thareja. It now became impossible for the legislative institution of the state to ignore what was happening. The fact that the member of parliament from Gujarat raised a question in parliament on their behalf is indicative of this, as is the fact that some of the randomly approached influential Delhi MPs also signed their petition, supporting their case against the NDMC.

The functioning of a party political system can, however, be a double-edged sword. On the one hand, it means that groups can at particular moments mobilize the support of one party against the other, creating for themselves strategic spaces that they might not otherwise have had, and on the other the need to mobilize votes to legitimize governance means that the parties and state institutions become complicit in not challenging the socio-economic relations that are counter to their own rhetoric. Caste, religion and gender relations are particularly sensitive socio-economic issues, as are those related to property and redistribution of wealth. The state organzations' embeddedness in civil society also reinforces this complicity.

Civil society is not an uncomplicated 'space of uncoerced human association and ... of relational networks – formed for the sake of family, faith, interest and ideology – that fill this space' (Walzer 1992: 89). The civil society is a deeply fraught space with hidden and explicit dangers lurking in the garb of national, religious and ethnic identities as fashioned by male-directed movements of various kinds (see Rai 1994). In this context, the 'embeddedness' of the state fractions in the civil society cannot be regarded in the positive light in which many developmental economists see it (see, for example, Charlton and Donald 1992: 7). For women the reinforcing of bureaucratic capacity by social norms can be a terrifying combination threatening any attempt to change their lived reality. In this context, however, the fractured nature of the state becomes important.

What we begin to piece together from our study of the struggle of the women on Janpath Lane, as far as the debate about women and 'the state' is concerned, is a highly complex picture. Indian post-colonial state formation can be seen in this case as fractured, with its different factions acting as oppressors, and also resources/supporters in these women's struggles to save their livelihoods. In conclusion I would argue that the relationship between theory and practice has to be foregrounded to be able to address the question of the political role that women can and need to play in the arena of state–citizen interaction.

Conclusion: in and against the state?

One of the most startling differences between the women in European liberal welfare states and those in India and most of the Third World is the extent to which they are directly 'touched' by the regulatory power of state organizations. In India the state organization is unable to provide the kind of safety network that the European liberal state does with its welfare provision, which depends greatly on social monitoring. Both upper-class Indian women and those of the lower classes do not fall within the ambit of state functioning. In health, education, childcare and employment the upper-class women have traditionally depended on the private sector, and so too the poorest women, the first group because of access to private, non-state resources, the second because the state can provide them with very little support.

Further, Indian women do not become aware of many areas of legislation and action. The dissemination of information about new legislation is extremely varied and patchy. Illiteracy and exclusionary social practices further exacerbate this isolation from the processes of state organizations. The lack of political will to disturb traditional family values is one manifestation of the 'weak' patriarchal state formations. Political expediency overrules the rhetoric of social justice fairly easily when state organizations perceive a threat to their continuance. Further, the lack of the infrastructural power of state organizations means that laws are altogether ignored in many parts of the country. So even though Indian women have constitutional rights of inheritance, divorce and maintenance, for example, the enforcement of these rights is at best patchy.

For most women in India, as we have discussed above, state institutions figure only marginally in their lives. They loom large only when women transgress the boundaries set by these institutions in various areas of public and private life over which they have jurisdiction. Therefore, for the majority of women the issue is not whether or not to approach state fractions; it is they themselves who are approached by state organizations, in many instances in a violent way. In that context, can one argue that 'to be "protected" by the very power whose violation one fears perpetuates the specific modality of dependence and powerlessness marking much of women's experience across widely diverse cultures and epochs'? (Brown 1992: 9) In the face of the exercise of violent state power, the 'protection' given by a court order prohibiting that violence can mean the difference between life and death to individual women (Williams 1991).

The question surely is not one of simply 'seeking protection', but of fighting state violence. The forms that this struggle might take may vary from country to country, state formation to state formation. But to focus simply on the regulating, structuring, constraining power of state institutions and to overlook the struggle against all these is to sell short the daily lives of millions of women. Worse, it is the road to inaction and nihilism. We can see from our brief study of the struggle of the women on Janpath Lane that without theorizing about state power they were quite aware of not only the huge importance state institutions have to their immediate existence, but also of their corruption and violence. They were also aware of the limited protection offered by legislation and court orders. They knew that they had to wage their struggle on many different fronts in order to create for themselves a protection that could not be ensured simply by administrative or judicial directives. This they did, and continue to do, by making themselves heard in the public arena, not simply directly in their own voices but also in others' words.

Finally, I would argue that the question of 'in and against' 'the state' has to be looked at afresh. Ehrenreich and Piven (1983) make a case for increasing women's involvement with state institutions by pointing to the radical potential of such a project for women both as individuals and as a growing collective. The London Edinburgh Weekend Return Group, in their influential book *In and Against the State*, made a different point: 'The state, then, is not "our" state. It is "their" state, an alien, oppressive state' (1980: 53). They reminded us, however, that 'we have made positive gains [under this hostile state] not by "winning power" in any formal sense but by taking a degree of control, counter-posing our forms of organisations to theirs' (ibid.: 147). I would argue, not in opposition but from a different standpoint, that if we do not regard the state as a unity we cannot look upon struggle as a unified strategy either.

My concern in this chapter has been to point to the lack of intentionality of a unified state structure, and also to point to the spaces that are available, and can and are created for and through struggle for retrieving, reconstructing and regaining control over the meanings and signifiers in women's lives. Women do this in different ways, taking into account their own experience, needs and situations, and they approach the various forms of state differently – in opposition, in cooperation, through subversion not simply of rules but of articulated intentions of state forms, and through negotiations. And they do all this actively, if not always with a coherence and intentionality of their own: 'It is because subjects do not, strictly speaking, know what they are doing that what they do has more meaning than they know' (Bourdieu, in Risseeuw 1991: 154). It is on this struggle – in all its myriad forms – that we must focus to understand the relationship that women construct with the state in which they live.

3 | Theorizing gender and democratization[1]

Democratization emerged as a strong political discourse in the 1990s. By some, this was seen as a long overdue examination of state institutions and processes, but for most it became rhetoric of the triumph of liberal values over socialist, of capitalism over socialism, of democratic political systems over authoritarian ones. Feminist scholars have contributed significantly to debates on democratization. In order to explore feminist perspectives on democratization we need to understand both feminist frameworks and methodologies. I outline what a feminist framework might be and then use this perspective to analyse feminist engagements with the theory and practice of democratization and the state.

Democratization can be defined as the process of 'making democratic' regimes, practices and discourses of public power. Luckham and White have identified four areas of inquiry for democratization analysts: 1) the nature of the particular institutional form of democracy; 2) causes and contexts of democratization; 3) prospects for the sustainability and deepening of democracy; and 4) the relationship between democracy and socio-economic development (1996: 2–8). Rueschemeyer et al. (1992) highlighted three factors that affect the actual working of democracies: 1) the international factors, such as interstate relations; 2) the individual state itself and its political institutions and leadership – the role of the military as opposed to civilian leadership, for example; and 3) 'civil society', which reflects the social and interest groups with a stake in society. It is, they argued, the constellation of these three factors which makes for the possibilities, or otherwise, of a successful democratization process. While valuable in themselves, both these explanatory and analytical frameworks share one fundamental characteristic – the focus is on spaces where actors, states and individuals act in the public political sphere.

In the following sections I present three insights arising from the work of feminist scholars which extend our understanding of democratization at the theoretical level. I then examine the specific field of gender and democratization and the nature of women's participation in politics. In the final section I reflect upon the wider socio-economic context in which men and women are engaged in democratization struggles. I conclude that democratization is an untidy and unfolding process and feminist insights are crucial for understanding it.

Feminist engagements

Public and private spheres of political action Perhaps one of the most enduring contributions of women's activism and feminist theorizing is the challenging of the boundaries between the public and the private as defining politics. In the words of Carol Pateman, 'the separation of the private and public is presented in liberal theory as if it applied to all individuals in the same way' (1983: 283). Feminists argued that public political life was built on the absence of women from it; that the exclusion of the private sphere was essential for the primacy of the public. By expanding the definition of politics to encompass both the public and the private spheres – indeed, by asserting that the two were mutually constitutive – feminists have been able to challenge the dominant understandings of politics itself, and therefore of democratic practice and discourse. For example, in the democratization movements against the military dictatorship, we saw the Chilean women call for democracy in the home as well as in politics (Navarro 1989). These struggles, however, have not always been successful. While the discourse about women's position and role within the family has been carried out in the public sphere, women's presence in the public sphere has continued to be a controversial issue.

Differences remain among feminists about the nature of the public/ private divide. While radical feminists have seen the obliteration of this distinction as necessary to democracy that is inclusive of gender-based difference, others have seen such a bridging of the public and private as a transitory phase – a phase that would allow the entry of women into the public arena as independent actors (Phillips 1991, 1993). Some feminist scholars have argued that, while democratizing the private domain is crucial for women's participation in the public, it ought not to be confused with issues of civic participation and rights (Dietz 1992; Mouffe 1992). Young, for example, has stressed the importance of maintaining the separation between the two spheres. She suggests that the private sphere should be thought of as 'that aspect of his or her life and activity that any person has the right to exclude from others. The private in this sense is not what public institutions exclude but what the individual chooses to withdraw from public view' (Young 1990: 119–20). Lister quite rightly points out the problems with this articulation of the public–private divide: 'it does leave open the question as to which individuals have the power to make their choices stick' (1997: 121). I would also emphasize, however, the need for a simultaneous but parallel democratization of both the public and the private spheres. Here I would insist, with Dietz, upon keeping the two domains separate. It is important, I would argue, to mark a conscious transition that women must make to politicize the issues that affect them within the private sphere. Rather than focusing on the issue of exclusion from the private sphere, I would emphasize the terms of *inclusion* in the public sphere. I would suggest that it is only through making the private public that we can move forward on this issue. While not entirely answering the question of agency raised by Lister, such a bringing together of the public and the private would happen in part through the social mobilization of women (and men) on particular issues in the public sphere. Such an analysis of the public–private divide not only allows us to focus on the importance of the private for the public, but it also provides us with a measure for assessing the processes of democratization. It is both a framework of analysis and a methodology for assessing political change.

Feminist methodologies Building upon this debate, the second insight that feminist scholars have offered is by paying particular attention to 'experience' as an important starting point of knowledge, which contextualizes the basis of politics itself (Scott and Butler 1992). Gender, as a social construction of sex, then, is reflected in the political roles that women and men are able to perform, and 'frames the very definition of politics, and by default, what does not constitute politics' (Rai 2000: 1569). From an analytical framework that challenges the public–private divide and insists upon experience as a valid form and basis of knowledge emerges a radical visualization of politics itself. This visualization sees the universalized language of politics, of citizenship and rights, for example, as marking the erasure of structurally embedded differences between individuals. As Blacklock and Macdonald argue, women's movements are 'exposing the limitations of a discourse which, in its universalism, conceals a gendered and racialised subject identity, a Western, ethnocentric conception of rights, and an ontology which denies heterogeneity and diversity' (2000: 19).

The importance of context has been the third intervention that feminists have made in the debate about democratization. Feminists have pointed to the diversity of women's histories, and the experiences of 'the public' in terms of class, race, disability and sexuality, to argue for the essentially contingent and contested nature of the debate on the distinction between the public and the private spheres (Lister 1997: 122–5). They have also quite rightly asked the question: What are the costs – social, economic and personal – of political participation for women? Who has the resources to be able to participate directly? (Phillips 1993). These costs are not the same, and quite often depend upon the social and economic resources that women are able to mobilize in order to access political life, to participate in informal and formal processes and political institutions. Religion, class and caste, ethnicity and sexuality, disability and language all mediate with gender to influence the outcomes of democratic participation for women and men.

Patriarchy and democratic politics And finally, feminists have theorized on democracy with regard to the meta-framework of patriarchy. Patriarchy can be defined as a systematic exercise of male authority over women through social, political and economic institutions. As a result it shapes, mediates and is dependent upon men's greater access to the public sphere and the resources that accrue from this access both inside and outside the home. While there are different feminist positions on the nature of patriarchy, broadly speaking the concept does define the feminist position on social relations. So when feminists have addressed the issue of democratization, they have asked different questions and sought answers that go beyond the mainstream debates on democratization. Questions of access to and participation in the political and the socio-economic spheres, the deepening of democracy within and outside the home, are therefore considered to be deeply gendered. In the next section of the chapter I build on these discussions to assess the nature and outcomes of democratization debates and initiatives from a gendered perspective.

Gender and democratization

Waylen, in her survey of the democratization literature, poses four questions about women's participation in the process of democratic transitions and consolidations: 1) why do women choose to organize or not?; 2) where they exist, what is the nature of these movements?; 3) what is the interaction between women's political activities and the process of transition?; and 4) what are the outcomes for women of transitions to democracy, as well as of further democratization of consolidated political systems? (1994).

Women's movements and democratization Social movements have been defined as 'organized efforts at the grass roots to represent interests excluded from or poorly represented in formal arenas of authoritative negotiation and value allocation' (Teske and Tetreault 2000: 9). In this sense women's movements have always been part of political processes in different contexts. It is through their participation in these movements that women and women's groups have been able to stake a claim to equal representation in political life and institutions (Jayawardene 1987), on the one hand, and on the other focus attention on the necessity of deepening democracy within the home as they negotiate the terms upon which they participate in social and political movements in the public sphere. For example, the Hudood Ordinances decreed in Pakistan by its military ruler Zia ul-Haq (1977–88) provoked a strong response from Pakistani women. They led to the establishment of the Women's Action Forum, which has not only mobilized against the ordinances, which were clearly discriminatory against women, but has also strengthened the struggle for democracy in Pakistan (Ali 2000: 46–50). The Mothers of the Plaza de Mayo movement in Chile against the Pinochet regime also shows how women have challenged the separation of the public and the private by building on their role as mothers within the home to challenge authoritarian regimes in public: 'Their refusal to acquiesce in the loss of their children was not an act out of character, but a coherent expression of their socialisation [as mothers] ... True to themselves, they had no other choice but to act, even if it meant confronting the junta' (Navarro 1989: 257).

An important and complex area where the overlaps between the public and private spheres create challenges for women is that of 'culture'. Feminist insights have insisted upon demythologizing an 'essential woman' through the study of difference – between men and women and among women – as a theoretical strategy that underpins women's struggles for empowerment (Fuss 1989). Even democracy movements create their ideal woman erased of all differences, however – authenticity of culture is inscribed on women's bodies and roles. Women have sought to democratize this discourse on two counts – first, by challenging the 'orientalist' and imperialist discourse of rescue of the women of particular (non-Christian/Western) cultures (Liddle and Rai 1998), and second, by challenging the codes of silence that their own communities impose on them in the name of anti-racism. As Mernissi writes about the Arab culture's imposition of restrictive codes of conduct on women, 'as Arab women are calling for change, we threaten the ahistoricity of the Arab identity imposed by society under the guise of authenticity, heritage, and using the past as a reference and as a model for the future' (1988: 37). By challenging both these positions women have attempted to open up and deepen the democratic debate. This has not always been easy and at times has sat uncomfortably with the mainstream public debate on democratization.

Nature of women's political participation Participation in political movements has been a crucial element in the struggles for democratization. It has contributed to the creation and expansion of civil society as well as having been critical to the claims of various marginalized groups to representation in national political institutions. Feminist scholars and activists have long been aware of the dilemmas of participation. On the one hand it is a powerful means of access and empowerment, and on the other it places differentiated burdens and costs on participants. Issues of difference are important when discussing the nature of political participation, as is its stabilization within specific political systems. While on the whole mainstream democratization theory has been sceptical about participatory politics owing to its unpredictability and long-term efficacy, feminists have embraced it despite the above reservations. Lynch has argued that 'theorising about social movements in the 1970s and 1980s made a double move – from a critique of capitalism to an interest in the "higher goals" of rights, peace, and democracy, and from a focus on "particularistic" movements ... to movements motivated by "universalistic" values and objectives' (1998: 162). For the women's movements this double move created new opportunities and solidarities within the broad framework of democratization. An arena of public politics where women's movements have attempted to bring together the public and the private is that of human rights[2] and citizenship. While rights, like the state, provoke different responses from feminists (see Rai 1996), human rights discourse was central to the struggles for democracy in the 1980s and 1990s. In Guatemala, for example, the exposure of human rights violations was the first step towards building the movement for democratization. The movement also tried, however, to motivate the popular masses with 'the longer-term goal of preparing *pobladoras* to become citizens by organising their communities ...' By raising awareness that 'all people are "entitled" to [human rights], the women's organizations are attempting to construct *pobladoras* as new "subjects of rights", new political actors, and new citizens' (Blacklock and Macdonald 2000: 22–3). It is through this linking of state-based rights and citizen-based motivation that the women's movements are participating in the creation of a civil society that might be able to sustain the expansion of formal rights, as well as to challenge a universalized understanding of rights themselves.

Women's movements have also reflected the unfolding nature of citizenship. They have pressed for different facets of women's lives to be represented in legal and constitutional arrangements – from the early-twentieth-century demands in many countries for universal political rights, to the current insistence upon mainstreaming a gendered perspective in political institutions. Thus, while feminists and women's movements have be wary of institutional power and discourses of universality, by opening up the issue of difference they have sought an intersection of the two. The interest in the 'third generation' of group-based human rights is evidence of this (Kymlicka 1995). In terms of democratization, this has led to some initiatives to secure women's participation in institutional politics through group-based quotas, with mixed and sometimes controversial outcomes (Rai 2002).

Women's participation in institutional politics While mainstream democratic theory has concentrated largely on representative as opposed to participatory politics, it is only relatively recently that feminists have explored the possibilities of representative institutional politics. Debates about rights and participation in movements for democracy have led women's groups to the recognition that it is imperative that the gains made through participation are institutionalized through laws, constitutions and political machineries and practices. Interventions of international organizations such as the UN also helped emphasize the importance of working with state institutions in order to improve the living conditions of women (UN 1996, 2000; Rai 2003).

Here we find significant variations depending on the nature of political transitions, political systems and political ideologies of leaderships, as well as different trajectories of change. Thus, during the period of transition to a democratic South Africa, the aim of the Women's National Coalition (WNC), which was the umbrella organization for ninety women's organizations representing about two million women, was to ensure that by participating in debates on the writing of the constitution they 'would be able to secure a consistent gendered perspective throughout this most important document' (Zulu 2000: 174). While the South African case is a success story for gender-sensitive transition politics, the experience of eastern Europe has raised important questions for women's movements, as well as for democratization struggles. The democratization of eastern European states did not lead to more representative political institutions.

On the contrary, there was a 'dramatic drop in levels of female political representation to 10 per cent or less in national assemblies after the first and second democratic elections in East Central Europe' (Einhorn 2000: 108). Given the enormous economic pressures that families have had to experience, and the abandonment of the earlier pattern of state-based participation in political institutions, women have largely stayed away from political institutions. They have continued to be active in some eastern European countries at the level of informal, civil-society politics, where they have channelled their energies into being lobbying and advocacy groups under 'severe limitations on their ability to shift state policies grounded in a culture of exclusionary ethno-nationalism' (ibid.: 109–10).

Within specific contexts, strategies for democratizing the state as well as civil society have thus been on the agenda of feminist democratic practice. A crucial context within which these strategies have taken shape and have been tried out, however, is that of economic liberalization.

Democratization and entitlements

Feminist scholars have long challenged the view that there is a positive correlation between political and economic liberalization (Elson 1989; Afshar and Dennis 1991). They have argued that the increased pressures arising from economic liberalization are exacerbating the burden that women carry in their daily lives and therefore reducing the time and space for them to be politically active. Globalization as liberalization is putting under pressure the idea of a stable social compact between citizens and the national states (Rai 2002: 157).

Cuts in state spending on health are adversely affecting women's health as families make choices about spending limited resources on men or on boy children, and are also increasing the care burden of women as they look after elders and children in the absence of state provision. Similarly, education of girls has fallen dramatically in countries where structural adjustment policies (SAPs) have meant cuts in state educa-tion budgets. According to UNCTAD, girl-child enrolment in sub-Saharan Africa has plummeted with the introduction of SAPs (2000). In terms of the development of human capabilities of poor women, and particularly the women of the South, this falling investment is resulting in the erosion of their future ability to contribute to the family income, as well as to participate in the wider political processes important to the development of their countries. Even the expansion of women's participation in the sphere of waged work in liberalized economies is no indicator of their empowerment. It could simply be 'the result either of progress towards the homogenization and equalization of the male and female employment roles, or be caused by persistence of differences in sex roles on the labour market, with demand for female labour protected by rigid patterns of sex segregation ...' (Rubery 1988: ix).

It could be argued that the dislocations in gendered power regimes at local levels caused by the expansion of female labour in export processing zones has led to women acquiring a higher status within the family, and the opening up of new spaces outside the home for their political mobilization. Women have participated in trade union struggles as well as in the wider anti-globalization/liberalization movements. In November 1998, for example, '182 women from 22 countries representing 104 organizations met in Kuala Lumpur to Resist Globalization and Assert Our Rights'. They argued that 'privatization of health care is a violation of women's basic human rights to total well-being', and asserted that Third World women have suffered most from globalization in Asia, where economic crisis has brought large-scale unemployment and displacement, deepening poverty, food insecurity due to increasing loss of biodiversity and the appropriation of land and water resources by large TNCs and the elite. They concluded, 'our governments, local elites and local businesses are the collaborators and implementers of this agenda' (50-years@igc.org).

Given the context of poverty and exclusion, such struggles are impressive. They also alert us, however, to the limitations of the democratization discourse if we do not take into account the socio-economic context of political processes. Indeed, attention to the question of citizenship entitlements of health, education and freedom from poverty is crucial if the democratization debate is to be inclusive of those on the margins of civil society. To facilitate women's active citizenship, argues Einhorn, what Amartya Sen has called 'exchange entitlement mapping' has to be enhanced through the strengthening of the economic as well as the political rights of women (2000: 113–14).

Democratization and globalization

As is evident from the above discussion, while focused on national states and political institutions and processes, democratization can no longer be discussed without attention to globalization. Thus, Held has asked: 'Whose consent is necessary, whose agreement is required, whose participation is justified in decisions concerning, for instance, the location of ... [a] nuclear plant? What is the relevant constituency? Local?

National? Regional? International?' (1991: 143). We have seen an exponential growth in financial and trade flows helped by a revolution in communications. The result has been arguments about deterritorialization of politics, the retreat of the nation-state, the convergence of economic policy, and a reflexivity about the world that we inhabit and whose citizens we are. Thus Giddens argues that globalization has led to the transformation of our daily lives. Feminist engagements with globalization theory also point out, however, that 'it is perhaps a particularly weak version of democracy that has been institutionalized on a global scale – liberal democracy in its most elitist, least developmental form' (Eschle 2001: 151). I have argued elsewhere that '[a]s the global reach of social and political movements increases through technological and information networks, and as the pressures of international trade and markets begin to impinge significantly on the national economies leading to a fragmentation and repositioning of nation-states, the relationship between local struggles, social movements and the national state is being constantly reshaped' (Rai 2002: 205; see also Stienstra 2000; Cohen and Rai 2000). Indeed, increasing attention is being paid to relations between women's groups across national borders, to networks of women straddling both North and South, and to the way in which cyber-technology is changing communications among and for women. Women are participating in struggles at local/national as well as local/global levels (Parpart et al. 2002). Movements of citizens' boycotts of particular transnational corporations or products, ecological struggles for the protection of biodiversity, the indigenous peoples' movements, and indeed the women's movement, have all had to operate across traditional national boundaries, and therefore to negotiate in the global political space. Issues of accountability, agenda-setting and interest representation as well as institutionalization have become globalized. Democratization is no longer confined within national boundaries, even though states continue to be the focus of the convergence of liberal democratic institutional politics. The pressures to liberalize economies as well as polities continue to be seen as markers of convergence of democratic practice, even while the outcomes of these pressures sharpen differences between states and among people.

In conclusion

As Luckham and White point out, the democratization 'wave had already begun to recede by the mid-1990s as entrenched regimes either resisted the trend, or merely went through the democratic motions, or as newly democratic regimes succumbed to various forms of authoritarian reversion' (1996: 1). Women's groups engaged in democratization struggles have been acutely aware of a need for constant vigilance in any engagement with state-dominated processes of democratization. Global economic trends also affect the processes and stability of demo-cratization. Feminist interventions in struggles for democratization have alerted women to view democratization as a context-bound process. State formations, the contours of particular civil societies, the possibilities of women's mobilizations, the entitlements that women have (or do not have) and institutional arrangements that give shape to particular citizen-ships have a profound impact on women's potential to participate in political life. As economic downturns affect different governments, issues about entitlements to citizenship become increasingly important.

Political practice has also clarified that democratization is not a wave that comes or goes – it is an unfolding and untidy process. Successes in one area are not suggestive of a completeness of the process. Issues are, and need to be, revisited with startlingly different results. Institutions that have been stable for decades, as well as new institutions of state power, need to be opened up for scrutiny. This is important because the dominant discourses of power have begun to engage with the struggles of marginalized groups, and need to be stabilized within old institutions put together in another historical context. Gains that have been made must be cemented within new institutions and old. The unfolding nature of democratization is also evident when we examine the question of entitlements. As transitions from one set of socio-economic relations to another make clear, political and social citizenships do not necessarily go hand in hand. The tension within liberal democracy – of individual rights embedded in a socio-economic context of unequal access to resources – continues to haunt the debates on entitlements. Newly democratizing nations and old democracies are both sites for the struggles for the democratization of politics.

Finally, we also need to emphasize the importance of comparative work so that women can view, analyse and perhaps use strategies for enhancing their participation in politics across the boundaries of nation-states. The debates on citizenship – in the universalist discourse as well as those focused on women's group rights – are particularly important in this regard (Young 1990; Lister 1997; Yuval-Davis 1997). The discourses of rights, of equality, of difference and of entitlements have all been employed by women as they strategize in their pursuit of greater freedom. International forums provide meeting places where women from differ-ent countries cross boundaries, create networks, confront constraints and explore democratic possibilities. Global frameworks, while necessarily limited, have also been utilized by women's movements to build bridges and create solidarities across national borders in their struggles to democratize politics. Feminist debates on democratization continue to contribute to such a rooted crossing of cultural, historical and political boundaries.

4 | Mainstreaming gender, democratizing the state?[1]

A key insight that emerges from the study of the state in Chapter 2 is that it is not unitary but fractured, as are its institutions and policy-making bodies, and that an engagement with state bodies is not a matter of option but an imperative for women, particularly those of the South, if their interests, however diverse, are to be at all represented in policies of the state. A second insight from Chapter 3 is that the democratization of the state requires that attention be paid to the gendered nature of the state, as well as the processes of democratization itself. In this chapter I incorporate these insights to study particular state institutions – the national machineries for the advancement of women. Certain themes emerge in the analysis that follows. First, are national machineries as state institutions the most appropriate instruments for furthering women's interests? Two sets of debates inform this issue – the viability of women's engagements with the state, and the nature of women's interests. The second theme is about the viability of national machineries as bodies promoting women's interests – do these institutions command the necessary resources to be able to promote women's interests? In this context I address issues of resources – economic and political – and the setting of goals and targets for national machineries, as well as political environments in which these machineries are embedded. Here, the stability of governance institutions, for example civil society, the relative strength of women's movements and issues of accountability of the machineries are also important. The third theme focuses on the processes of democratization that a state needs to undergo to mainstream gender effectively – the hierarchical nature of state bureaucracies and political parties, the presence or lack of auditing mechanisms within state machineries, leadership commitment to gender mainstreaming and, of course, increasing the presence of women within state bodies at all levels.

Institutionalizing women's interests in organizations and policies at all levels has been a concern of women's movements worldwide, as well as of international institutions such as the United Nations. Gender mainstreaming has emerged as a strategy for addressing this issue, relevant to all states and public institutions. National machineries for the

advancement of women are regarded as appropriate institutional mechanisms for ensuring that gender mainstreaming agendas are implemented
and issues of gender equality remain in focus in public policy. Gender
mainstreaming and national machineries have found added salience in
international public policy through UN-led and national government-
endorsed agreements on these issues, such as the Beijing Platform for
Action (1995) and ECOSOC Agreed Conclusions (1997).

Defining issues

What is gender mainstreaming? It can be defined as 'the process of
assessing the implications for women and men of any planned action,
including legislation, policies or programmes, in all areas and at all
levels. It is a strategy of making women's as well as men's concerns
and experiences an integral dimension of the design, implementation,
monitoring and evaluation of policies and programmes in all political,
economic and societal spheres so that women and men benefit equally
and inequality is not perpetuated. The ultimate goal is to achieve gender
equality' – with the aim of transforming structures of inequality (UN/DAW
1998: 4). In this book the term is used largely to address issues of gender
mainstreaming in public policy institutions, although the impact of such
policy shifts is expected to create a political context in which the process
of gender mainstreaming in private institutions also proceeds.

There has been a debate among those concerned with issues of gender
justice about whether to use the language of equality or that of equity. The
position of those concerned to emphasize issues of difference among men
and women is that the equality discourse tends to erase the differences
among women and men, that sameness becomes the focus rather than
an acknowledgement of different needs and interests of women and men.
The argument is also made that the language of equality is a language of
universalism, and that universal norms are really the norms of Western
hegemonic societies, which are inappropriate, or even counterproductive,
in different cultural contexts (Ali 2002). International bodies like the UN
and some other feminist scholars, however, have asserted the need for
universal rights to be made the centrepiece of gender justice strategies.
So, for example, it is argued that 'the term "equity", which is conditioned
by subjective criteria, cannot become a substitute for the fundamental
legal principle of equality ... [Further] that reference to the "dignity of
women" does not encompass and cannot be substituted for the principle
of the "dignity and worth of the human person and the equal rights of
men and women" enshrined in the Preamble of the Universal Declaration

of Human Rights' (UNHCR 2000: 5). The argument is that any dilution of equal treatment of women and men on grounds of culture undermines the very basis of gender justice. It also allows women of some countries and religious and ethnic groups to be left out of the discussions about refining and contextualizing the rights of women and men. Hegemonic cultural discourses often reinforce traditional gender roles, and the focus shifts away from the needs of women outside the boundaries that define these roles. Codification of women's social role within these cultural boundaries then gets in the way of processes of democratization of the state and within civil society.

What are national machineries? Despite attempts at a common definitional understanding of these institutions, differences remain in the ways these are conceptualized, which depend on political contexts obtaining in individual states. National machineries, also often called women's policy agencies, emerged as instruments for advancing women's interests after the World Conference of the International Women's Year in Mexico City (1975), but were particularly strengthened in the Platform for Action adopted at the Fourth World Conference on Women in Beijing (1995). They can be defined as 'the central policy coordinating unit inside the government. Its main task is to support government-wide mainstreaming of a gender equality perspective in all policy areas' (Platform for Action, para. 201). National machineries are thus 'catalysts' for promoting gender equality and justice (UNHCR 2000: 10). As Kathy Staudt has pointed out, however, 'we find vastly different institutional cultures, leaders and leadership styles, degrees of coordination, birthing periods, disciplinary specializations, missions, and staff demographics, gender and otherwise – all protecting their autonomy to likewise difference degrees' (2003: 46). The nation-state thus continues to be the focus of women's movements that remain embedded in particular cultural, historical and political contexts. In order to embed gendered perspectives into policy, the spotlight most often turns to how national states are performing on this score, though global institutions themselves are also increasingly under scrutiny in this regard.

Can state institutions promote women's interests?

I would suggest that one of the most important questions for analysing national machineries is whether state-based or -promoted institutions such as national machineries can be effective in advancing the interests of women given the embedded nature of these machineries in structures of inequality.

As I have argued in Chapter 2, the question of engagement with the state and state institutions cannot be seen in terms of binary opposites. Indeed, we need a position that allows for a mobilization of women's interests and their articulation within the space of civil society in order to challenge the gender status quo. In parallel, this would allow for an engagement with the policy-making machinery of the state in order to institutionalize the gains made through discursive and political shifts brought about through these mobilizations. I termed such a dialectical position 'in and against' the state. In terms of the national machineries for women, I would argue that an 'in and against' the state position allows us to consider mainstreaming gender through and within the state seriously, and critically. Thus, on the one hand, as the different case studies in this volume show, women's movements, NGOs and international institutions such as the UN have striven for state institutions in the form of national machineries committed to the gender equality agenda to be recognized, given political space and resources. This strategy has been seen as addressing the continued marginalization of women in the public sphere and continued gender inequality more generally. On the other hand, however, there has also been a concern that national machineries might well be used, especially where a strong women's movement does not exist, to coopt the gender agenda within state policy, thus divesting it of its radical edge. Holding these two positions, at times in tension with each other, together does not take away from the importance of the state as a significant arena for furthering gender justice. It also suggests that the state is a fractured and ambiguous terrain for women needing complex negotiation and bargaining by those working within its boundaries as well as those on the outside. So the answer to the question of whether national machineries can be effective in advancing women's interests must be yes, but under certain conditions, which include issues of location and resources as well as of strong democratic movements holding these bodies accountable. This position has not always been acceptable within women's movements or among feminist scholars, as will be evident below. If we examine the position of women in politics today, however, we can see that the scale of women's exclusion from political bodies needs to be addressed urgently if the nature of these bodies is to be changed.

Women in political institutions A headcount of the officers of the state in all sectors – legislature, executive and the judiciary – in most countries of the world reveals a massive male bias despite many mobilizations furthering women's presence at both national and global levels. An Inter-Parliamentary Union study found that the number of sovereign states with a parliament increased sevenfold between 1945 and 1995, while the percentage of women members of parliament (MPs) worldwide increased fourfold (Pintat, in Karam 1998: 163). The *UN Atlas of Women in Politics* (2000) shows that women form 13.4 per cent of members of parliament as a whole. The Nordic states lead with women constituting 38.8 per cent of members of both houses of parliament, while the Arab states have only 3.5 per cent (UN 1999). Furthermore, data show that there is no easy positive correlation between economic indicators and the presence of women in public bodies. While in Europe (excluding the Nordic countries) women constituted 13.4 per cent of the total number of MPs, the figure in sub-Saharan Africa was 11.7 per cent, in Asia 14.3 per cent and in the Americas 15.3 per cent. In recognition of the slow improvement in women's representation in national parliaments, enhancing women's presence within state bodies is now being pursued by both women's movements and international institutions. This suggests that an engagement with state structures is now considered an appropriate means of bringing about shifts in public policy.

The state response Most states have also undergone a shift in their policies towards accepting gender mainstreaming as a valid political agenda. This has been primarily due to the pressure from global institutions such as the United Nations (see Kardam and Acuner 2003). States' acceptance of the outcome of the world conferences on women, particularly the Beijing Platform for Action and the outcome document of the twenty-third special session of the General Assembly on Gender Equality, Development and Peace for the Twenty-first Century, has resulted in commitment to some form of institutional change. The political and discursive shifts within women's movements discussed above have added to this pressure on the state to engage with gender equality agendas. The support of global institutions through training sessions and particular projects, as well as political pressure from international non-governmental organizations and the women's movements, has also been helpful to move forward states' agendas on the issue of mainstreaming. Finally, practical issues such as filing state reports on the status of women under the Convention for the Elimination of All Forms of Discrimination Against Women have shown the need for a body to oversee the process (see Ali 2002).[2]

So, for a multiplicity of reasons, national machineries for the advancement of women are now in existence in many states. If these bodies raise issues about the nature of the state and women's engagement with it, however, they also raise questions about what and whose interests they are going to promote, mainstream and embed in political institutions. Identifying, aggregating and representing interests are thus core elements of the work of national machineries. National machineries have been envisaged as nodes for acknowledging, listening to, recognizing and articulating the interests of different groups of women within the national political community. Representing women's interest to governance circuits at different levels was one of the important tasks of national machineries. Thus, they are also seen as conduits between civil society and the state. What have been the debates on women's interests that need to inform this mandated function of the national machineries?

Representing women's interests What are interests? Interests can be defined as shared understandings and articulations of an individual or group's concern. The term includes both the objectives of the individual and group and the power of the individual or group to attract attention to their objectives. While traditional liberal theory has largely focused on individual interest, collective action and social conflict frameworks of analysis have shifted this focus to groups (Young 1995; Kymlicka 1995). These frameworks also allow us to reflect on strategies for pursuit of interests – demonstrating, lobbying, going on strike, or other such forms of collective action.

There is a comprehensive literature now about theorizing women's interests. The concept has been examined in two different ways. The first is a challenge to the view that equates women's interests with identity politics and particularistic demands. As Jonasdottir has emphasized, interests are formulated within particular contexts that frame the processes of making choices. She has also argued that women are not just another 'interest group' because they exist in a historically determined conflictual and subordinate relationship to men. There is of course the issue of difference among women which has challenged both feminist scholars and women activists. While women exist in a historically conflictual relationship with men, so do they with women of other classes, ethnicities, sexualities, dis/abilities, etc. So, for example, economic interests divide women, just as their subordinate position vis-à-vis men places them on the same side. Economic interests, especially in the contexts of global restructuring, have become important markers of difference among women, even as globalization is bringing women closer together across national boundaries through technological and global governance networks (Hoskyns and Rai 1998; Parpart et al. 2002). Whose interests, in this context, is not always an easy question to answer. There has also been some debate among feminist scholars on women's interests and gender interests, the latter addressing the structure of relations between women and men, the former concentrating on women's lives.

Maxine Molyneux has made an analytical distinction between women's 'practical' and 'strategic' needs. Practical interests reflect women's immediate and contained demands – for better conditions of work, equal opportunities, childcare, housing, water, etc. These interests do not challenge the wider framework of patriarchal structures of power. Strategic interests reflect the need to shift the paradigms of power. In the words of Molyneux, 'In the formulation of practical interests there is the assumption that there is compliance with the existing gender order, while in the case of strategic interests there is an explicit questioning of that order and of the compliance of some women with it' (1998: 235).

From a different standpoint, Chantal Mouffe (1992) and Mary Dietz (1992) have made the point that framing women's interests – both practical and strategic – in terms of the general interests of a just society can be an effective way of giving them greater salience in wider political debates and policies. This would be an effective way of mainstreaming – as opposed to adding on gendered analysis to existing paradigms of power. The current climate of global restructuring could be a good starting point for such reformulations.

Some have claimed that Molyneux has made too rigid a distinction between the two sets of interests. Molyneux argues, however, that the 'pursuit of particularistic interests ... is of course not necessarily at variance with strategies that pursue broader goals and interests and may be framed in terms of general principles ...' (1998: 239). The distinction also allows political strategizing to take place. As Molyneux points out: 'The political *links* between practical and strategic interests are ones which can only emerge through dialogue, praxis and discussion' (ibid.: 236). National machineries need to be able not only to participate in making these distinctions clear, but to strategize according to the specific contexts within which they function. If this is to happen, national machineries need clarity of mandate, sufficient resources and stability within governance networks. In the following section I examine the mandate and resources of the national machineries for the advancement of women.

National machineries for women

The mandate of national machineries places a great deal of stress on their agenda-setting role, while their legitimacy derives from the close contact they are able to maintain with women's groups. Finally, they represent national states at international bodies. The following is a survey of different issues that arise for national machineries in performing their roles.

A variety of national machineries National machineries vary considerably from country to country. In most countries the national machinery is part of the government structure. The particular issues here relate to the status of the governmental body, its closeness to the highest offices within the government, resources – both economic and political – available to it, and the access it has (or does not have) to other sectors and bodies of government. In some other countries, national machineries remain outside government, though the government recognizes their role as an important forum at both the national and the international level. Here the resource issue is critical at both the economic and political levels, as are issues of flexibility, voice and consensus-building across political boundaries. These bodies might be considered more autonomous, or less influential, depending on how they are able to negotiate political boundaries, to become effective in improving the status of women.

All national machineries are embedded in specific socio-economic and political contexts. Comparisons between them are therefore not always useful. We can, however, identify five elements that are critical for all: 'a) location [at a high level] within the decision-making hierarchy [and authority] to influence government policy; b) clarity of mandate and functional responsibility; c) links with civil society groups supportive of the advancement of women's rights and enhancement of women's status; d) human and financial resources' (ECOSOC 1999); and e) the accountability of the national machinery itself. I discuss these in turn in the following sections.

Location In a survey conducted by DAW in 1996 it was noted that two-thirds of all national machineries are located in government, and one-third are either non-governmental or have a mixed structure. Of those within the government, more than half are part of a ministry, one-third are located in the office of the head of state, with the rest being self-standing ministries. Of those within ministries, half are situated in ministries of social affairs and one-third in ministries of labour (ibid.;

see also Jezerska 2003; Kwesiga 2003). Why is there a preponderance of national machineries in ministries of social affairs and labour? What does it say about the assumptions about 'women's needs/concerns'? Does this indicate a 'low status' within the governmental structure itself – the high-status ministries being either the 'earning' ministries such as the treasury and industry, or regulating ministries such as home and foreign affairs, while social affairs is a high-spending area? (NGO Coordinating Committee for Beijing + 5 2000: 73). What does this mean for opening up or 'democratizing' the state through the presence and activities of the national machineries? Often we find that the comparatively low status of the national machineries for women has led to their frequent down-sizing and relocation in times of economic restructuring (Kwesiga 2003). Government portfolios that were traditionally considered 'soft', however – welfare, health and education – are also, under regimes of economic restructuring, where fundamental arguments about resource allocation are being had. It is at this time that national machineries can be most effective in insisting upon a 'reassessment both of priorities of states and of the normative social order' (Molyneux 1998: 242).

Free-standing machineries too have strengths and weaknesses. One danger of an autonomous entity is the lack of political clout and there-fore of political and economic resources. No ministry or politician need feel responsible for this body, and its achievements bring no benefit to ministers who might then develop a stake in the functioning of the machinery. As Marian Sawer has commented, 'Australian feminists de-cided against a self-standing bureau or ministry on the grounds that it might simply become a "waste-paper basket for women's problems" and an alibi for gender-blind policy in the rest of government ... [and] would lack policy clout ...' (2003: 245). Second, the resourcing of such a body would pose considerable problems. While project-based grants could provide it with some resources, this would not provide the stability of organization needed to develop medium- and long-term strategies. If the machinery were funded by international agencies, the political con-sequences of this resource might be unacceptably high in some political contexts, whereby the political system might label the machinery a 'tool of Western agencies'. Such a loss of legitimacy would make the work of the machinery extremely difficult indeed.

Location at the highest level raises the profile of the machinery, and arguably enhances its economic and political resources. In some countries the success of the national machinery derives from its cross-ministerial location (see Åskesog 2003). This is possible only when the head of government takes responsibility for opening up the governmental structure in this lateral way. To be effective at the highest possible level, however, several factors have to be considered, together with the location and the commitment of the head of government. The position of the head of government within the political system is crucial – the weaker this position (for example, as part of an unstable coalition), the less likely is the national machinery to be able to use this political resource (see Rai 2003). A more general political instability, military coups, for example, can also threaten the work of machineries at the highest level. As Honculada and Ofreneo point out, 'In the great divide between those for and against martial law [in the Philippines] the NCRFW was perceived by second wave feminists to be an ally of government' (2003: 33). Times of transitions, however, can also be moments of opportunity for the national machineries to strengthen their position (see Zulu 2000; Jezerska 2003). In other countries, such as Turkey, however, the number of women in the government has increased since the military intervention. The Algerian case also suggests that the political context in individual countries is of primary importance in any analysis of gender mainstreaming through institutional mechanisms (Mehdid 1996). While visibility provides resources, it can also be a burden. A head of state might adopt populist agendas that are not in the interests of women for immediate political gain. 'It is thus effective to create "alliances" with mid-level state personnel who are, in general, more open and more stable than appointed and/or elected officials at the top of the political machinery' (Vega Ugalde 2003: 125). In some contexts, location at the highest level within a governmental structure that is not accountable to the citizenry can lead to the alienation of the national machinery from civil society groups. 'In Chile, some civil society organizations saw the [National Women's Machineries] as an arm of a state which does not represent their interests' (Kardam and Acuner 2003: 103). An eight-country study by the UN in Africa also reveals that 'being located in the highest level of government does not guarantee national machinery influence and effectiveness ... An often ignored issue in the location debate is whether the location which is viewed as advantageous, because of its proximity to the powers that be, is also the best location when the mandate and functions of the national machinery are taken into account' (African Agenda 1999: 13, 15). Autonomy for the work of the machinery can be low at the highest levels of government. Cooptation thus remains a crucial issue for national machineries.

Location is also important for the role that national machineries might play at the regional and global levels. Here the national machineries function to participate in international forums, represent the governmental and non-governmental debates on gender equality, and collect and disseminate information, ideas and good practice from the global to the national level. Location at the top levels of government would provide the machineries with increased credibility at these forums, as well as the negotiating power to initiate strategic cross-border contacts and projects. This has happened rather successfully in South America. The South Asian experience, however, has not been so rewarding on cross-border contacts between state-based national machineries. The tense political situation between India and Pakistan dominates, although contact between women remains productive at the NGO level. National machineries are thus embedded not only in historical and cultural contexts, but also in more immediate intra- and interstate politics.

Clear mandates and functions Clarity serves a political purpose – it does not allow national machineries to be held responsible for areas that are beyond their remit. It also allows an assessment of why certain areas are outside the remit of the women's national machinery. Such an assessment can prompt questions about the openness of state structures to the agendas of gender equality. A review of the mandates and functions of various machineries illustrates this.

Some national machineries focus exclusively on their role as policy advisers and catalysts for gender mainstreaming, leaving the actual implementation of policies, programmes and projects to other bodies. Other women's machineries not only devise programmes but also monitor their implementation. An implementational role for the national machineries also has its merits. First, a successful project implementation raises the profile of the machinery involved, and provides credibility. The 3R project, carried out with the support of state funding and of the Equality Affairs Division by the Swedish Association of Local Authorities, which analysed the effectiveness of gender mainstreaming in local committees and boards, would be one such example (Åskesog 2003). Second, involvement in the implementational process could lead to cross-sector liaising that could spread the influence of the national machineries and open new areas for mainstreaming. Finally, taking responsibility for implementing policies could increase both political and economic resources as the process of implementation gathers pace. There are, however, also disadvantages of being involved in the implementation of policies. Under federal and/or multi-party political systems, for example, an implementational role can lead to confrontation and divisiveness within the civil society groups and the national machinery where these groups are affiliated with political parties not represented at the central level of government (see Rai 1997). Most studies in this volume show that national machineries for women do not take on (neither are they expected to) the role of implementing policies. It was for these reasons that the UN Expert Group Meeting on National Machineries in 1998 specifically recommended that national machineries 'at the governmental level [should be] a catalyst for gender mainstreaming, not [agencies] for policy implementation. [They] may, however, choose to be involved in particular projects' (UN/DAW 1998: 10).

A catalytic role for national machineries can be useful for strengthening their profile within the state and in civil society in the following ways: first, mainstreaming works through its 'ownership' by cross-ministerial structures of government. The responsibility for developing policy initiatives can involve the machineries in negotiations with other ministries that can expand the network of bodies involved in the process of mainstreaming gender equality agendas. Second, raising the profile of gender equality agendas is a more effective use of political and economic resources than trying to use scarce resources to implement policies that might best be tackled by individual ministries. Third, the role of national machineries as a catalyst within government allows these bodies to develop and conduct research on the policies being implemented, and feed these through into policy forums, and to develop methodologies and 'the political ability to anticipate and judge key opportunities and possibilities for effective political impact' (Vega Ugalde 2003). This would make machineries proactive, rather than reactive to state initiatives.

While approaches to the functioning of the national machineries vary, there are major functions that all these bodies need to carry out, though probably with varying degree of success. These are, in terms of their relations with civil society, making gender visible through media campaigns or other means, developing links with civil-society groups that support gender equality in order to strengthen the lobbying process, and to channel resources to community organizations, enabling them to participate in the processes of mainstreaming gender. While research and feeding through the results of the research into both civil society and policy-making bodies overlap, other state-oriented functions include the following: ensuring gender training for governmental officers; developing new initiatives and methodologies to ensure gender equality in government policy-making processes; reviewing proposed legislation in all appropriate areas; monitoring of government policy (insisting on gender-disaggregated budgets, for example;, and disseminating good practice. At the global level, the national machineries' function is to participate in international forums, represent the governmental and non-governmental debates on gender equality, and collect and disseminate information, ideas and good practice from the global to the national level.

Resources One could argue that the question of resources is fundamentally about politics. It is the political will of national leaderships which determines the resourcing of bodies like national machineries. Without a leadership commitment to gender equality, and to the mechanisms important for monitoring its pursuit, resourcing of these institutions is bound to be poor. An additional pressure is the economic restructuring of the state itself. The pressures of liberalization and the consequent shrinking of state budgets are resulting in cutbacks to budgets of bodies like the national machineries. This phenomenon is not confined to countries in the global South such as Uganda but is also prevalent in countries that are more economically secure, such as Australia (Kwesiga 2003; Sawer 2003). While resources can and need to be enhanced through project funding from multilateral bodies, the political costs of such support can also be significant. One way of enhancing the political resources is to link up with civil-society groups that have an important voice in the political system. While this strategy is not always feasible, it is important that we consider it seriously. Given that resources are political, the state elites' political will (or lack of it) can determine the extent to which national machineries are considered important political actors, and given access to policy-making and the implementational infrastructure of the state. The strength of the women's movement and the corporatist nature of the state can be important factors here, as is clear in the study of Nordic states (Åskesog 2003).

Links with civil society The relationship between national machineries and civil society is mutually reinforcing. 'Civil society groups have often played a crucial role in establishing national machineries. Support from civil society also strengthens the position of national machinery vis-à-vis other parts of government ... National machineries need strong links with non-governmental organizations (NGOs). Whenever possible, they should institutionalize their relationship with these organizations' (ECOSOC 1999: 18). While civil society is a crucial factor in the functioning of the national machineries, it is often not theorized enough to distinguish how it might support or in fact be a hindrance to the work of national machineries. Some clarificatory analysis is thus important in this context. First, 'it is necessary to hold together the constituent elements of civil society – including the system of needs (the market), the system of rights (the law) and non-state associations – rather than highlight one of these aspects of civil society at the expense of the other' (Fine and Rai 1997: 2). This is important, especially in the context of the growing need to assess how the globalizing markets on the one hand and legal initiatives of international institutions on the other are affecting women. Such an analysis would be important for national machineries in order to advise, strategize and make alliances with different groups within civil society. Without an understanding of how markets are gendered and how this affects their functioning, for example, changing labour markets and the shifting position of women and men within these would be difficult to map out (Evans 1993). Similarly, an assessment of how CEDAW might be used by national machineries to push the state to enact laws that are in the spirit of its aims, while at the same time embedded in local political culture, is needed. Non-governmental organizations (NGOs) would be useful participants in any strategizing by national machineries. An analysis of the variety of NGOs that are supportive of women's rights would, however, reflect both the political concerns of national machineries and the political positions of NGOs. As Stokes has pointed out, 'the question arises as to what extent there can be a shared point of view amongst such divergent groups. Are the Union of Catholic Mothers, Stonewall (a gay rights group) and the Women's Engineering Society ever likely to share an opinion?' (2003: 198–9). Strategizing to build on groups that are sympathetic and oppose those that are not requires a complex analysis that goes beyond categorizing all civil-society groups as beneficial to the work of national machineries.

Second, and equally important, 'we need to highlight the exclusionary aspects of civil society in relation to those who find no place in its system of needs or in its associational life, and therefore to question the description of civil society as a sphere of "uncoerced action" for all' (Fine and Rai 1997: 2). As the Pakistan's NGO Review of the Platform for Action states, 'increasing violence in society and violent conflict that has accompanied the rise of militant sectarian and conservative politico-religious and ethnic groups not averse to using violent armed tactics … to silence … those with different or opposing views' have militated against women's groups espousing the cause of enhancing women's rights. Third, 'in terms of the civil society–state relation, we should emphasize the importance of the state beyond simply maintaining (or not maintaining) the parameters of civil society itself, and of politics in mediating between the particular interests of civil society and the universalist claims of the state' (ibid.: 2). As the 'Recommendations to the Expert Group Meeting on National Machineries ...' suggest, governments are critical to the effective implementation of the PfA by encouraging NGO participation on policy agencies, in setting up accountability mechanisms, and indeed, '[w]henever possible, Governments should utilize NGO volunteer capacities' (UN 1998). The restrictive power of the state is also evident, however. Taking the above into account it is none the less important to note that women's groups that have organized outside state boundaries are critical to the continued strength and accountability of national machineries.

Democratization of the state

Democratization as a concept and process is informing the governance agendas of both international organizations and development agencies. Loans are often tied to democratization of state institutions and bureaucracies, and political pressure applied to ensure compliance in this regard. It is not always the case, however, that achieving gender equality is built into the definition of such 'democratization'. Considerations of cultural specificity often dilute the message of women's equal rights. As Goetz has argued, the hierarchical and undemocratic nature of bureaucracies, and their hostility to agendas which challenge accustomed organizational patterns is compounded by the high boundaries erected between different sectoral Ministries and by the patronage politics preserved by Ministerial boundaries (2003). In this context, national machineries need to be part of the process of democratization of the state from the outset if gender equality is to be made integral to it. If, as the PfA and subsequent recommendations on the issue suggests, there is a need for greater consultation between NGOs and national machineries, and the state bodies involved in policy-making, then the question of access to government becomes critical. There are five areas where a democratization of the state/government is required in this context. First, there is the issue of devolution or decentralization. This might be considered at two different levels of political devolution and of privatization.

While many states are considering devolved government under pressure of ethnic or regional movements and economic possibilities within their polities, we need to consider the gender-specific implications of decentralization, and whether such decentralization is beneficial to the work of national machineries. The particularity of political systems will have to be considered here. If decentralization takes place with a strong central bias then the national machineries for women at the devolved levels will have to consider their relationship with the central national machinery. Here, the relationship between civil society organizations and the national machinery takes on another layer of complexity. Given the paucity of resources available to national machineries in most countries, another layer of organization might not be the most efficient way of maximizing budget support and garnering influence for addressing gender equality agendas. On the other hand, decentralization in large, multi-ethnic and multi-religious states could benefit gender mainstreaming, as it would be more clearly 'owned' by not only governmental elites at the centre but also by local governmental and state elites. Decentralization under globalization is also occurring as privatization of welfare regimes. For example, as the state retreats from its role in the provision of health services in order to stabilize the economy under conditions of structural adjustment, two issues may arise for national machineries. First, how to campaign for an end to discrimination within the private sphere in terms of women's access to privatized health provision; second, how to influence the health machinery in terms of recruitment policies, as well as gender-sensitive provision of health facilities.

The role of political parties is also an important issue for the democratization of the state. As several chapters in this volume suggest, the place and ideology of political parties within the state system can either promote or hinder gender mainstreaming. A monopoly of state power poses difficult questions for gender equality. On the one hand, as Jezerska has noted, 'In a political sense, the women were officially equal with men under the communist system. For example, "the greatest number of women in the unicameral parliament [in Poland] under the Communist regime was 23 per cent in 1980–1985, far higher than in many Western democracies"' (2003: 171). The lack of political space in which women could organize, however, meant that this formal equality was not translated into gender equality agendas, and women who did attempt to push the boundaries of state policy faced threats of political persecution. In consolidated democracies such as India political parties pose different sorts of questions. The selection process of candidates for election has routinely favoured men, even when the gap between men and women in terms of their electoral participation has never been great (Rai 2003). In South Africa, this issue has been dealt with by encouraging political parties to introduce quotas for women on their party list, with varying degree of success (Zulu 2000). As many countries experience the 'Third Wave' of democratization and transitions from single-party to multi-party governance take place, the role of political parties in gender mainstreaming remains critical, and should be the focus of attention of both national machineries and the NGOs.

Democratization of the state is also needed in the area of monitoring and auditing mechanisms. These mechanisms have to be seen at different levels. First, in terms of democratic government elections, which would include a democratic audit of political parties and the functioning of state institutions. Second, in terms of intra-state accounting and monitoring mechanisms, which would involve the national machineries holding other areas of government accountable in terms of gender mainstreaming. As the Australian and Canadian examples show, 'gender budgets', also adopted by South Africa and the Philippines, require all government departments and agencies to prepare a budget document that disaggregates outlays in terms of their gendered impact (Sawer 2003; UN 1998). Finally, the openness of the state to civil-society scrutiny is required if gender agendas are to be monitored, implemented and audited. Strengthening the mechanisms of consultations with civil-society groups, including the establishment of formal channels for such consultation, where possible ensuring that the mass media carry the message of gender equality, or at least do not carry materials inimical to it, and including women's NGOs in international conferences, would be some of the ways in which this scrutiny could be carried out. The openness of the state to such auditing will be premised upon the openness of the political system in general, and critically upon the leadership of political parties and governments. The question of the political will of leadership remains extremely important, but also unpredictable in any equation regarding gender mainstreaming. Auditing and monitoring require training. This training must involve existing personnel and new recruits, and officers of the state at all levels. The training can be provided through national machineries – in which case the machineries need to develop in-house technical capacity – or through civil-society consultants at both national/local and international levels. The role of multilateral organizations such as the UN becomes critical in this context.

Leadership commitment to gender mainstreaming can be affected by different elements within the political system, as well as the personal commitment (or the lack of it) that leaders bring with them. Populist politics can work both ways – leaders can take advantage of a general civil-society mobilization by women to push for gender equality. This has been the case in many countries covered in this volume, such as Uganda (Kwesiga 2003). The reverse can also be the case, whereby civil-society mobilizations in the name of 'culture' or religion can undermine the leadership's commitment to gender equality (Karam 2000). Individual leaders' perception of themselves can also have an impact on whether or not they take up gender matters. In India and the United Kingdom strong female leaders – Mrs Indira Gandhi and Mrs Margaret Thatcher – did not choose to pursue gender agendas. Their understanding of their own meritocratic entry into public life did not allow them to see the social exclusion of women as a political problem (Rai 1997). Leadership commitment can also be affected by political instability. As Kardam and Acuner point out, 'Instability leads to job insecurity ... lack of motivation and ineffective performance ...' (2003: 102).

Democratizing the state also needs to address the issue of the presence of women within political institutions. Different states have addressed this in a variety of ways, or not at all. Quotas for women in political institutions (see Chapter 5) – in local and national representative bodies, political parties' lists and administrative recruitment – have been one strategy, and are increasingly being demanded by women's groups and being adopted in some states. The argument here is well rehearsed – the presence of women in state institutions allows women's interests to be considered at the time of political debates, policy-making and implementation. This presence needs to be at a 'threshold' level for women in state institutions to feel confident enough to take up issues across party and sectoral lines. While the evidence of the impact of a quota-based strategy is mixed (see Rai 2000), national machineries can benefit from these in two ways. First, they can lobby women more directly on women's rights, and second, they can use the expertise and access to state bodies of women parliamentarians or bureaucrats.

Democratization processes are therefore crucial for embedding national machineries in the architecture of governance. These processes include democratization of state and political systems, as well as gender mainstreaming within state and policy structures. As national machineries for the advancement of women become an established part of the political landscape of countries, their success will depend on the way in which they are able to address issues of governance and democratization both within the state and in their relationship with civil-society associations both at the national and global levels. One area where they have been relatively successful already is the idea of addressing political equality between men and women through quotas for women in political institutions, even though the outcomes of this strategy have been complex (see Chapter 5). The question that we continue to struggle with in our assessment of these important bodies is, however, whether, given their relatively weak structural position within the state system, they can deliver a more sustained socio-economic agenda of redistribution. As we have seen above, the capacity of these state bodies to deliver more broadly on gender equity remains diverse and is often undermined by the economic resources of developing states as the 'discipline' of economic restructuring bites, the lack of political mobilization and regular and productive contact with it, as well as the weak political will of the elites in terms of addressing issues of gender equality.

5 | Quotas in context[1]

WITH FARZANA BARI, NAZMUNESSA MAHTAB
AND BIDYUT MOHANTY

If national machineries for women have been the institutional form that women's engagement with the state has taken, then quotas for women in representative and other institutions of the state have been the single most important policy outcome of this engagement. Women's movements have been successful in making the gap between men and women in political institutions visible, and quotas have now been adopted by many countries to address this inequality in public life. Quotas have become an important part of the gender politics of development, with women's groups often making the connection between the politics of presence and the politics of interests. The argument often is that with the increased presence of women, also called numerical representation, in public life, women's interests will be better represented. This is called substantive representation. While few feminist scholars make a linear connection between the two, the presumption is that the first is the necessary, if not sufficient, condition for the second. This chapter examines the successes and failures of the quota strategy in the context of South Asian development.

South Asia has seen the world's first woman prime minister – Sirimavo Bandaranaike – come to power in Sri Lanka, one of the longest-serving prime ministers anywhere in the world – Indira Gandhi – in India, and the youngest woman prime minister – Benazir Bhutto – in Pakistan. In Bangladesh, two women have held the position of prime minister since 1991 – Begums Zia and Sheikh. And yet women's representation in politics in the region has been very limited and continues to be so at the national level. This chapter reviews the quota debates and provisions in three countries of South Asia – Bangladesh, India and Pakistan (see Table 5.1). While there has been some empirical work done on the process by which quotas for women were introduced and implemented, and on the outcome of the quotas for both women representatives and local government institutions in each of the three countries (Buch 2000a; Mahtab 2003; Bari 1997), this is the first comparative study of the issue.

TABLE 5.1 Quota types in South Asia

Country	Women in parliament (%) and number of seats (year of election)	Quota type	Year of introduction National	Year of introduction Local	Quota provision National	Quota provision Local	Electoral system
Bangladesh	2.0, 6 of 300 (2001)	Legal quotas (C)	2004*	1996	45 of 345 seats (13%)	At least three women (25%)	FPP
India	LH: 8.3, 45 of 541 (2004) UH: 11.6, 28 of 242 (2004)	Legal quotas (C) (local level) Party quotas (national level)	n/a	1992	Indian National Congress Party (15%) Assa People's Council (35%)	Not less than 33%	FPP
Nepal	LH: 5-9, 12 of 205 (1999) UH: 8.3, 5 of 60 (2001)	Legal quota (C) LH: Candidate quota UH: Reserved seats	1990	1990	LH: 5% of contesting candidates UH: 3 of 60 seats (5%)	20%	FPP
Pakistan	LH: 21.6, 74 of 342 (2002) UH: 17.0, 17 of 100 (2003)	Legal quota (L) (national level) Legal quota (Devolution of Power Plan) (local level)	2000	2000	Senate 17% National Assembly 17% Provincial Assemblies 17%	33% 29–33%	FPP
Sri Lanka	4.9, 11 of 225 (2004)	No quota					List PR

Source: Chowdhury (2003); Mahtab (2003); Rarran (2003); Reyes (2003); IDEA (2005).

Key: LH = Lower House, UH = Upper House; Quota Type: Legal Quotas, Constitutional (C) or Law (L); * No election has been held yet; Electoral Systems: Plurality-Majority: FPP = First-Past-the-Post; Proportional Representation: List PR.

While Bangladesh and Pakistan have quotas for women at the national level, there is a considerable discrepancy between the national-level and local-level quotas. The latter in all three countries examined here are 33 per cent of the total, while the quotas at the national level are much less – none in India, 13 per cent in Bangladesh and 10 per cent in Pakistan. The presumptions, which are not unproblematic or even accurate, that can explain the privileging of local institutions as sites for women's participation and empowerment have been the following: a) women are more comfortable participating in local politics than in politics farther away from home; b) that 'the local' is closer to the needs of the people than national politics; and c) that given the high levels of illiteracy among women, local politics is more within the grasp of women than the 'high politics' of parliaments. The debates on quotas in all three countries have also centrally taken into account issues of differences among women. Of particular concern has been the elite nature of representative politics in terms of both class and caste and of women in political life in particular (Rai 1997, 2002).

After reviewing the historical and socio-economic context in which quotas have been introduced in South Asia, and the evidence from the various studies on the implementation of quotas in local governance, the chapter concludes that quotas form part of a long history of constructing post-colonial citizenship, but that they are also part of current governmental strategy for addressing a complex set of issues relating to the status of the nation within the international community. The quotas in South Asia can thus be incremental as well as 'fast track' (Dahlerup 2006) in a historical context that is complex. We suggest that while quotas are important in addressing the exclusion of women from the public political sphere they can form only one part of a multifaceted strategy for empowering women, which must, together with increased political participation, also involve a redistribution of socio-economic resources within societies.

The context

The legacy of British rule, which led to the partition of India into India and Pakistan),[2] coloured the first debates on quotas in South Asia. The first quotas were part of the British administrative regime in South Asia. The official stand of the Indian National Congress under the leadership of Mahatma Gandhi was to oppose quotas – particularly quotas based on caste and religion. The British government, however, introduced quotas for a range of minorities under the Government of India Act of 1935.

Independence came with the partition of India in August 1947. In both Pakistan and India, the tradition of quotas continued. In India, the Dalit leader Ambedkar articulated the need for quotas for the lowest castes and tribes (Baxi 1995), and this was enshrined in the constitution. In India the women's movement came out strongly against quotas on the grounds of equal citizenship rights (Rai and Sharma 2000). Pakistan instituted a quota of 5 per cent for women under its first constitution, which was rather arbitrary and based on colonial legislation rather than on percentage of population (which would have given a parity position to women).

The mediation by the post-colonial state between discourses of modernity and nationhood and nation and culture informed the debates on the 'woman question' (Chatterjee 1993; Rai 2002). In India, Sarkar has argued that it was 'cultural' and not 'political' nationalism which enabled middle-class modern women to enter into the public sphere by 'domesticating' the nationalist project within the home (John 2000: 3822). As we saw in Chapter 1, Chatterjee's insight into 'presence without empowerment' helps explain what may have motivated those supporting the emergence of reservations (quotas) in India. While the constitution provided women with important rights – equality within the legal processes, rescinding of obviously discriminatory practices, the right to the vote, to education and in most cases to property, and laws against violence against women – the implementation of these rights was patchy and lacked state commitment. Further, the state's insistence on its secular character was mediated by its need to reassure Muslim minorities, which led to the recognition of 'personal law'[3] for religious groups. This created a context whereby the Indian constitution reflects the dominant (unequal) gender relations on the one hand while the state rhetoric on citizenship continues to insist on equality between men and women on the other (Pathak and Suder Rajan 1992).

In Pakistan the state negotiated its identity between what it means to be Islamic on the one hand and to be a modern nation-state that treats all its citizens (including women) equally, and therefore provides them with a political framework within which they can all be represented, on the other. In India, however, in both cases we find that tensions emerge early in these negotiated identities, which have repercussions for women's rights. The same tensions emerge in Bangladesh but in a very different context of civil war/war of independence. As Kabeer has pointed out, the tension is between religious and national identities where the language, dress and culture of day-to-day living of the Bengalis of

Bangladesh (formerly East Pakistan) rub against the grain of the Islamic framework that they share with West Pakistan (1988).

While the historical legacy of colonialism provided challenges for the post-colonial state in terms of its own identity – which led to the positioning of women in the political systems in particular ways – the economic legacy of colonialism and the continued struggle of the post-colonial states to address issues of modernization and development were also critical in framing the problem of women's empowerment. The levels of poverty for all the countries of South Asia were high, but women were particularly marginalized within the political economy. The vast majority of South Asian women are illiterate, in poor health, invisible in the system of national accounts, and suffer legal, political, economic and social discrimination in all walks of life. Women in South Asia (including Nepal and Sri Lanka) continue to have low rates of participation in the governance institutions where quotas do not apply. They occupy only 7 per cent of parliamentary seats, 9 per cent of cabinet seats, 6 per cent of positions in the judiciary and 9 per cent of those in the civil service (UNDP 2000).

The post-colonial state in South Asia has different political systems. India is a hybrid of centralized economic management of the country and a federal, multi-party, first-past-the-post electoral and political system which allows for political competition at both the national and the provincial (state) levels. In Pakistan, after a brief interlude, the military became a dominant force in political life, though it was challenged in different periods by democratic forces. In Bangladesh too this pattern of rule was seen until recently, when a fragile but growing stabilization of democratic government became visible.

Quota discourses in South Asia

We can identify three distinct phases in the unfolding of quota discourses that led to provisions of special measures for women in the region. Phase one was that of constitution-making after the achievement of independence in 1947. Here, debates on citizenship and the position of the state in society marked the period.

In India, the Congress Party's general commitment to addressing caste-based inequalities was translated by Ambedkar into specific measures, called 'reservations' or quotas, under the 9th Schedule (Articles 330 and 331).[4] There were also certain redistributive strategies initiated in tandem with the quotas, which were comprehensive – in education at all levels, in state employment, including the judiciary, as well as in political institutions. They were in the first instance provided for fifty years, but under the Sixty-second Amendment Act 1989 they were extended for another forty years, pointing up the political sensitivity of the removal of quotas once they have been established. As noted above, while there was discussion of quotas for women in the Constituent Assembly, they were rejected by women members representing the All-India Women's Congress as demeaning for women struggling for equality with men in all spheres of life. The precedent had been set, however, for using quotas as a means of recognizing historical exclusion.[5] In Pakistan, the recognition of women's exclusion and the symbolic importance of their inclusion in an Islamic republic led to quotas for women, but was not accompanied by a comprehensive approach to fulfilling women's wider socio-economic needs. Reservation of seats for women in the national and provincial assemblies, the senate and local government was agreed in the first constitution of 1956 at a minimal level of 3 per cent at both levels. Women were always elected to reserved seats through indirect election. The revised constitutions of 1962 and 1973 also provided reservation of seats for women at similarly low levels of 2.75 and 5 per cent respectively in the national and provincial assemblies. The insignificant number of reserved seats combined with the indirect mode of election to women's reserved seats, together with a failure to address the socio-economic and religious basis of women's exclusion, led to failure in terms of mainstreaming women in politics and providing an opportunity for them to play an effective role in politics. In Bangladesh the first constitution of the country, promulgated in 1972, provided for fifteen indirectly elected reserved seats for women in the national parliament for a period of ten years. This gave women a minimum representation of 4.7 per cent. Members elected to the general seats constituted the electoral college for electing candidates to the reserved seats (Chowdhury 2003).

The second phase of quota politics for women begins in the 1970s and 1980s. This, of course, is also the time when international organizations such as the UN were beginning to recognize the importance of women in public life, leading to the UN Conference on Women held in Mexico on the status of women worldwide and the declaration of the Decade for Women in 1975. Women's groups in South Asia were affected by these developments. Diffusion of ideas on women's participation in public life, however, had to be mediated within the nationalist context. Women's groups did not wish to be seen as 'Westernized' and cut off from their own culture. To negotiate the boundaries of tradition and citizenship was a challenge to the women's movements and groups in the South Asian region.

The state in India responded to UN exhortations and some unease about women's status within Indian society among women's groups by establishing the first Commission on the Status of Women in India (CSWI) in 1972. This once again debated the reservation issue. A majority of the CSWI members rejected the step as a retrograde one in terms of the equality conferred by the constitution. The CSWI recommended the constitution of statutory all-women *panchayats* at the village level to look after the welfare of women, though this was not implemented by most state governments. The National Perspective Plan for Women (1988–2000) recommended a reservation of at least 30 per cent of the total seats for women in the local government institutions. These developments towards a quota system for women's representation reflect some wider political processes in the country. As Gopal Jayal has argued, there was a growing concern over the 'failure of development programmes, and the perception that these would be able to perform better with local participation which would help to identify local needs ...' (2005: 1). By the 1990s the women's movement in India had begun to engage with the state at both the local and the national level, and women's groups were being consulted by the government on issues of women's welfare, culminating in the establishment of the Women's National Commission in 1992.[6] Attention to the mobilization of the women's vote came in the context of the collapse of the Congress-dominated political system and the beginning of coalition governments in India. Women were regarded as a new constituency by Rajiv Gandhi, the leader of the Congress Party, who addressed the issue of India's modernity by focusing on the position of women in the country. The 1992 provision of reservation of seats in local government for women under the 73rd and 74th Amendments to the Indian constitution was a key intervention by his government.[7]

In 1985 the number of reserved seats for women in the Pakistan national assembly was raised to twenty (10 per cent) for a period of ten years or three general elections, whichever came earlier. Women's mobilization came in the context of the enactment of the Hudood Ordinances in 1979 by the military dictator General Zia ul-Haq. These ordinances were a set of six laws, which were used to 'Islamize' criminal law.[8] Ali has sketched out the struggles of Pakistani women to find a voice that allowed them to be both secular citizens as well as Muslims (2000). A mature women's movement responded by organizing rallies against the legislation and by demanding equal representation. Women-only police stations, pressures on political parties to include more women on their lists and lobbying of the media to report atrocities against women constituted the background for arguments for higher representation of women in political institutions. Efforts to 'fulfil commitments in international treaties and conventions to promote women's free, equal and full political participation are summed up in the Report of the Commission of Inquiry for Women (August, 1997), the National Plan for Action (NPA) (September 1998) and the National Policy for Development and Empowerment of Women (March 2002)' (ibid.: 54).

In Bangladesh, the international donor agencies, working with/in the UN framework of Women in Development, were instrumental in pushing forward the discourse of gender equality (Goetz 1996, 1997; Kabeer 1994, 1995). It is estimated that 80–100 per cent of Bangladesh's national budget for development is underwritten by external funding, which makes donor pressure an overwhelming source of change. International pressure also comes from the UN and other international NGOs that support particular forms of initiatives – quotas for women being one – to address issues of gender inequality. The role of NGOs in Bangladesh in addressing the quota issues is also important. While many NGOs are involved in providing micro-credit (Kabeer 1995), others focus on political empowerment issues, particularly women's representation in political institutions (Kabeer 1999). They also mobilize women at the local level, and provide them with support and training, which is largely funded by international donor agencies and institutions. The 1986 constitution did not provide for quotas, but with regard to local government institutions Article 9 of the constitution stated that 'The state shall encourage local government institutions composed of representatives of the areas concerned and in such institutions special representations shall be given as far as possible to peasants, workers and women.' Reservation of seats was reincorporated into the constitution in 1990, valid for ten years. This provision lapsed in 2001, which means that the present parliament does not have reserved seats for women (Chowdhury 2003), though it was reintroduced in 2004 at 13 per cent of seats in the next parliament.

The third (and current) phase is characterized by several key elements. Economic liberalization has led to the further erosion of the welfare state in India and Pakistan. The latter has also felt the crushing burden of refugees on its Afghan border, as well as that of expenditure on security. At the international level, the 'third wave' of democratization has led to pressures on military regimes to democratize, while the 'war on terror' has led to Musharraf being courted by the USA on the other. Discourses of constructed modernity (democratic and liberalizing regimes) and fundamentalism (Taliban, al-Qaeda, jihad) have formed the backdrop to the region's most recent engagements with the changing international system. We have also seen a worldwide consensus emerging about the relevance of state feminism, especially after the Beijing Conference of 1995, and the emergence of an international discourse on the importance of women's empowerment through participation in the political institutions of the state as well as supra-state institutions (Bystendinzky 1992; Parpart et al. 2002). This phase has seen a debate on the extension of quotas for women to the national parliament in India and an extension of quota provisions in Pakistan and Bangladesh, where in the wake of the Beijing Conference the government 'announced a National Policy for the Advancement of Women in 1997. The Policy called for a larger number of reserved seats in the legislature for women through direct elections' (Chowdhury 2003). At the national level in Pakistan, in the senate and national assemblies, 17 and 18 per cent respectively of the seats are reserved for women. In the provincial assemblies 22 per cent of the seats are reserved for women (Reyes 2003).

Quota provisions in local government: a comparative perspective

This section examines the provisions of the local government quotas for women. The argument is that variations in the actual quota systems in the three countries influence the opportunity of women, once elected, to participate fully.

The new local-level quotas introduced during the 1990s were for directly elected reserved seats in all three countries.[9] The percentage of reserved seats was raised in India and Pakistan to 33 per cent and in Bangladesh to 25 per cent. These changes have been described by Raman, for example, as 'historic and one of the most significant attempts at transforming the Indian polity in the direction of greater democratization and decentralization of powers' (2003: 24). Assessing quotas in Pakistan, Reyes suggests that it has 'opened up not only an enormous political space but a strategic opportunity for women to make a difference in setting and implementing the agenda of local governments' (2003: 44). Chowdhury argues that in Bangladesh the direct election to local bodies 'has brought about a qualitative change in their role perception. On the whole they have claimed a space within the local bodies and have raised spirited calls to have their terms of reference and spheres of activity defined' (2003: 55).

How do the new local quota systems work? Even though the countries have a common political history the local political systems vary slightly from each other. In India, the 1992 73rd and 74th Constitutional Amendment Acts addressed the question of strengthening the role of local government and made provision for reserving not less than 33 per cent of total seats in local government for women (Mohanty and Mahajan 2003). A *gram panchayat* is meant to consist of eight to ten villages, though since the population is the criterion it can also serve just one village. The *gram panchayat* has about 12,000 to 15,000 inhabitants, though the Acts do not specify any such number, leading to variations across the country. The number of members in a *gram panchayat* is not fixed but varies from five to thirty members depending on the size of the population in the district. The *gram panchayat* members elect the *pradhan* (chairman) and vice-chairman from among themselves. The *Panchayati Raj* system is a party political system and the members are elected as candidates from a party list on a first-past-the-post basis and serve a mandatory term of

TABLE 5.2 The local systems in Bangladesh, India and Pakistan

Country	Level	Name	Number of councils	Elected
Bangladesh	District	Zila Parishad	60	n/a
	Sub-district	Upazila/Thana Parishad	450	n/a
	Union level	Union Parishad	4,500	Directly
	Village level	Gram Sarkar	68,000	n/a
India	District	Zila Panchayat	530	Directly
	Sub-district	Panchayat Samities	5,910	Directly
	Village level	Gram Panchayat	231,630	Directly
Pakistan	District	Zila councils	100	Indirectly
	Sub-district	Tehsil/Town council	330	Indirectly
	Union level	Union councils	6,000	Directly

Sources: Siddiqui (2002), Graff (2005).

Notes: a The urban local system consists of City Corporations and Pourshavas (municipal bodies) (Mahtab 2003). b According to the Local Government Reform Commission Report 1996, Bangladesh has a four-tier local government structure. However, until now nothing has been determined regarding the three-tier Zila, Upazial/Thana and Gram. No consensus has been reached regarding their composition, function or mode of election including the number of seats reserved for women, and no elections have been held at any of these levels. c The urban local system is a three-tier system: Municipal corporation (mega cities), Municipal Council (small cities) and Nagar Panchayat (transitional areas) (Sharma 2003). d The Tehsil Council is called Town Councils in the urban areas (Graff 2005).

five years in single-member districts. There is also a one-third reservation for women among the positions of the chairpersons (*pradhans*) of
these bodies (Baviskar 2003). There is a rotating system of reservations
for women, which means that if you have a *panchayat* with nine villages
and nine members, in three of these villages only women candidates
can stand for election. In the next election women will stand in three
other villages (ibid.).

In Bangladesh the local system consists of three tiers, but until now
continuous elections have been held only to *Union Parishad*.[10] The reservation of seats for women in local government institutions in Bangladesh is
stipulated under Article 9 of the Fundamental Principles of State Policy of
the Constitution of Bangladesh. Direct election of women representatives
to the *Union Parishad* and urban local government was provided for in
order to implement the constitutional provision. This also conformed
with the recommendations of the Study on the Institutional Review of
the WID Capability of the Government of Bangladesh 1996 and the Local
Government Commissions Report 1997.

The number of members in *Union Parishad* is fixed and does not
depend on the population size of the Union, unlike the system in India.
A union consists of five to fifteen villages with an average population of
24,500 people (Nathan 1998: 110; Thörlind 2003: 61–2). *Union Parishad*
consists of one chairperson, nine general members and three women
members in reserved seats, a total of thirteen persons. This means that
the percentage of women will be at least 23 per cent – not 25 per cent, as
there are no quotas allocated for the post of chairperson. All the positions
are directly elected, including the chairperson, on a first-past-the-post
basis in non-party-based elections (Siddiqui 2002). The chairperson is
elected from the whole *Union Parishad* and the post is open to both men
and women to contest. The nine general members are directly elected
from one of the nine wards the Union is divided into, and elections are
also open to both men and women. The women in the reserved seats
don't have any special ward of their own but are elected from three of
the general wards (Aminuzzaman 2003). In these wards (open to women
only) women candidates compete against each other but are elected by
votes from both men and women.

As Pakistan is a federal republic the local government has been viewed
as a provincial decision area. Therefore the reservation of seats for women
in local government has varied between the different provinces (Graff
2005). Women's rights organizations and activists have demanded the
restoration of the provision of reserved seats for women together with a

substantial increase to 33 per cent reserved seats for women to be filled through constituency-based direct elections by a joint electorate. The successive governments of Benazir Bhutto and Nawaz Sharif failed to respond positively to women's demands on the issue. In 1999 a military coup removed the civilian government and as part of a democratization process the military regime of Musharraf adopted the Devolution of Power Plan in 2000 to establish an identical set-up of local government bodies in all four provinces of Pakistan. This guaranteed a 33 per cent quota for women at all three levels of the local government; *Zila* council (district level), *Tehsil* council (sub-district level) and Union councils (village level). The members of the Union councils are elected directly but in the *Tehsil* and *Zila* councils the members are elected indirectly by an electoral college formed by the elected councillors in the Union Councils. The Union Council consists of eight to ten villages. It is composed of twenty-one members – one *Nazim* (chairman), one *Naib Nazim* (vice-chairman), eight general Muslim seats, four women Muslim seats, four Muslim peasant/worker seats, two women peasant/worker seats and one religious minority seat. This means that six out of twenty-one seats are reserved for women, and the actual quota percentage is 29 and not 33, which is the figure usually quoted. This is due to the fact that there were no quotas allocated for the *Nazims'* or the minority seats (Graff 2005). Elections to Union Council are on a first-past-the-post and non-party basis, as in Bangladesh, but contrary to the situation in both India and Bangladesh the Union serves as a multi-member ward for election of council members (block vote). The women elected to the reserved seats are elected by votes from both men and women, as in the other two countries (ibid.).

This comparison shows that the quota systems in the three countries are slightly different. In both Pakistan and Bangladesh quotas have been introduced at both national and local levels, while in India the quotas were introduced at the local level and the Bill to introduce quotas at the national level still languishes in the system (Rai 2000). In India there is a system of ward rotation for the reserved seats, which is not present in Pakistan and Bangladesh. In Bangladesh the wards for the reserved seats for women are three times bigger than those for the 'general seats'. This is not the case in the other two countries. In Pakistan the Union is not divided into different wards – as in India and Bangladesh – but serves as a single constituency for all the candidates. In Pakistan and Bangladesh the local elections are non-party-based in contrast to the system in India. In India the chairman's seat is included in the quota system, which means that one-third of the members are women. That is not the case in Bangladesh and Pakistan. There are also, however, some similarities in these different quota regimes. All three electoral systems have constitutional histories bound up with the British colonial past, are majoritarian political systems, and the women are directly elected by both male and female votes.

Further, the analysis of quota provisions in different countries shows some level of diffusion of ideas. Various elements can be evaluated here. All three states are signatories to CEDAW (though with certain opt-outs) and therefore have to report to the Committee on the Status of Women regularly. This, together with the Beijing and post-Beijing UN initiatives prioritizing women's participation in political institutions, has provided the impetus to examine quotas as a strategy for women's empowerment. A second element of diffusion is the role that women's movements and NGOs have played in demanding that women's exclusion from political institutions be addressed. Some of these demands have been the result of responses to state law, as in the anti-Hudood law movement in Pakistan. The women's movements in all three countries have been influenced by the shift in international women's movements from scepticism to engagement with state institutions. Finally, donor agencies are a source of diffusion of ideas on quotas. Familiarity with the Indian quota system, for example, makes donors suggest this pattern in Bangladesh, though it may or may not be suitable in the country's political context. There is also some evidence, however, that diffusion between these countries is limited. For example, critics in India have pointed out that seat reservation by rotation hinders the emergence of real leaders, because for first-time participants a five-year tenure is too short to nurture a constituency that reverts to being a 'general' constituency at the end of that period. In Bangladesh, however, critics of fixed constituencies for women have pointed out the benefits of the rotational system. Formal acknowledgement of 'best practice' exchange is absent in the context of the poor state-to-state relations.

Quotas in practice: do they make a difference?

Measuring the impact that the introduction of quotas may or may not have had is difficult. One clear measurement would be the increase in the number of women in local government after the introduction of quotas. This, however, can only be a quantitative assessment of the impact that quotas have made. A more complex issue would be whether the increased representation of women in local government has increased their active participation in local government bodies. Here we would need indicators such as attendance data, data about the number of times women speak in local government meetings, whether or not women have introduced and succeeded in getting through initiatives, and even empowerment indicators (training, travel and meetings with other women involved in local government, mentoring, etc.) would have to be examined. A further level of complexity will arise when we examine the context of women's participation – levels of education and health and the cultural and economic position of women, which has a crucial effect on their access to both the state and community resources needed for performing their roles as representatives in local government. Finally, of course, we need to factor in availability, reliability and the coherence of the data available, which in many cases are scarce.

Given the complexity of measuring impact, our conclusions are that issues of process and outcome, individual experience and systemic issues have influenced the implementation of the quotas.

Women's numerical representation Women's representation in local government has increased in all the three countries, and we suggest that this is because of the introduction of quotas in one form or other. In India, after approval of the constitutional amendments, two elections (in 1995 and 2000) have been held in almost all states, and today 1 million women occupy positions as members or heads in the rural and urban local government bodies (Baviskar 2003). It has been estimated that within a span of ten years about six million women have participated in the political process as candidates or elected members (Buch 2000b). While there are variations among the states in the magnitude of women's representation, most of the states have managed to meet the constitutional target of 33 per cent seats of for women and in some states this proportion has been exceeded. For example, in Karnataka women occupy 43.6 per cent of seats on local bodies. This means that a large number of women have managed to win general (unreserved) seats, defeating rival male and female candidates (Baviskar 2003). Bangladesh has held two elections under the new quota probation – in 1997 and 2003. In each of these elections over forty thousand women contested almost thirteen thousand reserved seats, which were all filled. In Pakistan, however, only 36,000 of the over 40,000 seats were filled, despite the fact that almost 49,000 women contested the elections held between 2000 and 2001. Most of the problems were reported from districts in the North West Frontier Province (NWFP), where many women were neither allowed to stand nor to cast their votes (Bari and Khan 2001: xii).

Challenges to participation Have the new systems with a higher percentage of reserved seats as well as provision for direct election not only increased the number of women but also improved the quality of their participation – in contrast to the previous, often criticized systems of indirect election? One indicator of the success of the quota strategy would be to demonstrate that women's increased presence within local government is resulting in the improved functioning of local government institutions in these countries. Our conclusion is that gender and class regimes mediate political participation in all three countries. State provision, formal and informal networks and customary laws prevent women from participating fully in local government. There is also a lack of education, training and resources for women representatives. Finally, their dependence on male members of the household and their inability to access economic resources (there are no salaries for local government representatives) are also inhibiting their performance. At the same time it seems that the new systems of reserved seats have created a social mobilization of rural women and changed their status both in the family as well as in society.

There is no consensus among researchers here. Any consensus reached would, of course, depend on differing definitions of contested concepts such as 'empowerment'. In India it is often reported that the reserved seats for women have been filled by 'proxies' – the wives of male politicians without any real power (Nanivadekar 1997). It is estimated that over 90 per cent of the elected women are first-timers. Even if the policy of reservation has helped some politically active women to be elected, these women have a lower political awareness, and as such their participation in politics does not disturb patriarchal family systems. No gender differences were found between the men and women representatives with respect to their priority issues (ibid.). Sharma is also critical, and argues that women are expected to adjust to the imperatives of party structures for their political survival (Sharma n.d.). Some micro-studies show that the elected women have not addressed any specific gender issues (Ekatra 2003; Ghosh 2003). At the same time, other studies suggest that elected women in *gram panchayats* are making a difference in shifting the focus of development policy by highlighting basic-needs issues like water, food security, education and livelihood, and are becoming effective supporters of women's interests (Mohanty 1999a; Datta 1998; Nussbaum 2003).

In Pakistan the impact of the new quota system is yet to be seen. Initial research shows that there are frequent complaints by women councillors that they do not receive invitations to the council meetings. They are not consulted in development planning at the district and union council levels. At the same time a study showed that female councillors have strong community contacts (Pattan Development Organization 2004; Rai et al. 2007). A case study on urban local government in Bangladesh shows that the elected women members can act as motivators and supervisors, and can be engaged in project planning, implementing, monitoring and evaluation processes. The participation of the ward commissioners in the activities of the city corporations is, however, low (Mahtab 2003).

The problems for the elected women can be explained by several factors. According to Kabeer, the northern plains of the Indian subcontinent

TABLE 5.3 Women's representation in local government

Country	Issues introduced by women
Bangladesh	Lack of good communication – damage of roads due to incessant rain during the rainy season, lack of maintenance of these roads and no plans to repair the roads or construct new roads
	Proliferation of urban slums, rise in urban population due to rural–urban migration; increase in urban poverty
	Lack of women's education – their limited participation in development activities, increase in violence against women, demand for dowry, lack of implementation of laws protecting the rights of women, child abuse and denial of justice
India	Speedy disbursement of rice and wheat through Public Distribution System (PDS)
	Widow pensions
	Low-cost shelters
	Encouraging girl child to join the schools
	Construction of bathing ghats
Pakistan	Education for girls
	Access to drinking water
	Price increase
	Access to health centres and trained health workers in communities, particularly for delivery of babies
	A say in spending the development funds assigned to local bodies
	Violence against women

Source: Interview with Shaheen Sardar Ali (first chair of Pakistan Women's National Commission) 29 November 2004; Mahtab (2003), Mohanty and Mahajan (2003).

and Bangladesh belong to a belt of 'classic patriarchy' characterized by the institutionalization of extremely restrictive codes of behaviour for women. They stand in contrast to societies of South India and much of South East Asia whose institutions and practices permit a more egalitarian system of gender relations. At the heart of this system of social arrangements is the institution of purdah or female seclusion, which defines and limits the personal and economic autonomy and social power of women and confines them in the private sphere of the home (Kabeer 1988). These patriarchal social relations are limiting women's ability to participate fully in the political life of the local community. In India the issue of caste-based discrimination forms an added layer of exclusion for women.

Further, in most states in India the role of *panchayats* is still principally confined to implementing centrally conceived schemes. The lack of administrative and financial autonomy prevents these institutions from fulfilling their role as institutions of self-government, and the elected women have been addressing gender issues within very narrow parameters set by the *panchayats* (Mohanty and Mahajan 2003; Matthew 2002; Raman 2004). A similar situation is reported in Bangladesh, where the lack of resources and authority is also a problem of the local government (Frankl 2004).

A third issue is the nature of representation by women within the reserved seats. In Bangladesh the reserved seats have no ward of their own. Instead one reserved seat covers three wards of the general seats, which creates problems when it comes to whom the elected women represent, access to development funds and campaigning, as they must cover a much bigger area (ibid.). Mahtab's study showed that the women commissioners in local government were undermined as they were deprived of their responsibilities and financial allocations for development of their constituencies (ibid.). In Pakistan all members are elected from multi-member constituencies, but despite this women are not given an equal share of development funds as they are not perceived to have any direct constituency or ward. In India the elected women have their own ward as they practise a system of rotation. This system has the advantage that the elected women have a clear mandate. At the same time it also works against women's interests. Women who have been elected from a reserved ward in the first election have to compete with men as well as women in the next election. And when the ward is 'open' no party wants to nominate a female candidate. Another option is to contest one of the other three wards that have been reserved, but then a candidate will derive no benefit from the work that she may have done before (Baviskar 2003).

Another issue is little or no special honorarium. In India a *panchayat* member gets between Rs10 and Rs50 as a 'sitting fee' for attending a meeting. In many cases, if she is an agricultural labourer, she will lose Rs50 as her daily wage and will not be able to feed her family (Baviskar 2003). In other studies (Rai 2007; Sharma 2003) several women pointed out that without members' salaries the *panchayat* is more open to corrupt practices and to being dominated by upper-class individuals who can afford not to be paid. The issue of payment also seems to be a particular one for women as being paid brings them status – *maan* – within the family.[11] In Pakistan councillors who gain reserved seats are not offered any honorarium, which forces women councillors to find transportation costs out of their own pocket, which causes difficulties as most of them are economically dependent on the male members of their families. In Bangladesh the members are supposed to receive an honorarium to cover transportation costs and so on, but not all members are able to get their money (Frankl 2004). The study undertaken by Mahtab (2003) showed that women commissioners do not have proper facilities, such as specific office space, transport and other facilities.

As noted before, local elections in India are party-based, in contrast to Bangladesh and Pakistan, where elections are non-party-based. More research is needed to examine the role of the political parties and how women's membership of these institutions might affect their work within the *panchayats* (Rai 2003). In local elections there is always a high number of candidates not affiliated to any political party (Nanivadekar 1997), and a study by the NGO Ekatra suggested that 70 per cent of women have succeeded in raising issues at various levels, even without the backing of political parties. In Bangladesh, elections are supposed to be on a non-party basis but, according to Ahmed, parties control and decide on their representatives even at local level. By doing so, they play an important role in shaping women's representation in formal politics (2003). In Pakistan Bari and Khan argue that party-less local government has provided the space for the poor to nominate their own candidates, as well as forcing the local elite to involve disadvantaged groups in the process of nominating candidates (Bari and Khan 2001).

The age, education, socio-economic status and political background of the elected women seem to have a crucial effect on their access to both the state and community resources needed to perform their roles as representatives in local government. In India studies conducted in several parts of the country show that a majority of the women belong to the lower socio-economic strata both in terms of education and class (Buch 2000a, 2000b). In India a majority of the elected women are from 'non-political' families with no previous political experience. The seats reserved for the Scheduled Castes and Scheduled Tribes (so-called 'backward' communities accorded special status) mean that the rich and politically dominant families are not able to grab the positions (Baviskar 2003). At the same time it seems that the percentage of women from lower incomes is lower at the leadership levels. When it comes to age, studies have shown that, in the first election, most of the women were aged forty or more (Datta 1998; Ghosh 2003). Studies have shown that in the second election, however, relatively younger groups have been elected (Panchayati Raj Update 2003). Similar findings from the survey undertaken in Pakistan by the Pattan Development Organization in 2001 show that more than half of the women were illiterate, very few owned land and a majority of them had never contested elections before, and neither had their families. And as in India, the percentage of women from the lower strata of society declined among the higher levels of local government. Almost 60 per cent of the elected women were aged forty-five or younger. In Bangladesh, however, a study undertaken by the World Food Programme in 1999 showed that the elected women had a better socio-economic status than the average rural women. Over 40 per cent were between thirty and thirty-eight years of age, and even though a majority of the elected women were housewives, most of them had at least a secondary education (86 per cent). Most of the elected women came from landowning families and 53 per cent owned more than five acres of land – a substantial amount in a country where half the rural people are landless. The study also showed that both the elected member and her family were very active in the village, where they were known for considerable social involvement even before the election (World Food Programme 1999). More research needs to be done to explain the differences between India and Pakistan on the one hand and Bangladesh on the other. According to Mohanty, the high proportion of women from lower social economic strata must be regarded as a success when it comes to decentralization, since women from all classes of society have been represented (Mohanty and Mahajan 2003).

The lack of previous political experience as well as a low level of education and socio-economic status underlines the need for training and capacity-building among the elected women. In Bangladesh training is offered by both the government and NGOs. A 2002 study (Democracywatch 2002) showed that the elected members had received a lot of training from different NGOs but also that they wanted and needed more training. The study also showed that effective training would need to include both men and women. In India evaluations have shown that the women want education and training continuously. So far most of the training programmes have focused on local government rules and regulations, but according to Raman the training also has to focus on problem-solving methodologies. People have to be trained for self-government (Raman 2004).

Despite the problems, however, quotas for women in local government have, together with other movements, such as, for example, the micro-credit movement, created a massive social mobilization in rural areas (Mohanty and Mahajan 2003). And the women's participation in the public sphere of *panchayats* has also enhanced their status in their families, castes and villages (Baviskar 2003; Sharma 2003). In Bangladesh, too, women's participation in local politics has led to a measure of increased freedom, and has reduced inequality and oppression (Frankl 2004). As elected members of *Union Parishad*, some women have been able to introduce change in the traditional village court. This, as well as membership of the *Union Parishad*, has made them well known in the village and given them a larger social network than before.

Conclusions

A comparative study of quotas for women in the South Asian region addresses several important issues concerning the gendered nature of political participation and representation. This study suggests that quotas for women in representative bodies at the local level came about as a result of many different factors – an internal debate about the ways in which marginalized groups can be compensated for historical exclusions from public life; external pressures from global social institutions such as the UN and the women's movements and the interaction of national women's groups with these; changes in the nature of state politics as well as the shifting positions of party and factional groups within national politics.

Here, some theoretical issues are raised about quotas. In terms of the politics of representation, quotas address the historical inequality that has kept women out of the public sphere. Both participation and representation have historically been hotly contested concepts. The politics of representation has reflected a wide variety of views towards quotas. From the justice argument to the empowerment argument, quotas have been seen as important elements in addressing women's historical exclusion from political institutions and processes. As is clear from the case study of South Asia presented here, the outcome of quota regimes is equally complex. On the one hand, we see quota-based representation in local government reflecting the gender regimes of inequality and worry about the cooption of women into state machinery without any significant shifts in their status, or indeed the status of local government institutions. On the other, however, we do see some clear indications that participation made available through quotas does have an impact on familial and institutional relations, even though this impact is rather fragile and will need further nurturing in order to be consolidated. Quotas in this sense are a start, and have the potential to kick-start other processes of empowerment of women.

Quota politics is also the politics of citizenship. As we have seen above, the constitutional debates in the three countries reflected the nature of particular citizenships, which meant that women's citizenship was formalized through equality provisions without necessarily providing the entitlements that were critical to operationalizing these. Women's movements had to struggle to make political rights real, and these struggles point to the dynamic and unfolding nature of citizenship debates and rights. While the early struggles demanded universal political rights, current movements have insisted on mainstreaming a gendered perspective in political institutions, as well as on the importance of entitlements to citizenship that include both socio-economic justice and a discursive shift from the earlier national citizenship rights to the demands for universal human rights. The introduction of quotas is the result of these struggles and a response to the limitations of the equality discourse when not backed up by social and political commitment to its implementation.

Through a multilayered analysis of the quota debate in South Asia, we become conscious of several issues. First, as economic restructuring of national economies under pressure from international economic institutions bites along lines of class, gender and race, debates about socio-economic entitlements to citizenship are increasing in importance (Fraser 1997; Coole 1996; Hoskyns and Rai 1998). In particular we find feminist theorists and policy analysts pointing out the importance of distinguishing between socio-economic and political bases of citizenship (Yuval-Davis and Pnina 1999; Lister 1997). It is in these debates on citizenship that feminists have also encountered yet again the issue of differences among women – the realization that if socio-economic contexts are important for women's citizenship to be actualized, then there needs to be an acknowledgement that not all women share the same economic and social space. Citizenship debates are important if we are to assess whether quotas open up space for the recognition of women's under-representation in politics, but also whether by making possible women's participation in politics they empower women. Local government quotas can work to empower women only when this wider context is taken into account. Second, empowerment is not the possession but the exercise of power – not simply power over, but power to. In the context of local governance in South Asia, 'individual empowerment, whether it be gaining skills, developing consciousness, or making decisions, takes place within the structural constraints of institutions and discursive practices' (Parpart et al. 2002: x). Third, measuring empowerment can be problematic. How will we measure the empowering effect of being elected *sarpanch*, or meeting other women in an institutional setting? It is the issue of keeping in view both the process and the outcome of policies which Nancy Fraser has addressed in her work on the 'politics of recognition' versus the 'politics of redistribution' (1997).

Fraser suggests that identity politics allows for recognition of inequalities within society but not necessarily for a 'politics of redistribution'. Redistribution of resources, unavailability of which underpins exclusion and lack of voice, cannot, she argues, be addressed simply through the politics of recognition. As we have seen above, issues of caste, class and religion continue to divide women and are reflected in the nature of local politics. Iris Marion Young, however, takes issue with this interpretation of identity-based recognition. She argues that in the very process of arguing for the recognition of hitherto excluded or marginalized groups there takes place a redistribution of discursive power (1997). The politics of recognition and of redistribution therefore unfold simultaneously. As Anne Phillips has argued in the context of political systems, however, the shift from the politics of 'ideas' (by which she means ideas organized within the structures of political parties) to the politics of presence (by which she means representation of identities in politics) is problematic. She argues instead that it is 'in the relationship between ideas and presence that we can best hope to find a fairer system of representation, not in a false opposition between one or the other' (1995: 25). In this sense, quotas have the potential to bring together the politics of ideas and that of presence. Where both Young and Phillips fail to address the point made by Fraser, however, is in the relationship between the structural inequalities of a socio-economic system and its impact on the politics of recognition as well as representation. Hoskyns and Rai have argued that '[the] feminist challenge is limited by a current lack of focus on the importance of redistributive policies that are rooted in the structural inequalities of capitalist production and exchange' (1998: 362). If quotas are to fulfil their potential for addressing women's exclusion from political life, women's struggles need to focus on the issue of redistribution of resources if power relations in society are to be fundamentally changed.

6 | Globalization, development and global governance[1]

In this chapter I move from a framework of state-based development to a globalized understanding of development. Specifically, I analyse the concept, framework and practice of global governance and reflect upon the importance of this shift for the gender politics of development. In my book *Gender and the Political Economy of Development* (2002), I mapped the globalization of development policy and its consequences for gender relations in developing societies. While the nature of economic globalization has been reviewed extensively by political economists, however – feminists and mainstream – only relatively recently have feminist critiques of governance been taking shape (Meyer and Prugl 1999; Waylen and Rai 2004; Rai and Waylen 2007). This is in part because the mainstream literature on global governance, which explains and analyses the neoliberal framework and how it is secured, not simply through the making of policy but also through legal and institutional forms at the global rather than the state level, is also relatively recent. In this chapter I take the debate forward by examining global governance in four different contexts – market, institutions, ideology and spectacle – and suggest that gendered global governance through regulatory laws and institutional practice is locking in modes of thinking, of working and, indeed, of being, such that challenging these seems to fly in the face of the self-evident, 'commonsense' nature of development itself. Such discursive primacy makes global governance an important concept for us to understand, critique and challenge. Issues of redistribution that have been key to the analysis of the gender politics of development thus far continue to be critical for understanding global governance.

Framing the global governance literature

Governance can be defined as a system of rules for public life. In this definition we go beyond the concept of government. Governance includes multiple actors as well as multiple sites. At the heart of the concept there is an assumption of a shift in the sources or 'spheres of authority' from the state to these multiple actors and sites (Rosenau and Czempiel 1992). In this context, the state becomes only one of the many institutions that regulate our lives – making rules, ensuring that these rules are accepted and implemented and that there are penalties attached to breaking these rules which are enforceable.

While there are discrepancies between different frameworks seeking to explain and use this term, some elements remain constant. The global governance literature has largely analysed the governance of polities as encompassing three different political arenas:

1. *Markets* The literature has focused on markets both in goods and services as well as increasingly on the markets of knowledge – information technology, patents on knowledge-based products, etc. The volume as well as the volatility of market interactions has been seen to be driving the need to transcend the bounded regulation of the state. The argument goes that global markets are now too big, the volume of exchange of goods and services too high and the complexity of interactions, especially in the sphere of finance, too great to be regulated by the state. The linking of local, national, regional and international markets has created multiple sites of both production and exchange, which perforce mean that the state is unable to exercise its authority over market processes. At the same time, the primacy of markets has the effect of leaching market norms into political institutions until they become institutional norms.

2. *Institutions* This has embraced the three levels of governance – local, national (sometimes regional and subregional) and international. It has focused largely on the way in which the national state has either been overtaken by or has had to transform itself in response to globalization. Here the argument is that institutions participating in the regulation of the global economy are increasingly of a wide range – from the national state to private agencies. This reflects the complexity of market interactions on the one hand, and changing patterns of political actors and their behaviour on the other. Transnational companies as well as transnational movements operate both globally as well as locally, using increasingly sophisticated media for their work, making it difficult for states always to be able to mediate between them or to exercise their authority over them. At the same time state institutions also participate in refashioning the interaction between institutions and regulation of the economy at different levels.

3. *Ideology* This has included analyses of how certain ideas attain the status of 'common sense', how the normativity of particular discourses

becomes entrenched as self-evident. It suggests the hegemonic dominance of certain epistemic communities – experts, policy analysts and
policy-makers, intellectuals. The literature also takes into account how
the ontologies of governance are promoted through networks of influence and authority of the richer countries, as well as how these are
embedded institutionally through international policies, conventions,
treaties, etc.

I would add another dimension of the governance of polities in order
to understand the interplay between these three arenas – markets, institutions and ideologies. To arrive at a more comprehensive picture of
how governance is being used in our political vocabulary in institutions,
we need to add a fourth arena to our analysis: this is the arena of the
spectacle.

4. *Spectacle* This refers to the modes of production of meanings through
a display of political power such that transgression and disciplining of
the other are seen as the exercise of legitimate power. Some cultural
norms then become human rights and others human wrongs. Acceptance
of and legitimacy of dominant relations of power are then produced for
us through performance – international summits, the military success of
'shock and awe', participatory modes of politics both violent and peaceful
at both local and global levels. The capturing of these spectacles and
their distribution is effected through both traditional and new means of
communication – the print and electronic media, which circulate images
of these spectacles that support the ideologies of power.[2]

Defining global governance

Hewson and Sinclair have outlined three shifts that have occurred in
international relations theory in response to global post-cold-war change:
first, in the work of Rosenau, the shift of authority from the state to
multiple arenas of governance. The second shift, seen in the work of the
UN Commission on Global Governance, Falk (1995) and the cosmopolitan
theorists like Held (1991), is the emergence of a global, rather than the
previously national, civil society. Finally, in the work of Cox they see a
review of the work of transnational economic and political elites and
coalitions of social forces (Hewson and Sinclair 1999: 5–8). This body
of work is a rich tapestry of analysis of the changing contours of the
international system and takes us out of the more narrowly focused,
issue-based analyses of regime theory of the 1980s. As such, this shift
is to be welcomed.

The various interventions made in the global governance debate predictably cover the entire spectrum – from realism to Marxism to feminism, from converts to sceptics. In this section we reflect upon some of these debates and the questions that they pose for us. We then examine whether these questions would be different questions, and the answers different answers, if feminist concerns were taken as central to these discourses rather than being marginal or even neglected entirely.

Brought into political currency by the Report of the UN Commission on Global Governance (1995), the concept of governance came to be identified with 'global values' – 'common rights' rather than the rights and sovereignty of the state in the international arena. The report addresses the role and potential of a transformative politics of civil society and non-governmental organizations (ibid.: 56–7). Its view of security is broader than the security of individual state borders, and encompasses people's human rights and the need for demilitarization as part of the security agenda (ibid.: 71–4). It also points out that globalization of the market is confined to the movement of 'capital (but not labor) flows ...', suggesting that attention to labour movement might allow us to review inter-state relations as well as create new agendas for global governance.[3] The Commission's approach falls within the liberal-internationalist school, which is concerned primarily with illuminating the rational (efficiency) calculus of international cooperation while failing to acknowledge the inequalities of power that tend to make democracy the 'captive of powerful vested interests' (McGrew 2002: 9). In his critique of the work of the Commission Baxi comments on the discrepancy between the assumptions of globality by the Commission, and the 'central facts of contemporary world disorder' (*Alternatives*, 21, 1996: 525–49, p. 530).

In his book *Governance without Government*, James Rosenau uses the term global governance to emphasize 'rule systems' through which 'we can trace and assess the processes of governance wherever they may occur ... the way in which authority is created, dispersed, consolidated and otherwise employed to exercise control with respect to the numerous issues and processes that states are unable or unwilling to address' (Rosenau and Czempiel 1992: 188). In this view, governance thus has been cut loose from the nation-state. Building on the Commission's dethroning of the state, Rosenau's focus shifts to what Held and McGrew call a 'multilayered ... structural enmeshment of several principal infrastructures of governance: the suprastate (such as the UN system), the regional (EU, MERCOSUR, ASEAN, etc.) the transnational (civil society, business networks and so on) and the substate (community associations and city governments)' (2002: 9; Scholte 2000). Thus, this understanding of global governance filters the debates on the changing nature of the state into a broader thematic ordering of the global political economy. Marxist scholars have shied away from the term governance but have had to engage with the concept. Marxists have looked to the earlier debates on imperialist competition to understand the current political economy. The crisis-ridden capitalist system is the arena where advanced capitalist states compete for markets and resources, leading to the current hegemony of the United States. Gill argues, for example, that global governance discourses and institutions are engaged in normalizing US regulatory power globally (1995). Developing further this interface of hegemony and imperialism, as well as of Marxist materialism and post-structuralism, Hardt and Negri argue in their book *Empire* (2000): 'In contrast to imperialism, Empire establishes no territorial centre of power and does not rely on fixed boundaries or barriers. It is a *decentred* and *deterritorialized* apparatus of power that progressively incorporates the entire global realm within its open, expanding frontiers' (pp. xi–xii; emphasis in the original). Others have noted that a convergence of institutional political discourses of governance embedded in global organizations such as the UN, the World Bank and the IMF secures the hegemonic position of the USA and provides the framework for the further expansion of the processes of capital accumulation worldwide (see Panich and Gindin 2005). One critical post-structuralist thinker whose work is increasingly making an impact on governance debates is Michel Foucault. His lectures on what he calls governmentality are being used to understand how state form, the processes of 'governing' and the 'mentality' that this generates are at the same time constitutive of and constituted by these practices (see Woel 2007). Governmentality thus allows us to reflect upon the effects of domination generated by the everyday governance of the state: 'It plays a decisive role in his analytics of power in several regards: it offers a view on power beyond a perspective that centers either on consensus or on violence; it links technologies of the self with technologies of domination, the constitution of the subject to the formation of the state; finally, it helps to differentiate between power and domination' (Lemke 2000). Critics have also pointed out, however, that governmentality, with its emphasis on individual subjectivity and technologies of domination, dilutes the place of the state in the theorization of governance (Hunt and Wickham 1994).

While these major strands of governance theory bring a great deal of sophisticated analysis to bear upon the changing nature of state and governance, we note that all are predominantly 'gender blind' or at best address the issue of gender in the context of the impact of the various political economic shifts on the lives of women. Thus, 'gender continues to be viewed as an issue of "special interest", whose incorporation into development analysis and program interventions has been at best piecemeal. Most discussions among development economists and policy makers (both in governmental and non-governmental forums) remain ungendered ...' (Agarwal 1997: 1373).

Feminist approaches to global governance have addressed this gap by engendering these debates. First, feminists have focused on institutional structures and processes: gender in global governance is seen as 'involving institutional structures in which women have found or carved out niches for themselves and their interests as women' and therefore 'introduce into global governance women-centred ways of framing issues ...' (Meyer and Prugl 1999: 4–5). Second, feminists approach global governance through critical gender politics, 'exploring the purposive, goal-oriented ... social-movement strategies to influence the United Nations ...' and Bretton Woods institutions (ibid.: 5; see also O'Brien et al. 2000). Finally, feminists have approached gender politics in the context of global governance as 'contestations of rules and discursive practices in different issue areas' (Meyer and Prugl 1999: 5). If these insights of feminist and critical scholars and activists are taken into account, it becomes possible to assess the nature of gendered global institutions as based on market principles, promoting market-based solutions to social and political problems, and stabilizing these solutions with the support of dominant epistemic elites (Taylor 2000). Thus, in analysing the constitutive parts of governance, as noted above, a feminist analysis can deepen, historicize and engender the debates on the governance of markets and the changing role of the state, on the ideologies of governance and of governance as spectacle.

Governance of markets Markets lie at the heart of capitalist social relations. These are the arenas of exchange of goods and services, and it is the globalization of these arenas which has posed challenges to regulatory systems, states and governance institutions. The dominant market actors, in the context of globalization, are those that control transnational capital, which is the motor behind much economic activity – through the circulation of money, through speculation on money markets and capital movements, as well as through tax evasion and money laundering. The market, then, though far from a level playing field, is given the primary political space in the discourse of globalization. While mainstream critical international political economy theorists have focused on the unevenness of the market arena in the context of capitalist social relations, feminists have argued that markets are socially embedded institutions and roles 'within market systems are structured by non-market criteria' (Harriss-White 1998: 201).

These non-market, though clearly not non-economic, criteria lead to specific gender-based distortions in the markets (see van Staveren 2001; Elson 1992; Palmer 1992). In the market system, participants come to specific markets with unequal capabilities, bargaining capacities and resources, which are the result of and inhere within unequal market structures, regulated and stabilized by gendered state formations, and characterized by more or less unequal power – class and gender are two bases for unequal power relations operating in the market. Evans argues that 'the power to threaten or disrupt economic relationships beyond the parameters of principal-agent relations is the kind of extra-economic coercion or influence that the neo-classical model fails to make explicit' (Evans 1993: 25). It thus fails to take into account the embedded nature of markets. It does not query the fact that individuals can pursue their economic self-interests in ways that have nothing to do with the 'best price'. Neither does it question the 'degree to which self-interest places economic goals ahead of friendship, family ties, spiritual considerations, or morality' (Block 1990: 54). Nor, indeed, how reproductive roles might change in the playing out of market roles (Harriss-White 1998). Finally, there is an assumption that instrumentality in decision-making goes hand in hand with obedience to rules, and with maximizing interests, rather than being a set of signals that can lead to conflictual economic and social behaviour in different groups of populations. The social embeddedness of markets is therefore not considered, other than as a distortion, by neoclassical economists. This brings into question the assumed neutrality on the basis of class as well as gender, and other cleavages of inequality of markets in terms of access, competitiveness and efficiency.

Markets, however, are stabilized and institutionalized not only in the functioning of global capitalism but also through the institutions of global governance. This, to quote Gill, is done through the process of 'new constitutionalism' – in contrast to the traditional constitutionalism associated with the state – which 'can be defined as the political project of attempting to make transnational liberalism and if possible liberal democratic capitalism the sole model for future development' (1995: 412).

It is in this project that institutions of global governance – the IMF, the World Bank and the WTO – become stronger vis-à-vis the state, presented as neutral players seeking maximum economic efficiency for all through attempting to ensure 'fair dealing' in the markets.[4] These institutions also symbolize the separation of the economic from the political, thus taking the heat out of macroeconomic policy-making. Indeed, the very term governance emerges because the increasingly important Bretton Woods agencies are not mandated to challenge the primary position of state actors. Governance then becomes a measure 'to refer to the capacity of governments to formulate and implement policies and processes by which authority is exercised in the management of a country's economic and social resources' (Faundez 1997: 6). Within the framework of neoliberalism 'good governance' is then associated with the qualities deemed by global governance institutions to emphasize the discipline of the market, and those that enhance that discipline through increasing transparency and accountability of the state. Law is an important framework for institutionalizing market neoliberalism, providing a set of enforceable rules known in advance, with mechanisms ensuring application of the rules. It allows conflicts arising between parties to be decided through the binding decisions of an independent body and ensures that 'there are procedures for amending the rules when they no longer serve their purpose' (World Bank 1992: 30). Rules, then, are critical to 'good governance' – rules that stabilize neoliberalism through state law, but which are disciplinary in the global sense.

In the current phase of globalization, markets are not seen as central only to resource competition and allocation in the sphere of private capital, but also to state and governance institutions more generally. This has led critical theorists to speak of marketized institutions (Hewson and Sinclair 1999: 17). Feminist scholars and activists have noted with alarm that even within public institutions there is a tendency towards adopting market principles of organization in the performance of their public roles. This in turn has various implications for public policy. First, without gender-sensitive indicators the allocative process cannot be an efficient one. Second, lack of gender-sensitive indicators signals failure to recognize the importance of the role of women in the labour market, leading to inequities that are overlooked and not addressed by policy-making (UN/DAW 1999: 7). Third, discrepancy between the increasingly unfettered flow of capital and the highly regulated movement of labour further affects the gendered nature of inequality under global capitalism.[5] Fourth, the development discourse under globalization, with the individual market agent central to it, also requires us to take seriously the ways in which men and women are able to access and play the market in order to enhance their life-chances, or standards of living. And finally, as we have seen above, the role of the state needs to be emphasized in the study of markets. We suggest that the state, far from being a passive victim of the global market, is an active player in restructuring not only the national gendered labour–capital relations in response to new pressures of globalization, but also in reorganizing its own regulatory and political boundaries to protect its position within the globalized political economy.

Governance institutions: a failing state? In the literature on global governance there is a great deal of interest in the shifts in the nature of the state in the context of globalization. The shifts in the nature and position of the state then pose the question of what replaces the state/government and the interstate world system. Writers point to various concepts, such as 'transworld' 'supraterritoriality' and, more narrowly, 'multilateralism' to describe the system of 'post-state' political economy and international relations (Scholte 2000). It is in this context that global governance takes shape. It is suggested that the state is no longer capable of addressing the issues arising from the global reach of capitalism, whether these are relating to competition in and regulation of the market, or to maintaining rules within its borders in order to resolve the collective problems of its citizens. From the argument outlining the 'leaking sovereignty' (Strange 1995) of the state to its 'lost' sovereignty (Cable 1995), the state is seen to be incapable of addressing the needs of the global capitalist economy. The diffusion of trade and finance is also diminishing the erstwhile centralized authority of the state.

This analysis of the 'leaking sovereignity' of the state is reflected in the discourse of the dysfunctional state in another context. One of the early interventions in the global governance debate was indeed made by one of the primary institutions involved in the 'governance' of global economic rules – the World Bank. In its 1990/92 World Development Report the Bank set out the case against the state. The state was, in line with the rhetoric of resurgent liberalism, the problem, not the solution; the state hindered the expansion and functioning of markets which was a key to the stabilization of the world economy. Too much government was stifling the energies of entrepreneurs waiting to take advantage of expanding markets. 'Weak institutions – tangled laws, corrupt courts, deeply biased credit systems, and elaborate business registration requirements – hurt poor people and hinder development ...' according to the World Development Report on Building Institutions for Markets (2002: <http://econ.worldbank.org/wdr/WDR2002>). This does not seem like a weak state, but a dysfunctional one. The question then was whether the state could respond to the new pressures of global political economy and, if so, what should be the parameters of its functioning? While the state continues to suffer within the hegemonic discourse of governance under globalization, both realist and Marxist scholars challenge this position.

The realists emphasize the continued centrality of the state by asserting 'the absence of a legitimate authority to which states are subordinate and give allegiance' (Gilpin 2002: 237). Upon this rather well-rehearsed position, the state and its interests – security and independence – continue to reign supreme and determine national behaviour. Therefore, the attempts by theorists of governance to disentangle (state) government from (supra-state) governance are misguided and do not reflect the power that states continue to wield. They also point to the 'democratic deficit' that will inevitably arise if such disentanglement is allowed, especially in the context of 'the increasing mismatch between the distribution of authority within and among existing institutions and the changing distribution of power in the international system' (ibid.: 242). The new medievalism of Hedley Bull, which argues that national sovereignty is at an end, is also rejected. While networks of policy-making bodies might challenge the monopoly over information that the states used to hold, realists argue that the role of NGOs and other policy-making bodies is so recent that the 300-year-old state cannot be effectively challenged, even though some of its functions might be supplemented by these new organizations (ibid.: 243–4). For the realists, the clearest rejection of the governance discourse comes from asking question of power: '... governance for what? What are the social, political and economic purposes that governance is to serve? Unless these issues can be resolved, proposals for international governance must be greeted with considerable scepticism' (ibid.: 246).

A similar question is asked by the Marxists and neo-Marxists, but from within a very different theoretical framework. They emphasize that class-based production and appropriation of value produced need regulation by the state. Such a starting point does allow the possibility of the state being displaced by governance institutions so long as they can play the same role in the global political economy as the state. Marxists do not find this a possibility: 'National states exist as political "nodes" or "moments" in the global flow of capital', and claim that their development is part of the crisis-ridden development of capitalist society (Burnham 1999: 8). In this view, then, the recent changes in the global political economy are analysed as being predominantly about reorganizing states rather than bypassing them, with 'state managers' actively attempting to restructure, and respond to, 'a crisis of labour/capital relations' (ibid.: 8). One of the most innovative analyses of the national state from a neo-Marxist position is that of Robert Cox, who argues that what we are witnessing is not the demise of the nation-state but its 'internationalisation'; not its destruction but its transformation. In brief, Cox argues that from being bulwarks against the global intrusions into national economies, today's states are becoming mediators, adapters and negotiators with the global political economy. To perform this changed role they have to reconfigure the power structures of government, giving far more emphasis to the role of finance and trade in economic regulation than to industry and labour, for example. The state's role, therefore, becomes one of helping to adjust the domestic economy to the requirements of the world economy (Cox with Timothy 1996). In a sympathetic critique of this position, Burnham points out that Cox's analysis 'underplays the extent to which "globalization" may be authored by states and regarded by state agents (both liberal market and social democrat) as one of the most efficient means of restructuring labour/capital relations to manage crisis in capitalist society' (1998: 5). In this context the nostalgia for a benign or at the very least powerless nation-state is clearly misplaced. And furthermore, this aspect of the internationalization of the state points to the current contradictions in globalization, as to extract surplus globally, capital depends on national and global public goods provision, while at the same time reducing the capacity of states to generate tax revenue, putting them under the discipline of neoliberalism through structural adjustment policies to provide those 'public goods'. Thus, Panich and Gindin argue, 'It is in these terms that we should conceptualize the "relative autonomy" of the capitalist state: not as being autonomous from capitalist classes or the economy, but rather in having capacities to act on behalf of the system as a whole (autonomy), while their dependence on the success of overall accumulation for their own legitimacy and reproduction nevertheless leaves those capacities bounded (relative)' (2005: 102). If the state is a participant in the reconstitution of its own relations with the global political economy, then it continues to be a focus for the struggles against this changing relation – whether initiated by (dis)organized labour in the urban or rural context, or other social movements.[6]

Engaging with deconstructing the concept of the state in the light of political engagements both with and against the state, feminist theorists have brought many insights to bear on the 'state debate' (see Chapter 2). One of the most important insights is that gendered social relations are constitutive of the state while at the same time the state is crucial to the continued dominance of the patriarchal relations of social production and reproduction (Pringle and Watson 1992b; Rai 1996; Randall and Waylen 1997). It has been argued that 'group interests do not pre-exist, fully formed, to be simply "represented" in the state ... they have to be continuously constructed and reproduced. It is through discursive strategies, that is, through creating a framework of meanings, that interests come to be constructed and represented in certain ways' (Pringle and Watson 1992b: 229–30). In this context, Polanyi's concept of embeddedness[7] becomes useful in analysing not only the market, his original concern, but also the state. In this context of embeddedness an examination of how different state fractions relate differently to each other, and to other civil and economic groups in different cultural milieus, becomes important (see Chapter 2). Women's movements have been grappling with this changing role of the state. As the sites of production and reproduction shift within states, as new regimes of production make for different forms of work – part-time, flexible, concentrated in Economic Processing Zones, migratory – women are having to organize differently. As global capital's presence is felt directly, mediated less through the state, and as local spaces are opened up to the forces of the market, the challenges to global economic forces and organizations are also posing issues of political discourse and mobilization for women. While the state continues to be a central focus of women's mobilization on various issues, supra-territorial strategies are being increasingly employed in order either to counter the state, to delegitimize its position, or to mobilize global discursive regimes in their interests. This is because the relationship between a modernizing state and a civil society within which it is configured is a complex one. In this context, to view the state as a unitary entity becomes paralysing, and regarding civil society as 'a space of uncoerced human association' perilous (Rai 1996: 17–18).

The analysis of the changing role of the state also gave impetus to the discourse of democratization of the state. As part of the liberal convergence of post-cold-war politics, democratization came to be linked to economic development. It built on a return to the classical liberal theoretical traditions in which markets were central and the free contracting individual the preferred economic actor. This literature did, however, pay attention to the multilevel analysis of the international system on the one hand and state and civil society relations, which was to become a hallmark of the governance debate, on the other (Rueschemyer et al. 1992). For Marxist scholars democratization is the form that the capitalist state takes under the current regime of globalization. 'Here, the separation of state from society within capitalism entails the constitutional distancing or political rule from the class structure. One aspect of this is the establishment of the rule of law as a liberal political framework for property owners. Another ... is the establishment of liberal democracy as the modal form of the capitalist state' (Panich and Gindin 2005: 102–3).

Feminist studies of transitional and democratizing states focused on the impact of liberalizing economies and the marketization of the state on women's lives (Einhorn 2000) as well as considering how women can engage the state in a globalizing context when the state is coming under multiple pressures and is repositioning itself in different ways in different contexts (Rai 2000, 2002; Jacquette and Wolchik 1998; Eschle 2001; Blacklock and Macdonald 2000; Waylen 2007). If the state is a participant in the reconstitution of its own relations with the global political economy, then it continues to be a focus for the struggles against this changing relationship. The nation-state as the focus of developmental struggles allows historical knowledges of traditions, cultures and political contexts to be mobilized with greater facility than the amorphous 'international economic institutions' peopled by shadowy figures not visible to the local oppositional struggles. Thus, state accountability and the space for political participation for both men and women form an important part of the understanding of governance for many women's groups (Tambiah 2002). Taking political institutions seriously has meant that feminist scholars and activists have taken seriously participation in political institutions. They have insisted upon the importance of representation of women in these institutions from different standpoints – arguing that women do politics differently/better, or simply that it is just that historically excluded groups should be allowed a say in the 'governing' that affects their lives. Strategizing for this, feminists have argued for quotas for women in political institutions in order to make them more visible and audible in political processes. They have also engaged with political institutions by participating in bureaucracies, policy-making bodies and representative organizations under the broad principles of gender mainstreaming (Miller and Razavi 1998; McBride, Stetson and Mazur 1999; Rai 2003).

If the realists, the Marxists and the feminists hold on to the state as a centrepiece of the international system and of global capitalism, the liberal internationalists do not shy away from cutting loose from the state, or at least from envisioning a post-statist world order. McGrew notes four presumptions of liberal internationalism. First, that reason and rationality are necessary and sufficient requirements for the effective conduct of international affairs. Second, the growing interdependence of states promotes international regulation. Third, international institutions promote peace by creating international norms to which both the powerful and the less powerful countries accede, and by creating new mechanisms for managing interstate conflict. And finally, liberal internationalism has aspirations towards 'the improvement of the human and global condition' (2002: 268).

The liberal institutionalist literature addresses some of these concerns by examining the consequences of the rise of global institutions. On the one hand, the various interventions focus on the need for conceptualizing alternatives to state institutions of government in the context of the global political economy. On the other hand, the literature focuses on addressing the democratic deficit of the global institutions themselves. How can these institutions be made more accountable in a context in which they seem to be usurping the power of the state (Woods 2002)? The effectiveness of global institutions, especially the UN system and the Bretton Woods institutions, is evaluated and found wanting, leading to prescriptions for reform. New governance institutions are recommended to regulate actors and issues emerging as key in a globalized world, such as mechanisms of consultation, surveillance and coordination of macroeconomic policies, an 'international financial architecture' stabilized through global institutions, and the regulation of capital (TNCs) and labour (migration) (Nayyar and Court 2002: vii–xi). The democratic deficit of old international institutions is identified as a reason for attempting to reform the global governance regime.

While engaging with important issues and providing some useful insights, the mainstream literature, from both the liberal and the Marxist positions, remains predominantly 'gender blind'. At best it addresses gender issues in the context of the impact of the various political economic shifts on the lives of women. There is no systematic analysis, for example, of the ways in which women's labour is crucial to capital accumulation under the pressures of globalization. Despite the existence of a rich literature, insights that feminist scholars and activists have brought to all these debates have remained on the margins of governance debates, which thus focus on questions and issues that do not centrally address social relations of globalization in a gendered way.

Governance as ideology The stabilization of markets, and also of marketized institutions, requires this third form of governance. Governance as ideology is produced and circulated through hegemonic discourses, educational institutions and media, both traditional and digital. Critical scholars have pointed to the ways in which epistemic authority secures the neoliberal discourse by evoking images of knowledge-based managerialism, which if allowed access to governance channels results in efficiency gains based on objective problem-solving approaches to the challenges of globalization (Gill 1995; McMichael 2000; Baxi 2002; Rai 2002). The hegemonic dominance of certain professional communities – experts, policy analysts and policy-makers, intellectuals – at multiple levels of governance can be assessed by focusing on the construction of epistemic authority. Such authority then reinforces the ideological message through research, and dissemination of that research through seminars, publications and policy networks (Rai 2004).

Governance emerges as a concept in the post-cold-war (some would call it a 'post-statist') period of the 1980s. We can easily pick up the threads of liberal triumphalism in the discourse of convergence that was articulated at this time. As I have commented elsewhere (Rai 2002), three texts were influential in the political debate on convergence, especially in the early period after the 'fall of the Wall'. These are Fukuyama's 'end of history' thesis (1991), Huntington's vision of the victory of the Christian liberal ethic over the Islamic in a clash of civilizations (1996), and Barber's lament against global capitalism and Islamic (and other) fundamentalisms that undermine democracy, and evocation of a revitalized liberal democracy within the national state structure (1996). In all three of these sketches of the world system in the late twentieth century, liberal values triumph over others; aspects of Western civilization over other cultures; and modernity's concerns are resolved through these triumphs. Struggles within the parameters of other cultures, religions and ideologies, in this envisioning, are doomed to failure unless they recognize the impossibility of reform from within. The logical conclusion, then, is that a liberal world is the only future that we can 'rationally' look forward to if we wish to live civilized, non-violent and democratic lives. The 'clash of civilizations' scenario takes on tremendous force in the context of the 11 September attacks upon the World Trade Center, and the idea of governance faces its first major challenge. The 'war on terror' has become a part of the governance discourse – Afghanistan and Iraq both become examples of an active engagement with the politics of convergence. Non-liberal regimes, especially those that defy rather than work with Western 'civilization', become legitimate targets of attack and reconfiguration. This Western civilization is also a 'market civilization' (Gill 1995: 399), where the individual competes for resources in the market and where the market civilization 'tends to generate a perspective on the world that is ahistorical, economistic, materialistic, "me-oriented" short-termist, and ecologically myopic' (ibid.). Democratic regimes, while being the only acceptable face of governance, are finding space to enact 'anti-terrorist legislation', which undermines the principles of democratic rights for individual citizens. At the same time, the image of the 'woman' behind the veil is constantly invoked to suggest the trope of rescue. The 'why now' question, then, is answered in two ways – first, the collapse of the 'evil empire' of communism allows the space for liberal values to spread, and new conversations about liberalization to take place. Second, and building on the first, the 'clash of civilizations' between Islamic fundamentalism and Christianity can take place in the context of resurgent global capitalism. One could argue that debates about convergence are being had today because of the one important convergence that occurred in the 1990s – the collapse of the Soviet Union and the statist social systems into capitalism. As Pieterse notes, 'If we would try to find a common theme among the disparate debates that are taking place ... capitalism remains the single framework that would be able to organize them' (1997: 367).

Thus, three different strands become visible when we examine the context in which 'governance' emerged as discourse. First was the collapse of the Soviet Union and the beginning of the post-cold-war period in the international system, and building on this was the convergence of economic policies under globalization within the liberal and neoliberal framework. Second, as a consequence of the collapse of 'communism' and the rise and dominance of the neoliberal framework in the global economy, was a re-examination of the role of the state in the context of the post-cold-war globalization. And third was the emergence of the discourse of democratization as the most appropriate framework within which both political and economic transitions could be accomplished – democracy became the bulwark against both forms of totalitarianism as well as the return to state-managed economies. The concept, indeed ideology, of global governance has come to take account of all these three strands.

For most critical governance theorists neoliberal economic theory is the ascendant framework for policy-making today. Building on classical liberal economic theory and challenging what Ruggie has called 'embedded liberalism' or the Keynesian welfare economics of the 1930s, which were the bases of the European welfare state models, the neoliberals posit the centrality of the markets in the economy. The discourse of neoliberalism, then, emphasizes, and indeed normalizes, the 'efficiency, welfare and the freedom of the market, and self-actualization through the process of consumption' (Gill 1995: 401), even though the outcomes of these policies are contradictory, hierarchical and inefficient in protecting human life and the world in which we live. This discourse of the market also has another message – if market-based competition is the most efficient way of allocating resources in society, then any attempts to interfere in its functioning would be per se inimical to the 'greater good'. As we have seen above, any attempts by the state to regulate markets then become scrutinized through the concerns of the economic actors that occupy the dominant positions within the market.

In his critique of the work of the Commission on Global Governance, Baxi comments on the discrepancy between the assumptions of globality by the Commission and the 'central facts of contemporary world disorder' (*Alternatives*, 21, 1996: 525–49, p. 530). Violence and poverty in particular are growing apace, and both affect women in particular ways. The feminization of poverty and violence against women in creating and policing new and old interstate borders have made this cooperative development a fraught discourse for women. In this context Baxi rightly comments that 'If governance is to be conceived as a process, it is well to recall that process is permeated by structures-in-dominance, both in states and civil societies' (ibid.: 532). The contradictions that arise out of capitalism's march across the globe are embedded in social relations of inequalities based on class, gender, ethnicities and religions, among others. The assessment of the processes and institutions of governance needs to be aware of these contradictions and the power relations that frame them.

Governance as ideology requires validation by epistemic communities – researchers, academics, policy advisers. They are key as gatekeepers of disciplines as well as the possible. What is feasible as an alternative needs to run the gauntlet of academic scrutiny, research developments and peer-reviewed publications. Feminists have long critiqued the parameters drawn around and by epistemic authority by challenging the definitions and recognized processes of knowledge production. Feminist critics have focused on how epistemological frameworks have been constitutive of the binaries of rational/emotional, universal/particular, objectivity/subjectivity (Hartsock 1997). Feminist work has also been undertaken on a more assertive project, however. This has meant rethinking the relationships between these binaries so that the historical identification of emotions, particularity and subjectivity with the subordinate or the subaltern is challenged by suggesting the mutually constitutive nature of these binaries (Jaggar 1997). So, for example, in terms of the central concerns of the regulatory regimes of global capitalism, and the role of global governance institutions in securing these regimes through TRIPS, feminist interventions in theorizing knowledge production can have a radical impact on our understanding of the roles that institutions play in stabilizing structures-in-dominance, and therefore can lead us to ask different and important questions about the nature of privatized knowledge and the application of this framework to global regulatory regimes. Indeed, some have argued that perhaps these insights should lead us towards exploring the merits of 'social patents', thus broadening the acknowledgement of knowledge creation. Thus regard to the gendered dimensions of knowledge production can provide insights into the nature of epistemic authority and practical policy shifts in terms of 'social patents', as well as critical evaluation of how 'disciplinary neoliberalism' works to entrench dominant social relations through legal provisions, such as TRIPS, regulated by institutions of global governance such as the WTO.

Feminist concerns with the politics of convergence have reflected the multilayered nature of the global economy, processes of democratic transition, as well as the changing nature of governance.

Governance as spectacle As noted in the introduction to this chapter, power displays through the production of spectacle are an important arena of governance that we need to analyse. This arena was first opened up for scholarly scrutiny by Guy Debord, who, in his *The Society of the Spectacle* (1967, 1998), argued that modern spectacle was 'the autocratic reign of the market economy which had acceded to an irresponsible sovereignty, and the totality of new techniques of government which accompanied this reign' (Debord 1998: 2). The spectacular power was, he suggested, concentrated (totalitarian state power such as in the Soviet Union) as well as diffuse (democratic systems such as the United States). In his 1998 *Comments on the Society of the Spectacle*, he expanded this to include the integrated power of the spectacle, through which spectacle has gone global: 'the globalization of the false was also the falsification of the globe' (1998: 10). Global capitalism, then, depended on 'the colonized social circuits that comprise spectacle – including confidence in the market and the state, and an identification with commodity culture – and that to disrupt spectacle may have great and unpredictable consequences' (Stallabrass 2006: 90). What we see, therefore, in media news 24/7 disciplines our senses as well as our understanding of this world; it makes our choices for us while at the same time giving the appearance of endless choice to us. Scholarly articles confirm for us the centrality of markets and marketized institutions, and our experience of the increasing commodification of social life – the care economy – becomes the norm rather than an aberration. Further expanding this discussion of the political economy of the imagery of power, Michel Foucault argued in his book *Discipline and Punish* (1991) that the spectacle of corporal punishment is a disciplining not only of the one being punished, but also of those who witness the punishment being meted out. Foucault sees the exercise of power as not limited within the boundaries of sovereign states, through the enforcement of law: 'We must eschew the model of Leviathan in the study of power. We must escape from the limited field of juridical sovereignty and state institutions, and instead base our analysis of power on the study of the techniques and tactics of domination' (1991: 102). The state is, then, only one of the sites of disciplinary power, which takes many forms, of which the enacting (together with the exercise) of disciplinary power is an important part (Woel 2007).

Building on this analysis of power, Judith Butler, in her book *Gender Trouble* (1990), argued that gendered power is a fiction that needs to be sustained in the domain of political economy through social performitivity. Through the enactment of dominant gender roles we recognize, circulate and reproduce the meanings of masculinity and femininity and thus perpetuate gendered social hierarchies. Though both these interventions have been challenged, they do open up an important analytical seam for the construction of governance theory. We have seen above how the concept of governance has evolved, embraced and challenged. The dominance of certain states and ideologies within international relations literature has led to an increasing acceptance of the term despite some unease about its political foundations. We would suggest that this dominance is embedded in the popular imagination and seen through political spectacles. Therefore we need to understand the importance of these spectacles and dissect them to lay bare their politics. Such analysis cannot replace the critical materialist analysis of governance presented above and elsewhere in this volume, but it adds another dimension to our understanding of the concept of governance. This dimension is particularly important to understand as increasingly the media – print, film and virtual – are becoming a battleground of ideas and spaces where ideologies of governance converge and contend.

If we examine the three arenas of market, institutions and ideology we find that all three are consolidated through and in the space of the unfolding spectacle of governance, whether it is 'the shock and awe' of the Iraqi war, the grey-suited men pictured at G8 summits surrounded by security barriers, the Abu Ghraib prisoners being carted around in shackles or, indeed, the counter-spectacles and alternative narratives of the Battle of Seattle, the World Social Forum and Live 8 concerts. Dominant states such as the United States put up hugely and purposefully aggressive displays of military power as well as the spectacle of a 'siege' of civilization through the media's coverage of radical movements – Islamist, but also in Cuba or on the streets of Seattle and Genoa. Both sets of images create a powerful visual medium through which the dominant modes of power are captured and circulated, and through which challenges to that power display are mounted through alternative modes of communication, largely on the Web, through blogs presented to new audiences. The cooption of journalists into militaries as embedded reporters, for example, shows us how the creation of spectacle and its distribution is organized, congealing markets, institutions and ideology into a visual manifestation of power. From Lynndie England in Abu Ghraib to images of burka-clad women in Afghanistan, women have both participated in and been the victims of repressive governance regimes. Feminist scholars and women activists have understood that gender discipline is enforced through economic dependence and political exclusion, and also through cultural markers of the subjugation of women by men. As such the challenge to patriarchal power has also been comprehensive. As Butler's work shows, feminist scholarship has ranged widely to understand the exercise of gendered power. It has always incorporated photography, theatre, poetry and art into mainstream feminist political analysis to 'display' the varied ways in which patriarchy holds sway.

Challenges by and for feminist politics

One could argue that global governance is a concept that hides as much as it reveals. On the one hand the shift from government to governance is presented as an explanatory framework seeking to account for global change, and on the other it is seen as addressing the problem of states' inability to respond to that change. In this concluding section

I look ahead to challenges that feminist scholarship and activism are raising for global governance theorizing, and also to what challenges they themselves face.

Feminists have built their engagements with governance institutions on some key concepts that emerged from women's struggles and scholarship:

1 a gendered analysis of the political economy and the relations between states and markets;
2 a challenge to the state-reproduced division between the public and the private; and
3 a commitment to the transformation of gender relations that form the basis of formal and informal politics.

If we take these insights into account when assessing key areas – markets, institutions and ideologies, together with spectacles – of global governance that we have identified above we stretch the boundaries of the governance debates.

One way of doing this, I would suggest, would be to analyse governance along two different axes in the different sites of governance. The first, and the one that we have focused on in this chapter, is the *governance of polities*. Governance of polities is about regulating economic and political life at different levels – markets and the state at local, national and international levels – and is also about the role that different actors play in this regulation – state and non-state (including market) actors, epistemic communities, social movements at the local, national and global levels. The second axis, which does not get much attention in the mainstream literature, but is equally important for the daily lived lives of women and men, is the *governance of communities*. There are processes and rituals as well as discourses and spectacles of violence that are deployed in order to police community boundaries and punish transgression. The parallel sovereignties thus created both challenge and work within the state. Feminist scholarship could make a tremendous contribution in bringing these two axes to bear upon theoretical work on global governance.

Broadly, the governance of community shows the following characteristics: first, the boundaries of communities are defined, policed and defended through education, through popular mobilization, through rituals, festivals and, in many parts of the world, through arranged marriages. Through all these, modes of thinking are given shape – of the Self and of the Other. In the name of culture the languages of hatred – racism, sexism and homophobia, for example – are aired, and those of alternative visions of community contained. The community's governance in this sense is aligned with the perpetuation of gendered traditions.

Second, the regulation of the realm of the community takes place through both formal and informal institutions, systems and discourses – caste, religious and ethnic local governing councils, modes of communication and excommunication – and also through spectacles of violence to subdue the rebels within communities. Whether this involves regulating sexualities at the local level or constructed civilizational clashes between Muslim and Christian worlds, these non-state governance institutions, mechanisms and discourses play a critical role in disciplining the way we live our lives. The state is mobilized in defence of the dominant social norms through constitutional, legal and policy frameworks, as well as through modes of policy implementation – police personnel, for example, are often implicated in religious riots, in participating in or at least ignoring violence perpetrated against transgressors of community norms.

Third, these boundaries are also defended and policed through demonstrations of violence, which, while not legitimized by all state fractions, is tolerated and even participated in by others. 'Crimes of honour' and of passion, for example, become more than just crimes: this is violence that regulates sexuality within communities. This means that such violence is seen as a 'legitimate' means of regulating communities, securing their cultural borders and insuring against transgression of their norms.

Fourth, these traditions bleed over time – diasporic communities everywhere take with them the burdens and the markers of community norms and rituals and diasporic 'legalities' that regulate their life away from home. Whether they are migrants within national borders or diasporic international communities, these traditions help define them in new contexts, and provide them with internal resources of solidarity to cope in situations of social exclusion. They help them make personal sense of politicized otherness in strange lands. From the local to the global, the governance of communities involves disciplinary modes of discursive as well as social power.

Finally, as with the governance of polities, however, the governance of communities is constantly challenged and reshaped by the struggles of individuals and groups both to cross critical boundaries of race, caste and religion, sexuality and class. These challenges tap into both internal sources of strength – a network of sympathizers – and networks of support from outside. Circulation of political vocabulary allows them access to alternative political languages, visions of society and of other imagined communities. What I want to emphasize here is that it is in the interplay between the two axes of governance – of polities and communities – that the concept is best understood.

Feminist scholarship and activism also face some other challenges. While feminists have posited a powerful critique to mainstream global governance literature, they also need to present an alternative articulation of what governance means (Pearson 2004). If they do not like marketized institutions, they need to be able to sketch the outline of governance institutions that they would like to see. Catherine Hoskyns and I (1998) have argued that '[f]or both strategic as well as practical reasons women have had to organize separately as women ... [However, the] feminist challenge is limited by a current lack of focus on the importance of redistributive policies that are rooted in the structural inequalities of capitalist production and exchange' (ibid.: 362). We posed the question: can gender recover class? Following Spivak, I would argue that a recognition of the importance of redistribution allows us '[b]oth in the economic area (capitalist) and in the political (world-historical agent) ... to construct models of a divided and dislocated subject whose parts are not continuous or coherent with each other' (ibid.: 276). And these dislocations and discontinuities are where women seeking transformation within the political economy as well as the discursive circuits of power can find agency. This is particularly relevant now when marketization and the retrenchment of welfare provision under globalization are creating tremendous pressures and inequalities across different social and spatial boundaries. We see, however, that feminists are engaging with institutions within the convergent ideological framework of neoliberal governance because the space for alternatives has been scaled down even as the recognition of gender-based inequalities has increased. This is not to suggest that these engagements are not important. Indeed, the solid ground of embedded liberalism has fractured so much under the neoliberal onslaught that the protection of the welfare state seems a radical project well worth participating in. A recognition of the limits of the strategies of engagement with 'constitutional neoliberalism', however, also needs to be taken seriously if we are to be effective in developing political strategies of empowerment for both poor women and men.

Feminists too are engaged in this debate as they see a 'general broadening of the field of international reorganization from a preoccupation with describing the output of intergovernmental organizations, their formal attributes and processes of decision-making to a concern with structures of governance' (Meyer and Prugl 1999: 4). These structures include organizations such as the UN and NGOs, as well as social and political movements in a 'global civil society'. A concern with issues of governance also helps explode the myth of consent that is a feature of the earlier globalization literature – a consent that is often juxtaposed with the inevitability of globalization and therefore conceals the power relations within which the process is developing. One could argue, as Palan does, that 'the language of global governance, with its attendant rather unflattering insinuations about the functions, legitimacy, and aptitude of the state (and society) ... makes sense only once an agreement is reached about some prior, if normally undeclared, common human goals, political functions and so on' (1999: 67). These a priori notions are themselves markers of closures – not the same as those operated under nationalist regimes, but new closures which make for new winners and losers – in both the public and the private spheres, taking both national and global forms.

In this chapter I have argued that issues of gender have particular salience in the debates on governance. Unless we use the insights that have emerged from feminist theory and practice we will not be able to encompass the needs of the future in conversations about the global present. To reiterate, feminist contributions to these conversations lie in the ways in which political activism and theoretical insights have been methodologically imbricated to develop insights on governance. These insights have examined the discursive as well as the material power wielded in embedding certain dominant explanations of governance in the mainstream literature, which have then shaped the agendas for 'governing' (Kooiman 2003) and paradigms of governance. Specifically, feminist interventions in the areas of knowledge creation, recognition and institutionalization have particular salience for the processes of embedding neoliberal marketized discourses of globalization and governance. Feminist debates on the state and democracy have relevance for the way in which political activism, as well as the relational understanding between the state and global institutions of governance, might be viewed. Gendered critiques of markets as not only uneven spaces of exchange but as inefficient and distorted mechanisms that build upon unequal gendered social relations subject the normalization of rationality of the market to rigorous scrutiny. The global governance debate needs to make a conceptual shift to embed these insights, developed through everyday struggle at local, state and global levels, as well as through engagements with and critiques of mainstream literature, if theories of critical governance are to fundamentally challenge the structures-in-dominance within this field.

7 | Knowledge and/as power[1]

WITH SHARMISHTA BARWA

This chapter focuses on the gendered nature of Trade Related Intellectual Property rights (TRIPS) as a way of exploring how the framework of global governance explored in Chapter 6 is translated into specific policies which then impact upon the way in which women and men access, create and distribute knowledge, and in so doing, depending upon their social position, either benefit or marginalize them. Against the backdrop of market liberalization and the transformation of the relationship between states and the global economy, TRIPS provide an important way of exploring not only the relationships between gender, knowledge, innovation and property rights but also the growing power of international regulatory institutions and governance systems. As we have seen in Chapter 6, though markets are today the hub of productive economic activity, to understand the interplay of different factors on the politics of women's work in the context of intellectual property rights, one needs to look beyond the market. The arguments presented in this chapter reflect a concern about TRIPS as socially embedded instruments of global governance. They reflect the 'unevenness' of globalization in terms of gendered locations, which must be unpacked, even as the global barriers to interconnectedness are being demolished. Feminist insights and critiques of TRIPS allows us to examine alternative forms that production and exchange might take in the global markets.

Women inventors, invented stories

This section begins with some stories – poignant, angry and illustrative. These stories are evidence of the assumptions about gender and invention: women do not invent. This is true even as we enter the second millennium and the third technological revolution. These stories are important because they show how women's contributions to the production of knowledge and the recognition of women as inventors have been historically denied on grounds of their sex, class or race. They also reveal that the exclusion of women from the discussions about regulation of knowledges through a denial of their work as sufficiently important to be counted as invention continues today. Any assessment of intellectual property rights (IPRs) that privileges intellectual production in the public domain needs to take the message of these stories into account. By doing this we can become aware of the limitations of the language of market-based rights, and therefore of a need for caution in promoting these as important to the individuation of women and a means for their empowerment.

> William is away, and I am minding the heavens. I have discovered eight new comets and three nebulae, never before seen by man, and I am preparing an index to Flamsteed's observations, together with a catalogue of 560 stars omitted from the British Catalogue, plus a list of errors in that publication. William says I have a way with numbers, so I handle all the calculations. I also plan every night's observation schedule, for he says my intuition helps me turn the telescope to discover star cluster after star cluster.
>
> Did you know that Hildegard proposed a heliocentric universe 300 years before Copernicus? That she wrote of universal gravitation 500 years before Newton? But who would listen to her? She was just a nun, a woman. What is our age if that age was dark? As for my name, it will also be forgotten, but I am not being accused of being a sorceress, like Aganice, and the Christians do not threaten to drag me to church to murder me, like they did Hypatia of Alexandria. *Source*: A letter from Caroline Herschel (1750–1848) (UNIFEM 1999)

> Eglui invented a clothes wringer, which she sold to an agent for US$18. He subsequently made a lot of money from it. When asked by a writer on women inventors as to why she sold for that amount, she replied: 'I was afraid to be known because of my colour in having it introduced into the market, that is the only reason.' *Source*: 'The innovative woman', *New Scientist*, 24 May 1984

> The year was 1933. Twenty-two years old Kamala Bhagwat, who had topped her BSc chemistry class from the University, was on her way from Bombay to Bangalore ... Kamala's father, a visionary, was determined to give his daughter an identity of her own. Father and daughter were on their way to meet Sir C. V. Raman, Director of the Indian Institute of Science at Bangalore who had rejected Kamala's application for postgraduate studies. The world renowned physicist told them clearly that Kamala could very well take herself back to Bombay as he believed that girls required 'weary persistence' and that he was himself fortunate to have only sons. He conceded only to give admission in the biochemistry

stream subject to a year's probation before she would be entitled to admission like her male counterparts. When she was able to get a lecturer to guide her, it was again on certain conditions – that she presented herself at the library at 5 a.m. each morning, worked diligently from then to 10 p.m. and read in the library in the night. She agreed if she was allowed two hours every evening to play tennis. By the end of the first year in which she published two papers, Sir C. V. Raman was so pleased with her dedication to research that he decided to throw open the Institute's doors to other female students and allowed Kamala to complete her research and take on the MSc degree course. She later obtained admission to the Sir William Dunn Institute of Biochemistry at Cambridge University as well as won the Travelling Fellowship of the International Federation of University Women. In 1939 she discovered the presence of cytochrome-C in plant tissue and submitted her thesis, becoming the first Indian woman to obtain her PhD from Cambridge – and in just 14 months! In 1949 she made an important discovery – the presence of vitamin P in green gram and also that when vitamin P and vitamin C found in lemon juice are consumed together, they help to strengthen the covering around blood vessels and thus stop haemorrhaging. (This discovery was made next in Russia in 1977!) *Source*: *Femina*, Bombay, India, 15 January 1998

'I may be illiterate but I am not stupid,' was the deep anguish expressed by Mrs Cgose Ntcoxo, a member of the dwindling San tribe from the borders of the Kalahari desert in Botswana, when she discovered that her painting of hyenas and trees had been used by British Airways to redecorate its fleet. Having spotted the work in a London art gallery, an emissary from British Airways flew to Botswana and got the 42-year-old bushwoman to sign away the copyright. Mrs Ntcoxo received 12,000 pulas for her efforts or £3,190. She promptly splashed out on seven cows, built herself a shack on the edge of the Kalahari desert and gave the rest of the money to her many nomadic relatives. Now bankrupt and living in the dust-blown town of Ghanzi in north-west Botswana, on the edge of the desert, she claims she is entitled to more pulas. Her husband has tuberculosis, her daughter is unemployed and she has a large family to support.

It was only when British Airways held a special ceremony that she realised that her design had ended up on the back of what she described in San language as a big fly – an aeroplane. The Kuru Development Trust, which sold the painting, claimed that the San people live in 'precash society' and have no understanding of the value of money and that the artist was happy with the money she had received. Incidentally the trust had pocketed half of BA's payment. *Source: Guardian*, 9 July 1998

These stories about women's erasure from formal scientific discovery on grounds of gender, race and class, of the obstacles that social mores and institutional prejudices place in the way of women achieving in the public sphere of knowledge creation, are not, as the above show, a thing of the past. While changes are reaching a breathtaking pace in the commercial and technological spheres, the evidence of gender inequalities involved in the field of science and technology continues to accumulate. It is in part to challenge this exclusion that feminist scholars and activists have questioned the very definitions of what counts as knowledge. Feminists have written about 'the extent to which traditional epistemologies worked to systematically exclude the possibility that women could be the agents of knowledge' (Kemp and Squires 1997: 142). Feminist critics have focused on how epistemological frameworks have been constitutive of the binaries of rational/emotional, universal/particular, objectivity/subjectivity.[2] The questions that they have asked have focused on two different aspects of knowledge production. The first is the interrelation between knowledge and power. Building on the work of Michel Foucault, feminists have asked, 'Is it possible for those long excluded from traditional institutions of knowledge and from conceptualizing theory, ever to gain the power that comes with these forms of knowledge?' (Gunew 1990: 22). The second aspect is how knowledge is exchanged and is reinforced through that process. Here, Christine Delphy has pointed out that knowledge is produced as 'learned discourse', which often prevents its use by those outside the circuit of recognition of knowledge (Delphy 1984: 15). We could also ask another pre-emptive question here, which has been asked by Vandana Shiva and Maria Mies in their book *Ecofeminism* – what power allows certain discourses to be recognized as 'knowledge' and others merely as conventions, mores or even superstitions? As Foucault has pointed out, 'For the State to function as it does, it is necessary that there be between the man and woman or the adult and child quite specific *relations of dominance* ...' (cited in Gunew 1990: 22). Power is thus reproduced every time those who claim to 'know' are able to exclude those whose claims to knowledge are not recognized. In the arena of international political economy the social relations of reproduction of knowledge become embedded in the relations of power obtaining in the market and are institutionalized through the procedures of law. The reproduction of unequal social relations is thus constituted by and constitutive of market relations backed not only by the state but increasingly by institutions of global governance. TRIPS, for example, reflects and reproduces the power relations in terms of both (non-)recognition of knowledge as well as the claim to ownership of that knowledge by invoking institutionalized market rules through the World Trade Organization.

The World Trade Organization and intellectual property rights

The World Trade Organization (WTO) was established on 1 January 1995 as part of the results of the Uruguay Round of GATT. TRIPS were also agreed upon in this round of agreements, setting out the obligations of member states to protect intellectual property rights within their borders.

What is the significance of TRIPS? First, TRIPS has for the first time brought into the arena of global trade the domain of ideas, knowledge and innovation. TRIPS are a set of agreements that regulate the granting of limited monopoly rights by the state to an innovator or inventor. 'They specify a time period during which others many not copy the innovator's idea, allowing him or her to commercialize it, and recoup any investment on research and development ... They trade off the welfare of the innovator, who deserves compensation for his or her efforts, against the welfare of society at large, which would benefit by unlimited access to the innovation' (Cosbey 2000: 3). The emphasis here is clearly on the trade-related aspect and monetary 'compensation' for investment; it does not take into account the value of the moral, ethical and non-monetary recognition of the innovator for an idea, invention or innovation. The problem of definition is thus twofold. On the one hand it is about what counts as 'innovation' and on the other it is about the recognized form of compensation. As we will see below, this particular reading of 'innovation' is particularly problematic for women as they bear far greater personal costs in terms of overcoming social prejudice to access the world of knowledge production.

Second, TRIPS define the nature of knowledge through identifying the boundaries of particular products and processes. There are three main types of intellectual property rights: patents, copyrights and trademarks. Copyrights cover literary and artistic works, as well as computer software, and trademarks are granted to names or labels denoting a particular quality that distinguishes them from other products. 'All patents involve invention, but not all inventions are patented. An idea need be neither patented nor patentable to be an invention' (Stanley 2000). Patents cover 'any inventions, whether *products or processes*, in all fields of technology, provided that they are new, involve an inventive step and are *capable of industrial application*' (our emphasis). Two things stand out here. First, that both product and processes have now been brought under the patenting regime. As a result, for example, farmers will not be able to keep seeds from their crops. As women constitute an increasing proportion of small and poor farmers, this provision is affecting them particularly. Second, patents privilege particular forms of knowledge – 'stabilizing' historically developed processes of production would entitle modern industrial companies to patent products and processes and deny nature's and people's creativity.

One of the most important issues to have emerged in the context of patentability is that of definitions of 'nature' and 'natural'. As Shiva points out, a patriarchal understanding of knowledge of nature has emphasized 'worked on' nature as natural: 'nature has been clearly stripped of her creative power; she has turned into a container for raw materials waiting to be transformed into inputs for commodity production' (2000: 4). Further, according to this view, 'to regenerate is not to create, it is merely to "repeat" which is the same as passivity' (ibid.). Women's and nature's regenerating role is then defined out of the sphere of innovation, excluding them from the regimes of patents and monopoly privilege. This is particularly evident in the case of the International Convention of the Union for the Protection of New Varieties of Plants, where 'microorganisms' have been excluded from the categories of plants and animals and therefore brought under the patents regime. This has allowed for changes in the genetic make-up of existing varieties of seeds, for example, to result in a patent being granted for products of the neem tree and basmati rice, among many other 'natural' products. This reading of innovation also goes against the recognition of the original reasoning for introducing patents, which was that innovation entails high costs of development and low costs of reproduction. By discounting time and the historically evolving nature of innovation, patenting institutionalizes privilege – those who are left out of the loop (very often poor women are the majority of those excluded) fall progressively behind in the race for ring-fencing products for monopoly exploitation. As Cosbey points out, 'there has been a steady and substantial transfer of resources from South to North as the valuable products of informal innovation have been appropriated cost-free' (2000: 8).

Third, TRIPS signify a major innovation in the global regulatory regime. Unlike other agreements, which define what member states may not do, TRIPS is proscriptive, in that it sets out what member states *must do*, thus encroaching upon the domain of national policy-making in an unambiguous way. Further, by making TRIPS part of the 'cross-retaliatory' regime under WTO agreements, the WTO has strengthened its regulatory power enormously. It now means that nonconformity in one area of regulation can lead to retaliation in terms of trade in areas covered by a different agreement. TRIPS are therefore part of an extremely powerful group of regulatory mechanisms that all members of the WTO must put in place. As we will see below, the poorest countries of the South suffer disproportionately from such a proscriptive and all-encompassing regulatory regime. Given what we have been arguing above in the context of the gendered nature of these regimes, TRIPS is important in stabilizing dominant discourses of knowledge/power through overriding nationally fought for and negotiated arrangements which might have, in some cases, protected the livelihoods of both poor women and men.

Women and inventions To invent is to find, but invention differs from discovery in terms of applications of discovery to practical use. Why are there so few women inventors? Some of the answers are obvious – invention usually requires money, materials and the opportunity to share ideas. Here, however, we also encounter the power relations that define, recognize and privilege only certain forms of knowledge. Women, and poor women particularly, stand outside the world of formal science and technology and far from the world of patents. They, together with other marginalized populations, inhabit a world where everyday processes of experimentation and adaptation lead to a problem-solving approach to knowledge (UNIFEM 1999). Though such processes are very much the result of logical and internally consistent frameworks of understanding, these knowledges do not get the status of scientific inquiry. Indigenous knowledge thus commands a weak price in a marketplace that privileges science and its methodologies.[3]

Historically, few women have been financially independent, and most have been excluded from sources of education and intellectual stimulation. This has meant that even though women have made several ground-breaking technological inventions, they have often been viewed as 'trespassers' in the field of invention and, as our stories above suggest, have often not been credited with the inventions they have made. Inventions such as Whitney's cotton gin (invented by Whitney's landlady), the jacquard loom, the fire escape (Ann Connelly), filter paper (Melita Bentz), the sewing machine and several other inventions that have made a profound impact on the quality of our lives were all made by women, but how many of us know this?

Patents, property and the global market Patents, as we have seen above, are forms of property. Women were responsible for only 0.8 per cent of the total patents at the US Patents Office in 1910 and 1.5 per cent in 1954. The range of women's inventions is now impressive: according to the United States Patent and Trade Mark Office (USPTO) Report, the most prolific woman originator of US patents from 1992 to 1996 was Jane Arcona, who was named inventor in eighty-two patents. According to this report, from 1977 to 1996 the corporate organizations named most frequently as owners of US woman-inventor patents were IBM (1,272), GEC (810) and Eastman Kodak (738). The US Navy topped the list of federal government organizations, owning 264 US woman-inventor patents! Patsy Sherman, commercial products development manager for the 3M Company, contributed to fifteen important patents, including 'Scotchguard', the widely used stain repellant for fabrics. Yet this list comprises only the few women who have been able to brave and overcome the unequal power relations operative in the marketplace at both the local and the global levels. Even these figures are skewed further when we consider that '95% of the world's patents are held in the North, and [in the sphere of] information technology it is estimated that 90–95% of the world's research goes on in highly industrialised countries' (Cosbey 2000: 11).

The inequalities persisting at different levels of the various market-places for women include access to, participation in and having an equal stake and appropriate bargaining power in relation to the acquisition/ invention of knowledge. Markets, it has been argued (Polanyi 1980), are embedded in dominant social relations. Discussing four dimensions of market power, White comments: 'The substance of market politics is characteristically about a number of issues: about the position of an agent or agents in relation to others within a market and their differential ability to extract resources through exchanges with other market participants; about the rules of the game and the nature of market institutions; and about the boundaries of the market' (1993: 5). The participants in the market include the state, market organizations such as trade unions, consumer groups and business associations, market networks, firms and individuals. The functioning of the market depends upon the politics of state involvement, the politics of market structures and the politics of social embeddedness – of the state and the market (ibid.: 6–10). In such a patterned market system, participants come to specific markets with unequal capabilities and bargaining capacities and resources, which results in widely different market structures, regulated by different state formations, and characterized by more or less unequal power – class and gender are two bases for unequal power relations operating in the market. The neoclassical model does not query the fact that individuals can pursue their economic self-interests in ways that have nothing to do with the 'best price'. As noted in Chapter 6, neither does it question the 'degree to which self-interest places economic goals ahead of friendship, family ties, spiritual considerations, or morality' (Block 1990: 54). Finally, there is an assumption that instrumentality in decision-making goes hand in hand with obedience to rules, and with maximizing interests, rather than a set of signals that can lead to conflictual economic and social behaviour in different groups of populations. The social embeddedness of markets is therefore not considered, other than as a distortion, by neoclassical economists. This embeddedness provides an explanation for the ways in which gendered regimes of patent-based property function. One can hardly be surprised that there are so few women inventors patenting their inventions. It is still more surprising that inventions made by women exist at all, and that they are not only patented but also commercially developed. As Cosbey points out, for example, 'large multinational plant breeders do not regard the South as a significant enough market to gear research towards varieties appropriate to the various regions ... It is to be expected that innovation done by Northern [funded] scientists will be in the interests of Northern producers' (2000: 11). The result is that not only are most women left out of the patents regimes, but also that the nature of research is typically skewed towards the needs of Northern trade and commerce rather than towards the needs of the poor of the South, and towards sustainability of life.

The Fourth World Conference on Women in Beijing in 1995 recognized that access to information prepares women to participate more fully in all stages of political and economic life. The *Beijing Declaration and Platform for Action* (UN 1996) called on states and organizations to increase women's participation in and access to new technologies as a tool for strengthening women's economic capacity and democratic processes. If we are to take the discussion regarding the constitutive and gendered nature of power relations seriously, however, we need to ask whether a system of knowledge-based property relations such as TRIPS can ever treat women, especially poor women of the South, equitably. On the contrary, it would seem that market power resulting from intellectual property might be used to extend these unequal relations of power into new and hitherto uncharted territories. Concentration of market power results from the increasing returns of scale for innovation patenting. So, as Cosbey points out, 'A decade after the passage of the US Plant Variety Protection Act of 1970, five companies – all with less than 10 years' work in plant breeding – controlled almost one third of the issued rights for American agricultural varieties' (2000: 3). The gap between biotechnology firms such as Monsanto occupying vast areas of agricultural markets and subsistence or small farmers in the South (increasing numbers of these are women) then increases the inequality in the marketplace. Further, agreements on the use of intellectual property may result in limiting the wider transfer or dissemination of technology or other knowledge – a situation called restrictive contracts or concerted practice – again dependent upon the intellectual and economic power of the owner and those seeking to use it (Acharya 1996).

The interrelationship between knowledge and property is reflected in TRIPS at two distinct levels: as multilateral development, affecting and being affected by multilateral trade liberalization and government trade policies, and as a microeconomic phenomenon driven by the strategies and behaviour of corporations where the changing dynamics of global competition and international competitiveness are the main concerns (Oman 1994). Added to these factors are two issues identified by the United Nations' Commission on the Status of Women, which further highlight the constraints faced by women with respect to intellectual property rights. First, inequality in women's access to and participation in the definition of economic structures and policies and the productive process itself, and second, the insufficient institutional mechanisms to promote the advancement of women in this regard.

Trade Related Intellectual Property rights – national and gender perspectives

Patent is property. The argument for patents is that inventors engage in the process of production of knowledge, which needs protection from piracy by others. The 'find' of an inventor is thus regarded as personal (or corporate, if the legal person is the group engaged in inventing) – something that is uniquely the property of the one who invents. To qualify for patent rights, the invention has to be novel, non-obvious and of practical use (Dasgupta 1999). Thereafter, the right confers on the holder a time-bound monopoly of the given product to enable the inventor to recoup the cost of development of the product and also to compensate for the risk undertaken. In addition, it is also expected that such rewarding of invention will encourage others to generate new inventions and thus help in the extension of scientific and technical knowledge that will benefit society as a whole. International protection of intellectual property rights has, therefore, been placed on the agenda of trade negotiations to safeguard the competitive position of some countries against intellectual piracy and the overly rapid diffusion of their comparative advantage.

Social knowledges, private patents: gendered and Southern challenges
Feminist understandings of knowledge and its creation have challenged the view that would allow intellectual production to be given the status of property. This is for several reasons. First, that such a view does not take into account the social history of the production of knowledge. The stories that we started this chapter with clearly indicate that the labour of women in the production of knowledge has been disregarded because the process of production has been linked with the public sphere, where women were not traditionally operative. Second, as we have argued above, the definition of knowledge itself has historically excluded the knowledges accumulated and produced by marginalized groups; hegemonic ideas about knowledge have defined out 'other' knowledges as unscientific, superstition and even witchcraft. Such defining out means that historical knowledges are treated as the raw material for scientists to work on without due recognition. Finally, feminists have pointed out that knowledges are evolving, not static – that fixing a moment that is then frozen in the form of a patent does not allow us to recognize the building blocks of previous work in the area. The rules regime that is now setting the boundaries of this fixity is itself highly problematic, given that it seeks to stabilize the unequal relations of power – within society, and between states.

Debates about the nature and processes of the creation of knowledge have also made TRIPS an increasingly important issue between and among states. While global in its formulation, TRIPS and its enforcement through the WTO is resulting in sharpening differences among states of the North and the South. Most developing countries feel that the attempt by the TRIPS Agreement (Article 65) at a global standardization of patent laws is in conflict with the thrust on 'diversity' by the Convention on Biodiversity (CBD) signed at the Rio Earth Summit in 1992. They feel that intellectual property rights must not be in conflict with conservation and sustainable uses of biodiversity, an issue that has been neglected by those who drafted the TRIPS Agreement (Swanson 1997). Questions have also been asked as to how far this patent regime would facilitate effective competition or dissemination of information. Some have even argued that that it departs from the competitive ideals and further restricts the access of the poorer countries to technology (Stewart 1993).

The two main objectives of an effective patent law are: promotion of technological innovation by enabling the inventor to enjoy the fruits of his/her creative activities, and the transfer and dissemination of technology in order to curb piracy. These views have been challenged on the grounds that they are Eurocentric views of culture. Take the case of the neem tree. Generations have built the knowledge about the uses of the parts of the tree in medicinal and agricultural production. Women have been central, as primary carers within the family, to the development of the medicinal developments from the neem tree. By attempting to patent the historically developed products through the property claims of the 'stabilization' technology of US biotechnology companies, the claims of these generations of women and men have been denied. So, the ordinary people who developed the use of the neem for medicine do not enjoy the fruits of their collective creative endeavour. Second, it has been found that about two-thirds of patented products are never produced but used to ward off rivals, which might inhibit further development of knowledge-based technologies. So, patenting can lead to restrictions being placed upon dissemination of knowledge to those in need of its products.[4]

The differential impact of the uniform patent legislation on less developed countries is a major contentious issue between the two blocs of countries, and it would seem that it is increasing the inequalities between the North and South. Vaistos estimated that in 1972 80–85 per cent of the patents were held by Northern interests (1972). According to a recent document of the World Intellectual Property Organization (WIPO) in the 1990s the citizens of developed countries held 95 per cent of African patents, 85 per cent of Latin American patents and 70 per cent of Asian patents (GRAIn 1998). According to another source, the majority of the biotech patents are in the name of companies originating in the West – in 1990, 36 per cent of these were in the name of US companies, 32 per cent in the name of European companies and another 23 per cent in the name of their Japanese counterparts – an aggregate of 91 per cent (Swanson 1997). Given that an overwhelming proportion of patents originate in the developed world, patent protection is likely to lead to a transfer of income from the less developed countries to the more developed countries and thereby widen the income disparities between the two (Deardoff 1993).

Biopiracy or value added? Patent dilemmas The issue of biopiracy concerning patent rights on seed varieties has been one of the most controversial issue in the TRIPS Agreement. It stipulates that plant varieties are expected to be protected by patents, by a *sui generis* system or by a combination of the two (Dasgupta 1999). As such, since the conclusion of the Marrakesh Agreement there has been an explosion in the activities of large multinational firms to collect germ plasms of different plant varieties located in the developing countries, and after some cross-breeding with other varieties they are producing new breeds of such plants and plant produce which are being claimed as unique and distinct and are being patented in the countries of the multinational firms. Once patented, these plants become the private properties of the patent-holder until the expiry of the patent right. Under 'exclusive marketing rights' (EMR), the patent-holder of a product patented anywhere in the world can drive out indigenous competitors from the domestic market in any other country as the patent is universally applicable. This places countries rich in biological wealth but economically poor in a very disadvantageous position. Instances of such patenting are numerous. The controversy has been over the issue of whether the materials created and developed by generations of innovation in the South, for instance the knowledge of agricultural products developed by farmers, are common heritage and should not be patented, or whether Northern corporations, by virtue of free access, can patent the same knowledge and product (Shiva and Holla-Bhar 1996). Beginning with the commercialization of products made from the neem tree in India, this issue has included other products – the vegetable bitter gourd (*karela*), the spice turmeric (haldi) and the fruit, jamun, a kind of blackberry, as well as the African soapberry and the patent covering all genetically engineered cotton varieties. In all such cases, the crux of the issue is whether the knowledge relating to the development of such items is a social product subject to local common rights or whether they should be treated as commodities in which the profits generated from the development of the products involved in commercialization are treated as property rights belonging exclusively to the patenting party initially. This is leading to an increasing feeling that national laws that protect domestic innovations will have to be altered to conform to the patent laws of developed countries.

An important consequence of the concentration of patents with multinational companies in the developed countries is the shift in focus in research and development from the public domain, universities and research institutions, to private companies involved in the maximization of profit. As the case of pharmaceutical companies in South Africa challenging the state's generic drug production to combat AIDS showed, this shift is inimical to the interests of the poor and of poor countries. With public subsidy, because of the low costs of reproduction, once discovered, an invention can be disseminated virtually without cost, and it can be shown that common knowledge products are efficient to finance publicly. If, on the other hand, private companies are allowed (as they are under TRIPS) to use the fruits of such basic research by making further investment in adaptive research for their commercial use, even though they cover only a small part of the total cost of research, they will claim patent (monopoly) rights to exclude others from accessing the knowledge.

Other challenges to people's access to and control of knowledge, technology and production processes include TRIPS' preference for product patents as opposed to process patents, especially in the field of pharmaceuticals and drugs, which would make developing countries' access to new technologies difficult and expensive. In the context of the pressures on the state to withdraw from the provision of health facilities, the increased prices of medicines are having a particularly inimical impact on the health of women and girl children. The 'classical pipeline protection' of Article 70.8 and the EMR of Article 70.9 for countries in the transitional phase of switching from process to product patents miss the desired impact in view of the 'long' transitional period. In addition, the fact that once a product is patented in any one country it becomes automatically and universally applicable to all WTO member countries denies the national governments the opportunity to impose conditions that safeguard the interests of domestic industry. The patent-holder is thus endowed with two types of monopoly arising from patents and EMR. Given that patents are for the most part owned by developed countries, the benefit would accrue primarily to the multinational companies of the developed countries. Developing countries argue that the TRIPS Agreement further forecloses the avenue to acquiring technology through the process of liberally using foreign technology or resorting to reverse engineering to enhance their own technological and engineering progress (Hoggard 1994).

Engendering the privatization debate Privatizing knowledge production is gendered in different ways. First, it has historically been a process of exclusion of women (as well as some racial and ethnic groups). In Europe research centres and hospitals became the domain of male scientists and researchers who denied the relevance of social knowledges to their work. In India lowest-caste people and women were excluded from education, and from even listening to the classical religious texts. Formalized education, then, has been a domain of denied opportunities for women. Further, in the global market systems dominated by hyper-masculinized values that recognize only certain forms of knowledges, work and competition, even the male populations of Third World countries are 'feminized' through economic emasculation in the marketplace (Ling 1997). This is evident in the case of the Warangal farmers of India, 500 of whom took their own lives in 1998/99, from a combination of local and global structural pressures (Vidal 1999: 10). The post-colonial nation-states have emphasized the need to develop indigenous strategies of modernizing their economies. This has led to two different strategies. Developing states have modelled their technological development on that of the West, at times by adapting existing technologies to their development needs. Patenting laws will result in the closing of this avenue of development. Without safeguarding the interests of the domestic industries, the price of goods has a tendency to rise. This has a differential impact on women and men, most startlingly in the sphere of health. A recent study by doctors in the All-India Medical Institute in New Delhi suggests that far fewer operations are being performed on women and girls than on boys and men (*Times of India*, 25 April 2000).

Second, there has been an emphasis on higher education rather than primary and secondary education. This has meant that girls have not been able to avail themselves of education – owing to lack of resources on the lower rungs of the educational ladder, and lack of expectation on the higher. Third, economic conditionalities imposed by structural adjustment policies on developing countries are leading to cuts in the public expenditure budgets of these states. These cuts are resulting in declining access to education and more health-related absences from school for girls and women. Between 1988 and 1990 expenditure was about 3.4 per cent of GDP on education and 3.7 per cent on health for all developing countries, on average, and only 2.8 per cent and 2.4 per cent respectively for the poorest countries (UN 1999: 52). Indeed, even in countries that had very high levels of female education, such as Russia and China, liberalization and structural adjustment have led to a dramatic fall in female education. In China, for example, 70 per cent of illiterates are female. Finally, it has also been noticed that among multilateral aid organizations 'less and less importance is being attached to training poor women – indeed some agencies have abandoned it altogether in favour of micro-credit and savings schemes' (<www.id21.org/static/4afl1.htm>: 1). Without training and with cuts in education, the levels of women's participation in creating formally recognized intellectual products will remain minimal.

A third important issue for the TRIPS regime is the unauthorized exploitation and appropriation of the full market value of the protected subject matter. Here, the inequality in market participation is important as both the protection of the inventor and subsequent commercial incentives are determined by the owner's position relating to market access and equal participation. As we have argued above, market access is socially determined, as is equal participation in the processes of production of intellectual property. We have also argued, however, that a feminist and gendered perspective makes us sensitive to the social history of knowledge production, and challenges the boundaries of privatized intellectual production. The market system, we would argue after Braudel (1985), can be understood only when it is placed within the context of an economic and social life.

Can well-designed intellectual property regimes try to balance a recognition of the social history of knowledge creation and of individual or corporate inputs that enhance the products resulting from existing knowledges? Can regulatory boundaries be drawn within an intellectual property regime around incentives for the creation of knowledge and the social benefits derived from it? We have argued that intellectual property rights affect women and men as well as developing and developed countries in different ways. Key issues determining these differences are: market access and competition policy, both at the national and international levels (Sell 1998). The endowments with which people enter markets and the structures of reproduction that govern domestic divisions of property and labour fundamentally influence market access and therefore also competition policy. According to Palmer, social constraints that distort allocation of labour and the rigid and socially sanctioned sexual division of labour that allocates the care of human beings to women function like a tax, further aggravate the gender blindness of allocative efficiency and have a bearing on women's participatory role in the market (1992). This is reflected in the TRIPS Agreement, whereby a new challenge is being posed to people's access, control and even knowledge of their livelihood resources.

In a world of unequal partners, it is not, therefore, surprising that the rules of the game (globalization) are asymmetrical, if not inequitable (Nayyar 1997). The gains go to countries that have participated most actively in setting the rules (Page et al. 1991). Developed countries of the West emphasize the close relationship between economic progress and protection and legislation on intellectual property rights, and feel this would further boost economic development in the developing countries through increases in employment and enhanced exports, as well as acting as an incentive for innovation and technological advance; on the other hand, the developing-countries view, as argued by Ramachandran, focuses on the double provision of patenting, which has led to several abuses, especially among developing countries (1977). According to Indian Patent Office statistics in 1998, the number of patents granted in India to foreign companies was 8,229, while the figure for Indian companies stood at 1,926. An UNCTAD report identifies the impact of the TRIPS Agreement on developing countries as 'ambiguous', reducing their access to technology developed in other countries while also imposing the cost of enforcement, which is particularly high in low-income countries (UNCTAD 1996).

The argument that in any society customary property rights are evolved to lessen transaction costs to individuals is valid generally, but this ignores the ideology of gender, which places differential values on male versus female ownership and rights (including intellectual property) (Mukund 1999). As such the intellectual property rights legislation has no provision for insulating the contribution made by women innovators, in the first place by acknowledging it as an innovation and thereafter protecting it from future unfair exploitation. Innovation for the universal formal sector signifies a proactive process in which opportunities are created or sought and risks taken or supported; in the context of women, however, innovation extends within a broader band of activities, which sometimes may not be linked to the market or to changes in the machinery or equipment. It can bring changes, however small, in the skills, techniques, processes, equipment types or organization of production which enable people better to cope with or take advantage of particular circumstances (Appleton 1995). Women are not generally high-profile users of technical hardware, but they have important technical skills and knowledge and are engaged in complex production processes. They constantly innovate and adapt or contribute to the innovations and adaptations of others, but under the protective legislation of intellectual property rights their expertise goes unrecognized and is less valued. The apparent 'invisibility' of women's technical contribution is not rectified by this new legislation.

TRIPS fails to recognize that the technological worlds of women and men differ according to social, economic, cultural and sexual relationships existing between them; that women's knowledge of processes of techno-logy *is* rational and *is* based on a coherent methodological framework; that the space in which women live affects their patterns of production and use of technology, as do circumstances such as national disaster, conflicts, environmental changes and market demands. TRIPS also does not recognize that women take different risks to men, but these are not acknowledged as such and are therefore not rewarded, and that they con-tribute significantly to enhancing the security of households through food production, processing and marketing on a daily basis. TRIPS also does not reflect the inequality that women experience in the communication of information and skills, education and selection owing to the socially embedded nature of national policy-making, and thus women use, adapt and adopt technology very differently to men (ibid.). 'We still live in a world where', as Dr Rosalyn Sussman Yalow, winner of the 1977 Nobel Prize for Medicine for the discovery of radio immunoassay (RIA), said, 'still a significant fraction of people ... believe that a woman belongs and wants to belong exclusively in the home ...' To advance women require competence, courage and determination to succeed. But this does not diminish the role of an enabling environment.

Institutional support mechanisms to encourage women to undertake the risks involved in innovative research and development continue, however, to be negligible. Facilities to run experimental trials, and re-sources to encourage such ventures make the access points still narrower. And while in some countries initiatives have been taken, empathy with the role women have to perform in society is yet to be developed to make the conditions facilitating them. Access to credit facilities or the lack of it has been a major deterrent to women's entry into this field. Formal financial institutions see a woman with an original creation to be tested in the market but without the conventional collateral as a double bad debt even before the loan has been approved. We need not venture farther into the details of monetary restrictions facing women at every step thereafter.

Acknowledgement and classification of women's contributions to many inventions are important aspects of the recogition of women's participation in the marketplace. Despite this, women inventors have generally been subjected to stereotypes – their inventions are 'domestic', mainly related to children, the home and beauty care. Venturing out, they advanced into 'nurturing' kinds of inventions for use outside the home, and finally entered a variety of areas not associated with traditional stereotypes – in biotechnology, including genetic engineering, etc. These assumptions, an integral part of any society's psyche, are a barrier difficult to surmount, and when overcome pose a host of problems before the inventions can be patented and subsequently commercialized.

Conclusions

This chapter has argued that though women – from both the South and the North – have participated in the processes of invention and knowledge creation, the TRIPS regime is reducing, not increasing, the space for women to reap the benefits of their efforts. This is because TRIPS is embedded in the global capitalist regime of individualized property, which is seen as of value only when traded in the marketplace. The market itself is a deeply implicated space where actors come with differential resources to trade, not freely, but under constraints that are both economic and cultural.

The TRIPS regime is institutionalizing the concentration of privilege – male and Northern – by operating according to a winner-takes-all market concept, and there is no in-built mechanism in the TRIPS Agreement to act as a safeguard in favour of the so-called 'underclass'. This is in spite of the fact that in 1990 estimated world sales of medicines derived from plants discovered by indigenous people and women amounted to US$43 billion. Only a small fraction of this went to the people and groups who had preserved the traditional medicinal plants. Countries of the South profit from the new technologies of the industrial world as much as they do from preserving and deploying the knowledge developed in the course of their own history. Their weak positions, however, cannot catapult them to a status similar to that of the Northern corporate groups which are quick to patent the age-old knowledge developed by and for the community, and make the same community pay a price for the products that have since posterity been in their custody. The technical interpretations of TRIPS in isolation would enhance the very inequality among nations and societies that it proposes to crase through the operations of the 'invisible hand' of the market.

The definition of knowledge itself needs to be expanded if the work of women and indigenous communities is to be recognized. It is important to note that the issues raised by the destabilizing impact of TRIPS on indigenous communities are leading many to engage with it creatively. Vandana Shiva, for example, has raised the concept of 'social patenting' rather than individual intellectual property to counter the possessive individualism embedded in TRIPS (2000). This would allow communities to patent historically developed knowledges and products for the use of the community. Shiva has acknowledged the difficulty of this position – by buying into the property discourse, is there a greater possibility of cooption of women and the indigenous population into the global capitalist property regime? If, however, we are to take an 'in and against' position (see Chapter 2) vis-à-vis the TRIPS regime, however, then expanding the concept of individualized property in this way might be one means of engaging with it creatively to protect vulnerable communities from the ravages of unequal property regimes. This does not mean that opposition to TRIPS through legal and political action should stop. As Martin Khor observed, 'there have been calls from some eminent economists and from some NGOs to study whether the TRIPS Agreement should be taken out of the WTO ... that it is a protectionist device and should have no place in an organization that is supposed to be committed to liberalization' (2000: 37). The questions that we have raised go beyond what Khor is arguing here, in pointing not only to the embedded and gendered nature of competitive markets, but also to the inequities that are built into the global property regimes.

It is perhaps useful to end with the story of another woman inventor. Marie Curie did not patent her inventions. She insisted that she wanted no profit from them but published them to promote the study of radium and its applications. We do have choices. The so-called obvious technology of age-old communities is usually the real leap in knowledge as compared to all the subsequent technology that is being patented with such enthusiasm.

8 | Networking across borders[1]

The developmental challenges posed by globalization have led not only to new forms of capital accumulation, exploitation and regulation, as discussed in Chapters 6 and 7, but also to new forms of resistance by the subaltern. These forms of resistance include developing new ways of communication, which are not bound by and thus challenge old state borders – through the speech acts of those involved, through technology that allows these acts to take place virtually, and through support that seeks to facilitate such contact in old/new ways of funding. These new forms of resistance are in turn faced with challenges of their own – of sustaining virtual contact, or resisting depoliticization and of creating and maintaining new solidarities across tense borders.

Key institutions and actors in the international knowledge networks, especially in the context of development, are too often assumed to be development agencies, foundations, think tanks and consultancy firms, as well as the individual experts and academics engaged by these institutions. This is evident also from the way knowledge networks are spoken of interchangeably as transnational policy research networks. As we have seen in Chapter 7, much of the literature on 'knowledge' and 'knowledge networks' is therefore framed within the context of engagement with institutions of power, whether at the international, global or national levels. Such a focus emerges from dominant discourses of power/knowledge as well as the economic underpinnings of the 'knowledge industry'. References to the agency of subaltern actors and institutions and to the work of academics who are engaged with these institutions remain few and far between.

Here I focus on a different approach to networks – a subaltern perspective – by examining the setting up and early functioning of the South Asia Research Network (SARN) on Gender, Law and Governance. I write here as a 'participant observer', as together with several other colleagues I have been involved in setting up this organization. In order to tease out some of the issues that I consider important, I will reflect very briefly upon the construction of discourses about 'knowledge' and 'knowledge-makers' and issues of access that emerge as a result of these discourses and practices. I will then describe the experience of setting up SARN and the issues that the founding members of the organization have been dealing with – examining our diverse starting points and political commitments. I will conclude by reflecting upon three aspects of a 'politics of network(s)-ing' – the politics of framing; the politics of process; and the politics of outcomes. The borders that we need to be aware of, I conclude, are not just national borders but borders of power.

Agents of knowledge, knowledge as power

In this section I argue that the 'archaeology of knowledge' needs to reflect upon both the material boundaries of epistemological power and the 'repertoires of collective action' in defiance of these boundaries (Cohen and Rai 2000). Knowledge and 'knowledge-makers', then, can be acknowledged as those engaged in historical transmissions as well as those in defiance of dominant epistemological flows of power. Further, a subaltern perspective on knowledge and knowledge-makers would, in line with critical feminist theory, 'reverse the traditional relation of dependence, deriving criteria of rationality and knowledge from substantive ideals of solidarity and community, rather than vice versa' (Braaten 1995: 139).

Feminist and subaltern epistemologies Much has been written about how traditional epistemologies exclude women as subjects and agents in knowledge production (Kemp and Squires 1997: ch. 7). Feminist critics have focused on how epistemological frameworks have constituted the binaries of rational/emotional, universal/particular, objectivity/subjectivity. As Hartsock has pointed out, 'the vision of the ruling class (or gender) structures the material relations in which all parties are forced to participate, and therefore cannot be dismissed as simply false' (1997: 153). Feminist work has also been done, however, on a more assertive project – it has suggested replacing old with new binaries. Feminists have not only disrupted frameworks of epistemological power by challenging the socially constructed binaries, but have also developed what came to be called 'standpoint theory'. Drawing upon historical materialist accounts of knowledge, standpoint theory argued that the sexual division of labour provides two distinct epistemological perspectives. It has been argued that focusing on a standpoint allows us to examine 'the real relations among human beings as inhuman' and points to the historicity of relationship, which can be liberatory (Kemp and Squires 1997: 143). While this materialist account of epistemological power disrupts the dominant discourse of objective, rational and universal knowledge, it does not acknowledge fully the divided and dislocated nature of the Subject. As Gayatri Spivak has pointed out, while an economic mode of life might determine the class position of the Subject, it does not encapsulate the Subject, whose 'parts are not continuous or coherent with each other' but are fragmented and contradictory (Spivak 1988: 276; see also Liddle and Rai 1998).

Feminist concerns about dominant epistemologies are echoed in radical historiography. The starting point of subaltern studies lies in its critique of dominant historiography and anthropology: '[the] entire field of transgressions, disorder and violence remains outside the anthropologist's privileged domains of enquiry ... [who creates] order by eliminating the chaos that the introduction of the subject might create' (Das 1989: 310). By examining the stories of the marginalized, through their struggles, not accounted for in the histories of dominant elites, the subaltern studies school makes an important contribution in 'establishing the centrality of the historical moment of rebellion in understanding the subalterns as subjects of their own histories' (ibid.: 312). It is also critical, however, to acknowledge that the Subject of colonial subaltern history is also a colonial Subject. The embeddedness within and engagement with the dominant legal and political frameworks of power simultaneously shows history as a 'moment of defiance' at the same time as it constructs 'the form of legal-rational domination' (ibid.: 314).[2] While a subaltern perspective allows us insights into the Subject position of the subaltern in the moment of defiance of the dominant power relations, however, it also often imbues the Subject with qualities that are ill at ease with his/her marginality. There remains an unanswerable tension in the dialectic of empowered and disempowered Subject which subaltern studies tries to answer by privileging agency at the same moment as it reminds us of the structural marginality of the Subject.

Those who were involved in setting up SARN approached the project after reflecting upon some of these debates.[3] What we were hoping to facilitate through this network was a conversation across borders in a region where such cross-border contact has been largely the preserve of political elites. Through SARN we were also hoping to develop new methodologies of agenda-setting for research which are not predominantly led by the funders but which emerge from the discussions of participants engaged in feminist research in Bangladesh, India, Nepal, Pakistan and Sri Lanka. And, finally, we were hoping to keep under review the relations between the researchers and civil society, the researchers and the funders, and between researchers and the end-product users. At every stage the acknowledgement of the power as well as a defiance of epistemological, political and historical boundaries was seen as critical.

Knowledge networks, nodal communications and democratic norms If 'knowledge' is a contested term, so is our understanding of networks. According to Manuel Castells, 'A network is a set of interconnected nodes' and 'within a given network flows have no distance, or the same distance between nodes' (1996: 470). Networks are, then, open structures, 'able to expand without limits, integrate new nodes as long as they are able to communicate within the network, namely as long as they share the same communication codes' (ibid.: 470). Such an understanding of networks allows us, one could argue, to evidence both the democratic impulse of networks and also their exclusionary power. The language of politics and the politics of the language of networks become critical here. Expansion and integration go hand in hand with recognition of 'the same communication codes'. The questions we need to ask here are: expansion to and for what? Integration with and into what? How can communication codes be made more accessible, and how are these used to assert the dominance of some codes over others? In sum, how do networks legitimize and/or challenge flows of power? This is a difficult issue at the local level, but more so when we consider global networks operating on an epistemological terrain reflecting the material power of global capitalism.

In such a context, do networks provide an integrative function by 'linking up' the sites of dominant knowledges as well as the organizations and individuals that seek and/or obtain recognition within this communicative field? The expansion of networks, in this context, would also be the further normalization of the dominant discourses of power – the example of Global Development Network (GDN) set up by the World Bank comes to mind here. The 'gateway to development knowledge' (<www.gdnet.org/>), through the incorporation of myriad local and global networks, attempts to systematize the knowledges generated by the individual and organizational actors that make up these networks. In so doing it seeks to impose a rationality that gives precedence to the 'conception of knowledge rather than ideals of community'. Expansion of networks is then integrated into the dominant development policy framework which legitimizes specific policies and ensures that the communicative codes are not challenged.

Further, such a systematizing framework of knowledge integration also casts a light upon the (lack of) distance between different nodes within the network. From agenda-setting to funding the nodal density of Northern-based organizations such as the Department for International Development (DfID), the Overseas Development Institute (ODI) and the Ford Foundation is far greater within integrative knowledge networks than among other constituent members. As Castells points out, 'network morphology is also a source of dramatic reorganization of power relations. Switches connecting the networks ... are the privileged instruments of power' (1996: 471). These switches can be seen as the nodes of concentration of economic and political power, which can be used simply as a threat or be operationalized to deflect and undermine the defiance of the dominant communicative codes. The distance between nodes, then, cannot be assumed to be the same, and indeed reflects the material relations within which networks are embedded. As Sperling et al. have argued, however, the resources that networks can garner are not only financial, 'but may also include access, reputation, influence and other intangible benefits' (2001: 1159). I would suggest that reputation could be a resource as well as a marker of particular moral politics. This could lead to the recognition of the world of the 'moral entrepreneurs'[4] and allow subaltern networks to approach this world with 'their eyes wide open'. While at times the power of privilege conflicts or competes with subaltern local networks and activities, at others access to tangible and intangible resources of transnational networks supports particular mobilizations and helps inform and/or expand the effectiveness of local networks. The desire of networks to secure their own reputation can therefore also be a resource for local networks.

These issues have been critical in the discussions leading towards the setting up of SARN. As outlined in the network terms of reference, the

> purpose of this network is three-fold. First, to allow a conversation regarding gender and governance to take place between organizations and researchers working in this area across national borders. This is important to share experiences both positive and salutary as women's groups and researchers make headway in individual countries. Second, to facilitate and strengthen the links between different groups within each participating country. This will allow for regular contact between researchers and activists for example, and consolidate the different but inter-related work on issues of gender and governance. Third, through these processes of conversing and networking we will undertake collaborative research on specific areas and aim to arrive at a regional perspective on issues of gender and governance. (SARN 2002)

All this occurs within a geopolitical context, which is diverse as well as historically anxious. The network comprises the already existing feminist research groups in the five participating countries of South Asia, but in their new configuration within SARN.[5] Thus only elements of the existing research groups that are working in the area of law and governance form part of the network. Does this reflect a similar distance between the network funders and the network partners?

The area of research (agenda-setting) within SARN formed part of intense discussions. The Norwegian Agency for Development Cooperation (NORAD), the initial funding body supporting SARN, has a declared interest in the promotion of women's human rights and would have liked SARN to focus on this area. In order to define women's human rights, however, a communicative code was needed that was decipherable by all the partners. In terms of the discourse of human rights in the UN Declaration, for example, many within the network would be placed at a much greater distance from that starting point than others would be. As the conversations about women's human rights in South Asia are informed by religions, political histories and specific gendered regimes of law and civil society, NORAD's broad commitment to human rights discourse was challenged by the experience of feminist activism and research in South Asia. The emphasis on law, in its broadest sense, then replaced a more pointed reference to human rights. A critical, subaltern discourse on the law and rights then became possible, as did the expansion of the communicative codes with which to converse across boundaries.

The 'diffusion of networking logic substantially modifies the operation and outcomes in processes of production, experience, power, and culture', writes Castells (1996: 469). In paying attention to this networking logic we can thus approach the process of the production of knowledges from different and overlapping standpoints, ever aware of the material inequalities built into such production and at the same time of the defiance of the constraints imposed by these. More positively still, through this ongoing critical dialogue we encounter vocabularies that might enhance the quality of conversations and expand the lexicon of feminist writing, and which might constructively interact with each other and 'emerge significantly altered' (Sperling et al. 2001: 1159). The permeability of communicative codes is thus moot here. Embeddedness of networks is, however, also reflected in the site of these conversations. I have already referred to the difficult geopolitical terrain upon which SARN is located. In the next section I wish to explore the meso-space that SARN occupies, between the local and the global.

SARN as a regional network: working across political borders

Regional networks are important arenas not only for conversing across borders but also for doing so in contexts that are more immediate and familiar to all involved. The strength drawn from regional collaborations can feed back into both the national and the global participation of women's groups. The starting point for SARN was an acknowledgement of the common history of the region, and at the same time of the significant resistance to border-crossing through state regulation.

Regionalization from below While the languages of nationalism and women's activism have long helped in creating communicative channels across borders in South Asia, keeping these channels open has not always been easy. It was also important to acknowledge that many activists and researchers that would form part of a regional network were already operating on a much wider global terrain. Globalization in this case formed the backdrop of this regional network. If, we had to ask, our partners were already participating in global policy forums, what would be the purpose of a regional network? It was evident that the political debates on globalization within the five countries involved in SARN had led to some communicative linkages on the ground. The 1990s saw a growing concern about women's work as well as women's political representation in all five countries. As we saw in Chapter 4, internationally supported strategies of women's empowerment, for example mainstreaming gender issues through institutional initiatives such as national machineries for the advancement of women, were also providing women's movements with a recognizable framework on the ground (UN 1996; Rai 2003). The Beijing Conference also pointed to the importance of global networking on the one hand and the difference among women on the other. The spread of technology, especially e-mail, allowed for building upon the contacts made at international forums, but the lack of hardware on the ground also suggested the limitations of this strategy for networking.[6] Finally, the question of power differentials in global networking as well as national politics was also an important starting point for us. Would a regional, meso-level articulation of issues allow SARN to contribute to democratizing debates at both the global and national levels, as it arguably has in other parts of the world?

Blacklock has argued that regional economic integration in Central America through the Central American Common Market poses questions for women at the regional as well as the national level. It allows the regional Foro de Mujeres para la Integración (Central American Economic

Integration Women's Forum) to engage the institutions of the common market as well as national states in debate (Blacklock and Macdonald 2000). No such regional integration exists in South Asia. Despite the framework of SARC (South Asian Regional Cooperation), South Asian states have not been able to overcome their considerable political differences to address the issues of globalization through developing regional perspectives. While all the five countries involved in SARN are members of SARC, we could not therefore build on already operative regional perspectives. At the inaugural conference of SARN in August 2002,[7] members discussed whether developing a regional perspective on specific issues of law and governance might provide us with the political resources to intervene more effectively in global forums and therefore to more effectively address the issue of power differentials among women's groups from the North and South. As Blacklock has argued in the context of CACM, 'Central American nation-states see in regionalization some potential to augment their power' (ibid.). I would argue that SARN could contribute to the political processes of regionalization in South Asia through creating common communicative codes, based upon cooperative research work, which might further enhance the common imaginings of/for the region. SARN could also contribute to the augmentation of the relative power position of South Asian women's groups within international organizations through the development of such a regional perspective on gender law and governance.

Democratic structures and practice: the setting up of SARN Working together across boundaries – national and regional – poses distinct questions of democratic practice. Many issues of the democratic structure and functioning of the organization, together with the focus of its research, were discussed among SARN members at the inaugural conference. The structure of SARN reflects our attempts to address the issue of power differentials.

The network works through three principal bodies drawn from within itself: partner organizations, the Conference Committee and the Coordinating Group. *Partners* have a commitment to participate in the network for a minimum of three years. The partners propose, discuss and assess the research agenda of the network at the annual conferences. They also propose specific projects to be undertaken within the agreed research agenda. This ensures that the responsibility and the power to shape the comparative work of the network rest not with the funders, or even the Coordinating Group, but with partner organizations already involved in women's groups and contributing to debates in individual countries. The funders will thus be 'offering opportunities for ... networking' but less so 'models for effective local action' (Sperling et al. 2001: 1160), which will emerge from discussions and conversations of the partner organizations. I will address the question of how competing research and political agendas might be answered in the concluding part of this chapter.

The *Conference Committee* of SARN comprises the partners who will host the conference in a particular year and the Coordinating Group. The membership of this group will therefore rotate annually, with the Coordinating Group providing continuity. The *Management Committee* will also provide the local point of contact for that year, and will be responsible for publishing and disseminating the proceedings and outcomes of the conference. One of the strengths of this model of organization is that the Conference Committee will be able to draw upon the expertise and knowledge of local women's groups and to invite them to attend the conference. The potential for the extension of the network is also enhanced. With such a rotation in the work of SARN, this management model will also allow for the sharing and transferability of technologies and skills. An important aspect of this rotation is that it addresses regional sensitivities. Dominance of bigger countries, which also have greater resources, will be avoided in terms of management of contact between partners.

The *Coordinating Group* continues to help secure funding and coordinate the projects of the network and in the initial phase of SARN manage its website. A *Panel of Advisers*, which includes academics, activists and policy-makers from South Asia but also from other countries, publicizes the work of SARN and helps to further its international links. The role of the Coordinating Group is both critical and sensitive within the organization. Its members are all, so far, based in the UK (Warwick University). They also have the most direct contact with the funders on the one hand and the partners on the other. Issues of coordinator accountability have been important during the functioning of the network. While the group is a resource for partners, it also occupies a more privileged position (switch/node) than do the partners. The resources of the group, however, are also based upon the cooperation of the partners and of their existing national networks. The partners in this case, while looking to enhance their credibility at the regional level, are already resource-stable organizations. This dialectic of privilege and dependence was discussed during the inaugural conference. The partners were convinced of the importance of having a coordinating group outside South Asia to act as a catalyst as well as the organizational hub for SARN. The political situation on the ground, as well as the existing responsibilities of partners in their local spaces, meant that none of the partners wished to dilute the role of the Coordinating Group. The Coordinating Group also suggested, however, that eventually its membership needs to widen and change in the interest of stabilizing the organization.

The various bodies comprising SARN work not only through the annual conferences, but more routinely through the SARN website (<www.sarn-glg.net>). The website occupies a unique place in the structure of SARN – a virtual office, the site of the various databases developed by SARN, and a communicative space. In order to create a communicative space within which all partners feel empowered, an extensive questionnaire seeking their views was circulated prior to the inaugural conference. The development of the website thus reflects the priorities of the partners and extends the possibility of developing democratic practice through working in a safe space. The website is divided into two parts – the intranet, which is accessible only to the partners, and the internet, which is the 'public face' of the organization and carries the products of its work, such as databases on law and governance in all five participating countries. It is the intranet which carries the work calendar for the various projects and where the partners liaise while working together.

Does such an organizational structure and the methodologies of working together make SARN a non-hierarchical network? This is a difficult issue to address. As a research network one could argue it already occupies an elite position within the region. While there are national women's networks, these are largely of activists or at least self-consciously occupy a dual space of activism and policy-oriented research. The partners either occupy this dual space (CWDS, New Delhi) or are clearly academic institutions involved in research (Human Rights Study Centre, Peshawar University). Second, the structure of SARN, though conceived of on a horizontal plane, is already marked by difference between the relative nodal power of the funders and the Coordinating Group and the partners. Third, while the agenda-setting process is envisaged as a 'bottom-up' project, it is difficult to predict whether the broadening of this agenda to address issues that funders/coordinators or even some of the partners have not anticipated (a cross-border peace initiative, for example) will result in conflicts of interests, and how these will be resolved. After the inaugural conference one could, however, say that the beginnings were positive – different research agendas were discussed openly and passionately and a way was found to resolve issues of precedence and focus. Finally, there is the question of relations with nation-states and with global institutions. On the one hand, there was an expectation that national policy networks will be accessed by partner organizations, with augmented regional authority gained through comparative work within SARN. On the other hand, SARN also expected to develop critical and subaltern perspectives on issues concerning gender law and governance, which might not support such an engagement with governmental organizations. This tension will need to be addressed, if not resolved, if the network is to be sustained over time.

'Critical and creative' research agendas Much has now been written about the engagement of women's and feminist groups in the debates about globalization as well as engagement with global economic and social institutions (Peterson 2003; Rai 2002; O'Brien et al. 2000; Marchand and Runyan 2000; Peterson and Runyan 1999). The literature has covered not only issues of discursive and economic power relations between women's organizations and global institutions, but also the changing relations and differences among women's groups and movements. The process of engagement itself has been reviewed within the context of issues of access to policy-making institutions, agenda shifts and the resources available to various groups in this process. I have argued, for example, that 'Attempts to leap-frog the nation-state by approaching multilateral organizations can also result in the undermining of democratic politics or struggles towards a democratic politics on the ground' (Rai 2002: 176). Often such undermining occurs as a result of lack of resources of time, technology and money. NGOs often find themselves committing to the agendas and programmes of funders without enough discussion about the politics or processes attached to the funding in order to pursue goals of organizational sustainability (Cohen and Rai 2000; O'Brien et al. 2000). This lack of time to focus on the politics of projects becomes more difficult if organizations are working across borders, and do not have the technological and financial support to do so – project-based funding imposes a disciplinary framework which is often not conducive to democratic practice. These were also some of the issues discussed at the inaugural conference.

At the conference it was decided that SARN would contribute to the debate about the relevance of regional economic linkages on the one hand and the nature of these linkages on the other. These debates will necessarily include the question of peace across borders, as attempts to focus on economic and trade relations in favour of boundary issues between countries have thus far been unsuccessful. Issues of conflict and security, then, will form an important element of SARN's research and policy work. Definitions of conflict and security will have to be explored and expanded to include violence against women within and between communities, food security and women's contribution towards resolving these conflicts through both political participation in community organizations and participation in food production and knowledge creation to support this role. Another area where we were able to map regional policy transfers from global/local perspectives was that of addressing women's under-representation in the political institutions of the countries of South Asia. National machineries for women's advancement exist in all participating countries. Conversations across boundaries between members of these machineries, as well as women's groups engaging with them, have already occurred on a regular basis, and there is some evidence that these conversations can contribute towards a regional understanding of the constraints as well as the benefits of these institutions. Quotas for women in local as well as national institutions is another area where there is some cross-fertilization. The Indian legislation in this regard has led to debates about the efficacy of quotas as a means of addressing gender inequalities in *panchayats* in Pakistan, for example (see Rai 2007). A sharing of lessons learned from different experiences of a similar strategy could be a useful starting point for a South Asian contribution to this debate globally. Local governance, then, formed the third research focus for the first phase of SARN's work (SARN 2002). SARN will be the catalyst for exploring regional perspectives in these areas through partner research.

Network sustainability: the challenges before SARN Scholars have identified three types of relations that go towards making a stable network and are crucial for the sustainability of social action. First, interpersonal networks, which facilitate recruitment and participation; second, links between individuals and organizations based upon their multiple allegiances; and third, inter-organizational links that allow for a degree of trust between the participants in a network. I would add here the importance of trust between participants and funders. In the coming together of SARN all these four have been operative, but they also need to be continually nurtured and critically assessed.

Interpersonal networks have been crucial in the setting up of SARN. The crossing of national boundaries, which is at the heart of the network, was made possible through the members of the Coordinating Group establishing close professional and then friendship ties. Two members are originally from India, one from Pakistan and one from Oslo. A common interest in issues of gender and governance was the basis of this relationship, as has been a commitment to the development of a regional perspective on these issues. Personal histories of transnational forced family migrations across borders at the time of the partition of India have contributed to this commitment (Rai 1997). Involvement in national politics as well as in women's movements has also secured the interpersonal networks upon which SARN has been built. Academic contacts as well as collaborative projects between institutions and individuals have nurtured existing networks and allowed SARN a credibility base critical in the establishment of a new project. Finally, interpersonal networks have been used to draw the particular membership from among a rich tapestry of women's activist and research groups in South Asia. The challenge has been how to build upon these important interpersonal networks without personalizing the long-term trajectory of the network. It would not do to create the sense of a club that hangs together through these interpersonal threads. There is also the need to establish norms to guide us in the processes of expansion or reconfiguration of network membership. Issues of transparency and democratic accountability will have to be discussed and working procedures established in order for future recruitment to take place without the original interpersonal contacts being necessarily dominant.

The links between individuals and organizations within SARN are based upon their multiple allegiances – NORAD is funding not just SARN but a myriad of projects. While this project, with its emphasis on governance, is currently important to NORAD, it might not remain so in the future, NORAD will need to communicate to the network the extent and length of its commitment, to help build resources that will be self-sustaining and engage SARN members in dialogue that will allow the development of sustainability strategies. SARN will need not only to establish its rules of organization and functioning but also establish new organizational relationships through its individual members (partners, the Panel of Advisers, new funding organizations). Though SARN partners are committed to developing regional (rather than a comparative) research and political perspectives, this will not be easy. Most partners are grounded in their own countries. To gain a comparative perspective might be of great value and immediate relevance to the participating organizations. To engage in developing a regional perspective needs a further commitment of resources of time and effort, which will only gradually begin to bear fruit. Will the Coordinating Group be able to provide a sustained focus to partners on this crucial issue? Its interpersonal skills and the trust of partners will be crucial here.

Different relationships need to be secured through the development of trust. First, though partners have established a framework of working with each other which is open, deliberative as well as respectful in order to sustain long-term collaboration, this will need to be nurtured – at a distance; face-to-face contact through annual conferences might prove critical here. Then there is the relationship between SARN members and NORAD, its initial funding body. How far can NORAD exercise agenda-setting influence without compromising the autonomy of the network? One example of this has already been provided in the context of the human rights/governance focus of the network. Another area that we have struggled with is that of registration of the network. NORAD, together with many other Northern funders, has strongly favoured SARN being registered in a Southern partner country, while being more sanguine about the registration of financial accounts in the North. While political sensitivity necessitates this approach, responsibility and accountability issues for the coordinators of SARN make it imperative that institutional recognition through charity status is gained in the UK, where the Coordinating Group is based. At the inaugural conference it was decided that SARN will not pursue a strategy of registration as a charity but instead will concentrate on nurturing inter-organizational links between partners to enhance the sustainability of the network.

Conclusion: understanding the politics of knowledge networks

In this concluding section I reflect upon the politics of knowledge networks in three ways: first I examine the politics of process by assessing the possibilities of deliberative politics; second, I examine the politics of outcome by reflecting upon issues of access and the dangers of circularity of knowledge and policy networks; finally, I examine the politics of framing by assessing the relevance of cosmopolitics in understanding the global/local space that knowledge networks occupy.

Politics of process, outcome and framing The politics of process is critical to building trust and also to legitimizing the outcomes of deliberation. Deliberative democracy has been put forward as one important model for addressing issues of process in decision-making (D'Entreves 2002; Elster 1998; Bohman and Rehg 1997). Deliberative democracy involves three elements – process, outcome and context. Its starting point seems to be that 'democracy revolves around the transformation rather than simply the aggregation of preferences' (Elster 1998: 1). Feminists have argued for a similar process/outcome-based politics when they have spoken of 'rooting and shifting' or 'transversal politics', of situated deliberation leading to democratic outcomes as being particularly suited to the way women do (or are predisposed to do) politics (Yuval-Davis 1997). Deliberative democracy scholars have defined deliberative democracy in the following way. As a *process* it includes:

1. Collective decision-making with the participation of all those who will be affected by the decision or their representatives.
2. Decision-making by means of arguments offered *by* and *to* participants who are committed to the values of 'rationality and impartiality'[8] such that they are able to argue in terms of public rather than simply particular interests.
3. Conversing such that individuals speak and listen sequentially before making collective decisions (Knight and Johnson 1997).
4. From the perspective of participants, ensuring that some interests are not privileged above others, and no individual or group can dictate the outcome of the actions of others, which means that outcomes are not known before the deliberations are conducted and completed (Elster 1998).

In this view, equality becomes a central theme in the deliberative democratic argument.

Having reflected upon the need for equality of distance among network nodes on the one hand, and the undermining of this parity through inequality of resources on the other, developing the process of deliberation is indeed a challenge for transnational knowledge networks such as SARN.

A second challenge to the stability and sustainability of SARN emerges out of the politics of outcome. I have already referred to the tensions that might arise between activists and policy advisers for SARN partners, and also between comparative and regional perspectives. We have also reflected upon issues of agenda-setting and the power differentials between funders and the funded. The question of access here is of particular relevance. The terms upon which access to policy-making institutions is granted is crucial. Following Rounaq Jahan, I have argued elsewhere that most of the 'initiatives taken by these institutions under pressure from women's groups are "integrating" rather than "agenda-setting"' (Rai 2002). Further increasing evidence of women's engagement with policy-making institutions, especially international financial institutions, suggests that such engagements do not generally favour women. Not only are there significant differences between policy-making institutions and women's NGOs or networks, but the differences among women's groups and networks also suggest that different actors bear differential costs of (non-)engagement with policy networks. Not only do these issues of difference go towards building or undermining trust within networks, they also point to the dangers of circularity. Working against the grain can be difficult; access to influence can exact the price of losing control of agendas for research and around which to build a political argument. In this context, the processes of deliberation can lend themselves to legitimization of outcomes – whether agenda-setting, research or the choice of political campaigns. The seduction of influence can blunt the critical edge of subaltern politics.

Finally, transnational networks are constituted by and constitutive of the politics of framing. The global space has become the terrain for transnational politics. This has become possible through the expansion of flows of information, resources and technological change. This new politics (or old) has been captured in the discourse about globalization. As discussed above, globalization is, like most political phenomena, a contested concept. One of the important issues related to globalization is that of democratic politics. One the one hand we have the anxiety about the 'hollowing out of the nation-state' and consequent lack of accountability of state institutions to their citizens; on the other, we have a limitless vista of a new global politics made possible through technology and the agency of global social movements in a global public sphere. Gupta and Ferguson contend that 'Something like a transnational public sphere has certainly rendered any strictly bounded sense of community of locality obsolete. At the same time, it has enabled the creation of forms of solidarity and identity that do not rest on an appropriation of space where contiguity and face-to-face contact is paramount' (1992: 9). More cautious voices warn us, however, that 'the discursive spaces through which transnational actors move are socially structured' (Guarnizo and Smith 1998: 21). A new form of politics beckons at the same time as we become aware of the enduring power of capitalist social relations which also frame this new political space. So, while Stone (2003) is correct in pointing to the discourse structuration of development economists, I would argue that this discourse is indeed embedded in the dominant social relations, as is evident from the minimal shifts in the macroeconomic framework of development economic policy-making. The question then arises: what can subaltern networks do to produce not only a methodology of social practice but also outcomes that are democratic? Cosmopolitics has been one answer to this question.

Archibugi defines cosmopolitical democracy in the following way: 'Cosmopolitical democracy is based on the assumption that important objectives – control of the use of force, respect for human rights, self-determination – will be obtained only through the extension and development of democracy' (2000: 143). It builds on the assumption that issues such as the environment, migration and use of natural resources are no longer contained within national boundaries, that technology allows communicative networks to be globalized and therefore democratic politics to become possible, including the re-envisioning of non-coercive international institutions without abolishing the national states. A world parliament is suggested, as is the extension of world assemblies, which are representatives not of the states but of the people. Critics have, however, pointed out the naivety and indeed the danger of such cosmopolitan envisionings: socially structured spaces of world politics do not, Chandler argues, allow for sovereign equality among states. The hegemonic power of some states (particularly the USA) is evidence of the embeddedness of the dominant discursive agency of some in the face of the diminishing autonomy of others (Chandler 2000). In this context, subaltern knowledge networks see the spaces for negotiations and deliberations leading to radical outcomes decreasing. This cautionary stance is important if networks are not to transform themselves into 'systems that create themselves' (Riles 2000: 173). The seduction of networks in providing a sense of agency against all odds, at times through emphasizing the process over outcome, at others through emphasizing 'empowerment' that denotes changes in power relations without the transfer of resources, also provides cautionary tales.

As I reflect upon the current state of play for SARN I am aware that borders of nations, resources – both human and financial – and the variations of framing among the partners have not been crossed as we hoped, leading to a state of limbo within the network. The work has progressed, but in unexpected ways. The network members continue to work, but not always together. The hope of using technology to cross borders has not been fully realized because of lack of hardware, broadband facilities and sometimes even office space. Political instabilities in partners' countries have meant that their agendas have shifted radically and unexpectedly, and they have not had the time to take the others with them. Dangerous choices have had to be made – support of 'outsiders'/insiders might not always be desirable in such moments of political rupture. Does this mean that networks are simply integrative? I am not suggesting any such thing. What I am arguing is that networks, like any other structure/agent, are implicated in the many nodes of power in our global society; that they are politically heterogeneous. For subaltern networks to be sustainable not only of their organization but also of their politics they need to be self-reflective. Without such critical self-reflexivity the consequences of network failure can be enormous, not only to those directly involved but also to those who depend upon the work of such networks.

Conclusion: what hopes, why despair?

This book reflects the gender politics of development as it has evolved over two decades in which the world has changed fundamentally. Globalization has become the dominant frame within which we discuss issues of development. Modes of production and exchange have globalized, as have the modes of governance and resistance. As is clear from the discussion in Chapters 7 and 8, there has been speculation about whether the terms of political participation are shifting in the light of the changing relations between state and supra-state institutions. Questions have been asked about how we might participate in supra-territorial institutions when national institutions have proved to be so distant and unaccountable to politically marginal groups. As we saw in Chapter 6, women's engagements with global governance have built upon the insights derived from the debates on the market and the state as well as on processes of democratization in innovative and productive ways.

And yet, many things remain the same – and this poses challenges for those of us who want to change gendered social relations under globalized capitalism. These challenges, however, are not just posed by us but also to us – to our theoretical framings and strategic priorities; to our solidarities as well as our differences; to our commitment to a politics of recognition as well as to one of redistribution. Here, I reflect upon these challenges as I look forward from the issues discussed in this book to the old/new challenges facing feminist work. As the Shona saying goes – 'paths are made by walking'; the directions we tread leave imprints for those who follow just as others' footsteps can make it easier for us to walk a difficult and contested terrain.

Despite the progress in the lives of women that I have charted above, the recognition of the structural power of both patriarchy and capitalism that has framed my analysis has often led me to hold on to my pessimism about the future possibilities of transformation. My optimism regarding the 'progress of the world's women' has constantly been challenged, and sometimes undermined, by the ferocity of violence, inequality and injustice that take different forms and frame the agency of women within the local, national and global space. According to the World Bank,

Women in low-income countries have less access to formal jobs now
than they had 25 years ago: the female labor force shrunk from 53% in
1980 to 49% in 2005, while men continue being employed at roughly the
same level, around 86%; [the] share of women in non-agriculture wage
employment has barely budged in low-income countries since 1990,
from 23% to 25% in 2003; in all developing countries, women still earn on
average about 22% less than men after taking into account differences in
observed skills; women in Africa receive less than 10% of all credit going
to small farmers and 1% of the total credit to the agricultural sector,
while they make up a majority of agricultural workers and each year,
600,000 to 800,000 people are trafficked across international borders;
women and girls make up the majority trafficked for sexual exploitation.[1]

Despite this evidence, women continue to encounter 'the travel metaphor'
(Skjeie 2006), which assumes that it is only a matter of time before wom-
en's equality becomes a reality and implicitly chides activists for being
too impatient for change. Policy-makers and mainstream economists
continue to insist that there is a continuing 'slow but steady progress'
on the path to gender equality. The implication here is that in the face
of deep-rooted historical barriers to gender equality women should yield
in their insistence on changing gendered policy frameworks all at once,
in the interests of incremental change. This is women's 'duty to yield'
on gender equality. When we examine the debates on nationalism we
encounter similar impatience with women fighting for equality (see
Chapter 1) as we do today in terms of paradigmatic and policy shifts in
political economy; my pessimism doesn't seem so misplaced!

My optimism at the ways in which women have been able to challenge these structural impediments to their progress is also dented
by the terms of the debate on women's empowerment. The worries of
socialist feminists about cooption if they worked with the state and of
marginalization if they didn't seem to be valid today as gender politics
is increasingly depoliticized. On the one hand gender has become much
more visible in public policy, and on the other the space of transformation of social relations has become increasingly hostile.[2] As I pointed out
in the Introduction to this book, these worries have been articulated by
Nancy Fraser in her delineation of the 'politics of recognition' versus the
'politics of redistribution' (1997). This is a sophisticated and nuanced
argument, but at its heart lies the worry that the postmodern turn in social
sciences and gender studies has allowed us to take our eyes off the ball
where the fundamental transformation of social relations is concerned;

that the recognition of identity-based inequalities and injustices has not always translated into the redistribution of resources needed to address these. Fraser is not only critiquing the postmodern position, however, which sees social power in particular ways, but also reminding us of the structural power of capitalism, which closes off spaces of contestation even as it opens up markets in the name of extending choice. Fraser's analysis can take us in many different directions. For me, this concern about redistribution of resources as well as the transformation of structural inequalities it involves has underlined the fact that women's agency cannot be assessed without assessing the risks that they take in challenging their oppression. Measuring agency in the empowerment literature, for example, needs to be accompanied by measuring vulnerability; to do one without the other can only be politically irresponsible and ethically dubious.

Take, for example, the question of women's work. Feminist economists have long been arguing that domestic work needs to be counted; methodologically there has been the development of time-use surveys to measure women's work in the home. They have also been arguing for making employment markets more accessible to and equal for women. There has been a concern about childcare, health and safety issues at work, equal opportunity, equal pay for equal work; the argument has been made about the sharing of domestic work; there has been talk of the double burden that women carry (and sometimes of the triple burden – organizing as well as working inside and outside the home). But there has been little work done on what the economists would call depletion in terms of women's lives. In a recent article, Catherine Hoskyns and I have argued that despite small and, for those involved, critical gains, the fundamental shifts in policy frameworks are not happening; that the disconnect continues (Hoskyns and Rai 2007).

We noted that the states concerned are only just beginning to realize that there might be social consequences as a result of the increased employment of women, especially in the South. The gaps in social provision resulting from the inadequate recognition of social reproduction in wages as well as in state services are met by the unpaid work in households and communities in both North and South. This creates a depletion of resources unless support is given from elsewhere. This depletion is at the moment unmeasured. While economists talk of the depletion (depreciation) of machinery, capital goods and the environment, however, they rarely talk about depletion or depreciation in terms of the household and social reproduction. Depletion of household and social reproduction, if counted, could include increasing concerns about 'food security' in Southern countries, variable access to health as commercialization kicks in, and the patchy nature of child and adult care. While UNICEF has initiated some discussion about the social costs of economic adjustment, these have not so far been represented in the economic accounting upon which economic policy is based. And yet the consequences of globalization in a situation where these factors are not measured seem to warrant concern and further investigation, and not just by feminists. This gap in statistics also makes accurate research difficult – child and adult care, household maintenance and health provision in the domestic sphere are not measured in formal statistics, which leaves the measurement of depletion of energy resources of those engaged in these services not only unacknowledged but also not systematically addressed in policy.

If we take another example, that of violence against women, we find that overlooking the costs of 'empowering' women through development programmes can be catastrophic. Uma Chakravarti has written a moving as well as a politically sophisticated analysis of the Women's Development Programme in Rajasthan, India. The tensions resulting from the important but flawed WDP came to a head with the gruesome gang rape of one *sathin*[3] – Bhanwari Devi – in 1992. Bhanwari Devi was paraded naked through the streets of the village and her husband was also beaten up for not being able to keep his wife under control. Chakravarti concludes from this that 'The government wants empowerment without breaking into the power of those, including themselves, who have power over the disempowered ... while the *sathin*s struggle ... for the statutory minimum wage of workers and the survival and expansion of the scheme, the government claims credit for the "success" of the *sathin* programme in Beijing, Vienna and Geneva' (2006: 18). This story raises many questions about the levels of risk involved for women in doing their work without adequate support, as well as about how to translate conscientization into practical politics when the structures of power are supported by political elites at every level.

So, when analysing or measuring empowerment, can we afford to overlook the risks? When developing programmes that might empower women, can we overlook the perils of participation? When seeing women as agents, can we afford to overlook their vulnerabilities, which make them victims as well as actors in their struggles for empowerment?

My final thought on the issue of measuring risks in the search for empowerment is this – often what is presented as empowerment is really a struggle for survival. I started thinking about this distinction some time ago when I read the Indian Canadian writer Rohinton Mistry's epic novel *A Fine Balance*. What he describes in that story can of course be easily represented as a triumph of spirit over adversity; of agency over structures of oppression. What I could not escape while reading this account of survival, however, was how the nature of Indian politics and economic inequalities was such that so much energy is often expended for short periods of calm before the next crisis once again threatens the survival of the poor, the weak and the marginalized. A 'cost–benefit analysis' of this expenditure of energy would perhaps show us that the costs far outweigh the benefits, even though we celebrate the survival of some of the characters and shed tears for those that go under. So, does this distinction between empowerment and survival strategies, and the risks and costs attached to these, make a difference to our analysis? I think it does. By insisting upon counting costs, whether as depletion or more qualitatively in terms of violence, fragility, etc., we are also insisting upon the recognition of structural barriers to empowerment; we repoliticize the concept. Such a cautious approach would then allow empowerment strategies to focus not only on individuals but also on the contexts within which individuals function; a recognition not only of disadvantage but the redistribution of resources.

Another issue that continues to challenge us is that of addressing difference. While Fraser's concern about the politics of recognition remains valid and confronts us with difficult issues of structural power, it is also important to note that in the post-9/11 world gendered, racial and religious discrimination continues to consolidate. When we examine the geographies of exclusion we are simultaneously examining the politics of inclusion. The needs of metropolitan centres attract populations to them, but also contain and shape this inclusion. Women from all over the world are travelling to distant and terrifying landscapes, escaping from other frightening spaces – as domestic and care workers, as brides and sex-workers, as factory workers without any rights. The ghettos of subalternity that emerge in metropolitan centres tell us about both the expanded needs of metropolitan power and its servicing by the subaltern other. And yet, the flourishings in the ghetto do challenge as well as serve the needs of the metropolis. The question then, following Spivak, is not only 'can the subaltern speak', but also 'can the metropolis hear'?

'Hearing' often takes the form of illustrative engagements. This approach often leads to museum-like displays of the gendered, exoticized other – teaching us about declined civilizations, peripheral but colourful examples of weakness in one or other form. Such exoticization, as Said has so powerfully argued, is the result not only of conquest of/through state power but also of a refashioning of systems of thought to which the conquered elites might have access. Education and knowledge as power, as Foucault observed, are the key to the reproduction of exoticized cultures. Illustrative power holds sway in curricula through which metropolitan power teaches its own as well as the elites of emerging economies – both servicing the needs of the metropolis. When the day is done, the glass cabinets – in museums as well as of metaphoric spaces in educational institutions – with their displays of decline can be locked away in darkened rooms, having created value in instruction as well as the fees charged for entry to the space of that instruction.

But what of the voices of the ghettos? Peripheral and contained, perhaps, but also escaping and disturbing the dominant flows of communications. Worried by all sorts of internal demons – accountability, authenticity, representation – their engagement with the dominant flows of communication displays post-colonial anxieties that don't make for the 'easy listening' of neat composition. The internal disturbance resonates in the fractured, sometimes tortured articulations of anger, but also in alternative visions of changing landscapes. If this mapping of exclusion and inclusion resonates at all with feminist challenges, then where do we go from here?

Raising this question in the academy is in itself critical – what we teach, how we teach and who teaches are all questions that need repeated airing. The issue of structure and agency that I have been wrestling with continues to dog our collective footsteps. If we accept the power of the metropolis as shaping our lives, then our alternative visions will continue to reflect that power despite the challenges that the ghetto and the museum pose by their presence in the metropolitan landscape. These alternative visions provide a promise of empowerment, through ambiguity rather than certainties; through struggles to create new spaces where they can think 'other-wise'; where there is a proliferation of many voices rather than a few and where we continue to create knowledge as we resist by avoiding 'paradigmatic conceit' (Ashley and Walker 1990). We do this because we crave not only interpretative autonomy but also a transformative politics that addresses both the exclusions and terms of inclusion in the metropolitan centres of power.

What continues to unfold, therefore, is not only the consolidating power of the metropolis, but also the challenges posed by women and men seeking to transform the world that they inhabit. The tensions between structure and agency that I referred to in my introduction to this book cast long though shifting shadows in which both globalized and gendered power are exercised and the resistance to oppression takes shape. It is this productive tension which is the central concern of this book and which continues to inform my work.

Notes

Introduction

1 The ILO annual jobs report says that global unemployment continues to grow; young people now make up half of those out of work: <www-ilo-mirror.cornell.edu/public/english/bureau/inf/pr/2006/1.htm>.

2 Oxfam, *Gender Equality*: <www.oxfam.org.uk/resources/issues/gender/introduction.html>.

1 Gender, nationalism and 'nation-building'

1 First published in *Gender and the Political Economy of Development*, Cambridge: Polity Press, 2002.

2 This emerged as a popular term after the Second World War, often used interchangeably with 'modern', especially in economic usage, and therefore associated with industrialization, urbanization, and in the 1970s with representative democratic political systems (see Rostow 1979; Huntington 1968: ch. 2). During the colonial period many of the ideas central to development were cast in terms of 'progress', which encompassed an understanding of modernity – both economic and sociocultural.

3 Nationalism continues to play an important role in the promotion of policies loosely defined as either liberalization, or more broadly as globalization. Indeed, some have argued that a nationalist backlash against globalization cannot be ruled out if liberalization does not (and there are many reasons why it might

not) deliver high growth rates in Third World countries.

4 Here I argue with the grain of the quite different argument that O'Hanlon and Washbrook (1991) make in their study of approaches to Indian culture (see *Histories in Transition: Approaches to the Study of Colonialism and Culture in India*). They suggest that the 'political economy' approaches are important to the understanding of culture, whereas I am suggesting that the 'political economy' approach in development would benefit from extension into the field of cultural history to embrace some of the important impulses and starting points of national development. Thus, a theoretical framework that is not too narrowly focused on one or the other is perhaps more able to demystify issues of culture and development.

5 It is fascinating to note, for example, that Dahbour and Ishay (1995) does not include a single feminist piece, not even under the section on 'The Contemporary Debate on Nationalism'. The only woman whose work is included is Rosa Luxemburg.

6 Hobsbawm points out that during the early period of theorizing the nation (1830–80) there were only three criteria which allowed a people to be recognized as a nation: its historic association with a current state or lengthy recent past; the existence of a long-established cultural elite, and a written literary and administra-

tive vernacular; and a proven capacity for conquest (1990: 37). While the later theorizing may no longer see capacity for conquest as essential to the assertions of nationhood, cultural and historical capital remain necessary to the formulations of the yearning for selfhood of nations and peoples.

7 As it has been used to frame women's role in the state since the birth of nationalism itself in the eighteenth century.

8 Indeed, some have pointed to this resurgent nationalism as evidence of the continued salience of the nation-state in the face of the forces of globalization (Anthony Giddens, speaking on 'The Third Way' at the University of Warwick, 9 October 2000).

9 Western European states had invested in colonial and semi-colonial states more than the entire wealth of Britain (Cairncross 1975: 3).

10 Modernity, writes S. C. Dube, 'may be understood as the common behaviourial system historically associated with the urban, industrial, literate and participant societies of Western Europe and North America. The system is characterised by a rational and scientific world view, growth and ever-increasing application of science and technology, together with continuous adaptation of the institutions of society to the imperatives of the new world view and the emerging technological ethos' (1988: 17).

11 In other cultures, such as Spanish America, this concern with purity was less evident. Indeed, the Catholic priests were continually dismayed by the lack of concepts of honour dependent upon the sexual purity of women.

12 Indeed, in India nationalist Congressmen tried to keep prostitute women and 'Congress ladies' apart from each other on political marches so as not to offend the sensibilities of upper-caste/class women and their male relatives (Desai 1989).

13 It is important to note, however, that the colonial state also provided opportunities for women to register their protest against the traditional social relations in Africa. As Bayart notes, 'Neither "women" nor "minors" submitted passively to the law of the elders ... women were feared for the efficiency of the sorcery ... ' However, 'their actions were not "revolutionary", and they were as often individual as collective' (1993: 112–13).

14 In India the cultural articulation of *ghare/baare* (inside/outside) served the same purpose (Chatterjee 1989).

15 In the case of Kenya, for example, the link between nationalism and African socialism was made on the premise that all Africa had a single traditional culture, 'that of communalism. The common colonial experience, it was argued, subdued communalism and exploited resources in Africa for the benefit of non-Africans. To achieve post-colonial economic advancement or progress, rational planning of resources would be required' (Cowen and Shenton 1996: 316). The role of the state elites thus remained central to the project of African socialism.

16 For an analysis of Marxist regimes, see below. The political situation in post-colonial Latin America was also different.

17 In countries like China, where Marxism was embraced by a major part of the oppositional elites, class

politics subsumed the economic rights of women, while the political agenda was similar to the one outlined above (Evans 1997).

18 For an analysis of similar debates on culture and constitution in Algeria see Cherifa Bouatta in Moghadam 1994. The arguments about Islamic propriety and the citizenship rights of women are discussed, as is the eventual compromise between the FLN and the Muslim clerics in the shape of the Family Code of 1984. See also Mehdid 1993.

19 Nehru writes in *The Discovery of India*: 'The very thing that India lacked, the modern West possessed and possessed to excess. It had the dynamic outlook. It was engrossed in the changing world, caring little for ultimate principles, the unchanging, the universal ... Because it was dynamic, it was progressive and full of life, but that life was a fevered one and the temperature kept on rising progressively. ... India, as well as China, must learn from the West for the modern West has much to teach, and the spirit of the age is represented by the West' (1990: 384–5).

20 While in principle Islam provides women with the right to inherit the father's property, in practice the right is often overlooked in favour of male heirs (Ali 2000).

21 In China, Mao Zedong wrote 'On Contradictions', which systematized the Communist Party's demand for loyalty. He stressed that in each context, in each period, each crisis, the role of the communist leadership was to identify the main contradiction, and devote all resources at the command of the party to its resolution. All other (secondary!) contradictions were subordinate to the primary contradiction. Any disturbing

of the hierarchy of contradictions identified by the Communist Party was therefore divisive and unacceptable.

22 Similar personal characteristics continue to define women politicians today. For India, see Rai, and for Chile see Waylen, in Goetz 1996.

23 Bereswell and Wagner, writing on the women's peace movement in Europe during the First World War, quote the leader of the Federation of German Women's Organisations, Gertrud Baumer, who said, 'For us it is natural that during a national struggle for existence we, the women, belong to our people [*Volk*] and *only* to them. In all questions of war and peace we are citizens of our country, and it is impossible to negotiate in an international circle ...' (1998: 236).

24 For a discussion of contradictions arising from the coexistence of African Customary Law and nationalist, secular legal regimes, see Stewart (1993).

25 The Shahbano case, which opened up the debate on women's rights and cultural rights in the 1990s, shows the intractability of this constructed binary on the basis of 'ideal' home/nation. (See Pathak and Suder Rajan 1992.)

26 For a 'colonization' of nationalism that yokes it to women's agendas in the form of the radical idea of a women's nation, see Dworkin (2000). Dworkin argues, 'women cannot be free of male dominance without challenging the men of one's own ethnic group and destroying their authority. This is a willed betrayal, as any assault on male dominance must be.' In an interview she comments, '... it is an incredible thing to overlook as a possibility. We've never dealt with the issue of sovereignty ...'

('What I believe', *Guardian Weekly*, 13 May 2000).

2 Women and the post-colonial state

1 This chapter was first published in *Social and Legal Studies, an International Journal*, 1995, 4(3): 391–410. Though the environs and economy of New Delhi have changed considerably (there is, for example, lighting on Janpath Lane now and the information industry has become a key export), the issues raised in this paper remain largely the same. I have, therefore, not 'updated' it.

I would like to acknowledge the support of the Nuffield Foundation, which facilitated my research in Delhi by means of a grant. I also gratefully acknowledge the tremendous support of the women on Janpath Lane during my research. They opened themselves to me with courage and generosity, without which this research would have been impossible. I also thank Livleen Sharma and Mr Thareja for sharing information and opinions with me. I would like to thank Jeremy Roche, Ann Stewart, Sol Picciotto and Peter Burnham for their support in writing this paper.

2 Durga and Kali are two forms, benevolent and angry, of the goddess Parvati, the consort of Shiva, the god of death in Hindu mythology, and signify *Shakti* or female energy in their different forms.

3 Theorizing gender and democratization

1 This chapter was first published in Peter Burnell (ed.) (2003) *Democratization Through the Looking Glass*, Manchester: Manchester University Press.

2 It was only in 1991 that Amnesty International put the violation of women's rights on its agenda. Prior to this, feminist activity was not a recognized 'political' category except when integrated into the programme of a political party or trade union (Ashworth 1986: 11).

4 Mainstreaming gender, democratizing the state?

1 This chapter is reproduced from UN Division for the Advancement of Women (2003), *National Machineries for the Advancement of Women: Mainstreaming Gender, Democratising the State?*, Manchester: Manchester University Press.

2 The implications of CEDAW for states party to it are potentially far reaching indeed. Not only must they abolish all existing legislation and practices that are discriminatory, they are also under a positive obligation to eliminate stereotyped concepts of male and female roles in society. 'Traditional customs and practices' as an argument is not considered valid. There is no provision under CEDAW, however, for one state to complain of a violation of the Convention carried out by another state. Neither do individuals have the right to complain about a state on the grounds of violation of the Convention. The approach taken to enforcement of the Convention is one of 'constructive dialogue' and 'progressive implementation' rather than a requirement for immediate action on the part of party states.

5 Quotas in context

1 This chapter was first published as 'Gender quotas and the politics of empowerment: a comparative study',

in Drude Dahlerup (ed.) (2005), *Women, Quotas and Politics*, London: Routledge.

2 Pakistan was further divided in 1971, when Bangladesh came into existence after a civil war.

3 This allows people of different religions to follow their own religious rather than secular state law in the area of marriage, divorce, custody, etc.

4 Article 331 stipulated a reservation of seats for the Anglo-Indian community for two years if the president thought it to be underrepresented in parliament.

5 Class-based exclusion, however, was not taken on board in the quota regime. Rather, this was to be addressed through equal opportunity provisions on the grounds that class mobility allows a way out of the poverty trap, which the caste structure does not allow. This approach to reservation has led to the charge that the 9th Schedule creates sub-elites within the scheduled castes and tribes, limiting the redistributive role of quotas.

6 Rai's interviews with women activists suggest that quotas were largely the result of government initiative. The 'seven sisters' (important women's NGOs) were consulted at the stage when the decision to introduce quotas had been taken, but it was largely femocrats within the government who formulated the policy. In India, said Veena Mazumdar (of the Centre for Women's Development Studies), 'reservations have generated a debate, not a movement'.

7 There have been discussions about introducing the same type of legislation at the national level in an 84th Amendment Bill but it has not yet passed (Rai 2000; Raman 2003).

8 'The Hudood Ordinances disregard the testimony of women for inflicting *hadd* or punishment ... evidence of four, adult male Muslims is required of the actual act of penetration as proof of adultery or rape ... Women also stand discriminated against because these laws fix a lower age of criminal responsibility for girls than for boys' (Ali 2000: 47).

9 As outlined in the Introduction, it is important to make a distinction between 'reserved seats with indirect election' and 'reserved seats with direct election'. Systems with indirect elections have a certain number of seats that are reserved for women but they are nominated and elected by, for example, the directly elected representatives at a lower level. In systems with direct elections there are certain seats reserved for women which only women are allowed to contest.

10 Below *Union Parishad* there are about 68,000 so-called *Gram Parishads*, which consist of one village. No elections have been held at this level (Mahtab 2003).

11 *'Maan'* is an important concept here. It can be translated in many different ways but essentially denotes respect, though this might be underpinned by pride. A woman's place within the family might be enhanced if she is bringing in some income and gains recognition for a 'job' that can be characterized as 'public service'. This also supports Amartya Sen's contention that paid work outside the home is a prerequisite for women's improved status within the family.

6 Globalization, development and global governance

1 A version of this chapter first appeared as 'Gendering global

governance' in the *International Feminist Journal of Politics*, 2004, 6(4).

2 There are, for example, deep and growing anxieties regarding blogging in not just authoritarian states, such as China, but also militarized institutions and systems. US soldiers in Iraq are being discouraged from blogging and therefore sharing their experiences and analysis of the war on the ground.

3 The debate on the provisions and rules of GATS is extremely relevant here. See Gill (1995), who argues that GATS negotiations have three main elements: 1) expanding market access commitments; 2) placing new constraints on state regulation of the domestic sphere; and 3) expanding GATS' rules and disciplinary framework to include emergency safeguards, subsidies and government procurement.

4 One could argue that this disciplinary neoliberalism is clearly evident in the increasing convergence between the economic policy frameworks of the World Bank and the UNDP, especially in addressing the anti-poverty agenda, as well as in initiatives for the management of capital–labour relations through the Global Social Compact, which builds on the idea of 'corporate social responsibility' – one way of privatizing social governance.

5 The impact of the globalization of labour markets in this particular way has, of course, enormous implications for women's work and migration.

6 It is fascinating to note how global economic institutions such as the World Bank are clearly recognizing this participating state in particular political ways. Thus, the 2000 World Development Report clearly states,

'Poverty is an outcome not only of economic processes – it is an outcome of interacting economic, social and political forces. In particular, it is an outcome of the accountability and responsiveness of state institutions' (p. 99). The economic forces are then depoliticized, while the state becomes associated with maladministration (non-accountability) as well as with politics (lack of responsiveness to its 'clients'' interests).

7 Polanyi, of course, sets up a dichotomy between pre-capitalist embedded markets and the capitalist unembedded price-setting market of a 'modern society' (1957). The idea of the embedded market, however, is now widely used to understand the different ways in which different sectors and regions experience the market, and how markets are 'distorted' by or enmeshed in cultural and historical spaces (see also Braudel 1985).

7 Knowledge and/as power

1 This chapter was first published as 'Knowledge and/as power: feminist critiques of Trade Related Intellectual Property Rights' (with Sharmistha Barwa) in *Gender, Technology and Development*, 2003, 7(1). Despite further developments in this field the framework of TRIPS has not changed, obviating the need to 'update' the chapter.

2 As Hartsock (1997) has pointed out, 'the vision of the ruling class (or gender) structures the material relations in which all parties are forced to participate, and therefore cannot be dismissed as simply false'.

3 It is interesting to note that indigenous knowledges do command a good price in the marketplace once

they have been packaged by business for mass consumption. States contribute to this process of marketization through the regulatory regimes of 'standards' and standardization. For more on how branding makes the product, see Klein (2001).

4 On the issue of compulsory licensing, while TRIPS is not very particular on this, several national patent laws (in China, Argentina, Brazil) use it effectively to prevent the patent-holder from denying access to the patent product and make it possible for others to apply for permission so to use it for a fee (Keyala 1998).

8 Networking across borders

1 This chapter was first published in *Global Networks*, 2003.

2 For more on subaltern studies, see Guha (1982–87).

3 The initiative to establish SARN emerged at a meeting on gender and law at Peshawar University, Pakistan, in 1996 (Rai 1997). At the time, of the three colleagues involved, one was based in Pakistan, one in the UK and one in Norway; all three are academics. Two carried with them histories of personal/political engagement in South Asia, and one long experience of setting up a network on gender and law in southern Africa. Another colleague later joined the group in the UK, and the colleague from Pakistan also moved to the UK. So now all three members of the Coordination Group of SARN are based in the UK, and the colleague from Norway is a member of the Panel of Advisers.

4 Moral entrepreneurs are defined by Sperling et al. as 'those who contribute to building organizations and discourses that have moral implications ... [and] in the process

they develop a greater or lesser degree of international prominence and credibility' (2001: 1159). I would suggest that both transnational and local organizations can be moral entrepreneurs. For a discussion of 'knowledge management' as means of NGO accountability, see Smyth (2002). Accountability here is to funders and investors, while knowledge management also contributes to securing reputations through cornering the market in specific areas of 'systems for learning', which could be either through activities in 'the field' or 'institutional learning' within the NGO sector.

5 The feminist organizations that are partners in SARN are largely research organisations. These are: Centre for Women's Development Studies (India), Intermediate Technology Group (ITDG) (Sri Lanka), FWLD (Nepal), Ain o Sailesh Kendra (ASK) (Bangladesh), National University of Juridical Sciences (India), Human Rights Study Centre, University of Peshawar (Pakistan), Hamdard Law University (Pakistan). Some of these organizations focus on legal issues. They provide legal aid to individual women and lobby governments on specific legal issues. Others work on a variety of women-related issues such as employment, violence and security. Almost all combine research with activism at both the grassroots and policy levels.

6 In an interview with Brinda Karat the author ascertained that an all-India organization of more than 100,000 women had to make do with fewer than ten computers.

7 The conference was originally to take place at Peshawar University, Pakistan. The move to the UK was made because of the difficult political

situation between India and Pakistan during the months leading up to the conference. At one stage there were no flights between the two countries, visas were being denied to citizens of the other country, even war seemed imminent. While the move from Pakistan to the UK posed significant challenges for SARN members, it also underlined the need for cross-border cooperation in the region.

8 Both these terms have been contested by feminists. Here, however, I offer them within the theoretical framework of deliberative democracy and with the caveat of plural rationality and embedded impartiality.

Conclusion: what hopes, why despair?

1 <web.worldbank.org/WBSITE/ EXTERNAL/NEWS/0,, contentMDK:20 127207~menuPK:34480~pagePK:343 70~theSitePK:4607,00.html>.

2 For example, while placing emphasis on gender equality the World Bank formulates its approach in terms of Smart Economics, which simply translates as 'Economic empowerment is about *making markets work for women* (at the policy level) and *empowering women to compete in markets* ... The Action Plan targets four key markets: land, labor, product, and financial, chosen because of their potential to produce rapid and sustained increases in women's productivity and incomes': <http://siteresources.worldbank.org/ INTGENDER/Resources/GAPNov2. pdf>.

3 *Sathin* can be translated as either friend or companion. *Sathin*s in this context were the women development programme workers.

Bibliography

Acharya, R. (1996) 'Intellectual property rights and information technology: the impact of the Uruguay Round on developing countries', *Information and Communication Law*, 3(2).

African Agenda (1999) 'National machinery for women ... can the state deliver?', no. 1, pp. 13–27.

Afshar, H. and C. Dennis (eds) (1991), *Women and Adjustment Policies in the Third World*, New York: St Martin's Press.

Agarwal, B. (1997) 'Editorial – resounding the alert: gender, resources and community action', *World Development*, 25(9): 1373–80.

Agnihotri, I. and M. Veena (1995) 'Changing terms of political discourse: women's movement in India, 1970–90', *Economic and Political Weekly*, XXX(29).

Ahmed, K. U. (2003) 'Women and politics in Bangladesh', Paper prepared for the International Conference on Women and Politics in Asia, Halmstad, June.

Alavi, H. (1972) 'The state in post-colonial societies: Pakistan and Bangladesh', *New Left Review*, 74, July/August.

Ali, S. S. (2000) 'Law, Islam and the women's movement in Pakistan', in S. M. Rai (ed.), *International Perspectives on Gender and Democratisation*, Basingstoke: Macmillan.

— (2002) 'Women's rights, CEDAW, and international human rights debates: towards empowerment?', in J. Parparat, S. M. Rai and K. Staudt (eds), *Rethinking Empowerment, Gender and Development in a Global/Local World*, London: Routledge.

Allen, J. (1990) 'Does feminism need a theory of the state?', in S. Watson (ed.), *Playing the State*, London: Verso.

Alvarez, S. E. (1990) *Engendering Democracy in Brazil: Women's Movements in Transition Politics*, Princeton, NJ: Princeton University Press.

Amin, S. (1974) *Accumulation on a World Scale: A Critique of the Theory of Underdevelopment*, New York: Monthly Review Press.

Aminuzzaman, S. M. (2003) 'Strengthening the UP: problems and prospects', Paper presented in a workshop on Local Government and Reforms: Issues and Prospects, Dhaka, April.

Amos, V. and P. Parmar (1984) 'Challenging imperial feminism', *Feminist Review*, 17, Autumn, pp. 3–19.

Anderson, B. (1991), *Imagined Communities: Reflections on the Origin and Spread of Nationalism* (revised and extended edn), London: Verso.

Anthias, F. and N. Yuval-Davis (1989) *Woman-Nation-State*, London: Routledge.

Appleton, H. (ed.) (1995) *Do It Herself*, London: Intermediate Technology Publications.

Archibugi, D. (2000) 'Cosmopolitical democracy', *New Left Review*, 4, July/August, p. 143.

Ashley, R. and R. J. B. Walker (1990) 'Reading dissidence/writing the discipline: crisis and the question of sovereignty in International Studies', *International Studies Quarterly*, 34(3): 367–416.

Ashworth, G. (1986) *Of Violence and Violation: Women and Human Rights*, London: Change.

Åskesog, B. (2003) 'National machinery for gender equality in Sweden and other Nordic countries', in S. M. Rai (ed.), *Mainstreaming Gender, Democratizing the State? Institutional Mechanisms for the Advancement of Women*, Manchester: Manchester University Press.

Bamat, T. (1977) 'Relative state autonomy and capitalism in Brazil and Peru', *Insurgent Sociologist*, Spring.

Barber, B. (1996) *Jihad vs McWorld: How Globalism and Tribalism are Reshaping the World*, New York: Ballantine Books.

Bari, F. (1997) 'Discovering female representatives in local government', Unpublished report.

Bari, S. and B. H. Khan (2001) *Local Government Elections 2001. Phase III, IV & V*, Islamabad: Pattan Development Organization.

Barrett, M. and A. Phillips (eds) (1992) *Destabilizing Theory: Contemporary Feminist Debates*, Cambridge: Polity Press.

Baviskar, B. S. (2003) 'Impact of women's participation in local governance in rural India', Paper presented at the Rural Network Conference, Inverness, June.

Baxi, U. (1995) 'Emancipation as justice: Babasaheb Ambedkar's legacy and vision', in U. Baxi and B. Parekh (eds), *Crisis and Change in Contemporary India*, London: Sage, pp. 122–47.

— (1996) '"Global neighborhood" and the "universal otherhood": notes on the Report of the Commission on Global Governance', *Alternatives*, 21: 525–49.

— (2002) 'Global justice and the failure of deliberative democracy', in O. Enweror et al. (eds), *Democracy Unrealized*, Kassel: Hatje Cantz Publishers, pp. 113–32.

Bayart, J.-F. (1993) *The State in Africa: The Politics of the Belly*, London: Longman.

Ben-Amos, A. (1997) 'The uses of the past: patriotism between history and memory', in D. Bar-Tal and E. Staub (eds), *Patriotism in the Lives of Individuals and Nations*, Chicago, IL: Nelson-Hall.

Bereswill, M. and L. Wagner (1998) 'Nationalism and the women's question – the women's movement and nation', *European Journal of Women's Studies*, 5: 233–47.

Bianco, L. (1971) *Origins of the Chinese Revolution 1915–1949*, Stanford, CT: Stanford University Press.

Blacklock, C. and L. Macdonald (2000) 'Women and citizenship in Mexico and Guatemala', in S. Rai (ed.), *International Perspectives on Gender and Democratisation*, Basingstoke: Macmillan.

Block, F. (1990), *Postindustrial Possibilities, a Critique of Economic Discourse*, Berkeley: University of California Press.

Bohman, J. and W. Rehg (eds) (1997) *Deliberative Democracy, Essays on Reason and Politics*, Cambridge, MA: MIT Press.

Bouatta, C. and D. Cherifati-Merabtine (1994) 'The social representation of women in Algeria's Islamist movement', in V. Moghadem (ed.), *Identity*

Politics and Women, Cultural Re-assertions and Feminisms in International Perspective, Boulder, CO: Westview Press.

Braaten, J. (1995) 'From communicative rationality to communicative thinking: a basis for feminist theory and practice', in J. Meehan (ed.), *Feminists Read Habermas: Gendering the Subject of Discourse*, London: Routledge.

Braudel, F. (1985) *La Dynamique du capitalisme*, Paris: Flammarion.

Brown, W. (1992) 'Finding the man in the state', *Feminist Studies*, 18(1).

Buch, N. (2000a) 'Women's experience in new panchayats: the emerging leadership of rural women', Occasional Paper 35, Delhi: Centre for Women's Development Studies.

— (2000b) 'Panchayats and women', in G. Mathew (ed.), *Status of Panchayati Raj in the States and Union Territories of India*, New Delhi: Concept, p. 150.

Burnham, P. (1999) 'The politics of economic management in the 1990s', *New Political Economy*, 4(1): 37–54.

Butalia, U. (1998) *The Other Side of Silence: Voices from the Partition of India*, New Delhi: Penguin.

Butler, J. (1990) *Gender Trouble: Feminism and the Subversion of Identity*, London: Routledge & Kegan Paul.

Bystendinzky, J. M. (ed.) (1992) *Women Transforming Politics: Worldwide Strategies for Empowerment*, Bloomington and Indianapolis: Indiana University Press.

Cable, V. (1995) 'The diminished nation-state: a study in the loss of economic power', *Daedalus, Journal of the American Academy of Arts and Sciences*, Spring.

Cairncross, A. K. (1975) *Home and Foreign Investment*, New York: Harvester Press.

Castells, M. (1996) *The Rise of the Network Society*, Oxford: Blackwell.

Chakravarti, U. (2006) 'Rhetoric and substance of empowerment: women, development and the state', in M. E. John, P. K. Jha and S. S. Jodhka (eds), *Contested Transformations: Changing Economies and Identities in Contemporary India*, Delhi: Tulika Books.

Chandler, D. (2000) 'International justice', *New Left Review*, 6, November/December, pp. 55–66.

Charlton, R. and D. Donald (1992) 'Bringing the economy back in: reconsidering the autonomy of the developmental state', Paper presented at the Annual Conference of the Political Science Association, Belfast, 7–9 April.

Chatterjee, P. (1989) 'The nationalist resolution of the women's question', in K. Sangari and S. Vaid (eds), *Recasting Women: Essays in Colonial History*, New Delhi: Kali for Women.

— (1993) 'The nationalist resolution of the women's question', in K. Sangari and S. Vaid, *Recasting Women, Essays in Colonial History*, New Delhi: Kali for Women.

Chaudhari, M. (1996) 'Citizens, workers and emblems of culture: an analysis of the First Plan Document on Women', in P. Oberoi (ed.), *Sexuality and the State in India*, New Delhi, Sage.

Chazan, N. (1999) 'Gender perspectives on African states', in J. Parpart and K. Staudt (eds), *Women and the State in Africa*, 2nd edn, Boulder, CO: Lynne Rienner.

Chhachhi, A. (1991) 'Forced identities: the state, communalism, fundamentalism and women in India', in D. Kandiyoti (ed.), *Women, Islam and the State*, London, Macmillan.

Chowdhury, N. (2003) 'Bangladesh's experience – dependence and marginality in politics', in IDEA, *The Implementation of Quotas*, Asian Experiences Quota Workshops Report Series, Stockholm: International Institute for Democracy and Electoral Assistance, pp. 50–58.

Cohen, R. and S. M. Rai (2000), 'Global social movements, towards a cosmopolitan politics', in R. Cohen and S. M. Rai (eds), *Global Social Movements*, London: Athlone.

Cohen, S. (2000) 'Social solidarity in the Delors period: barriers to participation', in C. Hoskyns and M. Newman (eds), *Democratizing the European Union: Issues for the Twenty-first Century*, Manchester: Manchester University Press.

Coole, D. (1996) 'Is class a difference that makes a difference?', *Radical Philosophy*, 77, May/June.

Cooper, J. (1993) 'Poverty and constitutional justice: the Indian experience', *Mercer Law Review*, 44.

Cosbey, A. (2000) *The Sustainable Development Effects of the WTO TRIPS Agreement: A Focus on Developing countries*, <www.wtowatch. org/library/admin/uploadedfiles/ sustainable_Development_Effects of_ the_WTO_TRI.htm>.

Cowen, M. P. and R. W. Shenton (1996) *Doctrines of Development*, London: Routledge.

Cox, R. with J. Timothy (1996) *Approaches to World Order*, Cambridge: Cambridge University Press.

Crenshaw, K. (1993) 'Whose story is it, anyway? Feminist and antiracist appropriations of Anita Hill', in T. Morrison (ed.), *Race-ing Justice,*

En-gendering Power, London: Chatto and Windus, pp. 402–40.

Crush, J. (ed.) (1995) *The Power of Development*, London: Routledge.

Dahbour, O. and M. R. Ishay (eds) (1995) *The Nationalism Reader*, New Jersey: Humanities Press International.

Dahlerup, D. (ed.) (2006) *Women, Quotas and Politics*, London: Routledge.

Das, V. (1989) 'Subaltern as perspective', in R. Guha (ed.), *Subaltern Studies IV, Writings of South Asian History and Society*, New Delhi: Oxford University Press.

Dasgupta, B. (1999) 'Patent lies and latent danger', *Economic and Political Weekly*, 17–24 April.

Datta, B. (ed.) (1998) *And Who Will Make the Chapatis? A Study of All-Women Panchayats in Maharashtra*, Calcutta: Stree.

Davis, K., M. Leijenaar and J. Oldersma (eds) (1991) *The Gender of Power*, London: Sage.

Davis, M. (ed.) (1987) *Third World, Second Sex*, London: Zed Books.

Deardoff, A. V. (1993) 'Should patents be extended to all developing countries?', in R. M. Stern (ed.), *The Multilateral Trading System: Analysis and Options for change*, New York: Harvester-Wheatsheaf.

Debord, G. (1995 [1967]) *The Society of the Spectacle*, trans. Donald Nicholson-Smith, New York: Zone Books.

— (1998) *Comments on the Society of the Spectacle*, London: Verso.

Delphy, C. (1984) *Close to Home: A Materialist Analysis of Women's Oppression*, London: Hutchinson.

Democracywatch (2002) *Assessing Training Program for the Female Members of the UP*, Dhaka: Democracywatch.

D'Entreves, M. (2002) *Democracy as Public Deliberation*, Manchester: Manchester University Press.

Desai, A. R. (1989) *Social Background of Indian Nationalism*, Bombay: Popular Prakashan.

Dietz, M. (1992) 'Context is all: feminism and theories of citizenship', in C. Mouffe (ed.), *Dimensions of Radical Democracy*, London: Verso.

Dube, S. C. (1988) *Modernization and Development: The Search for Alternative Paradigms*, London: United Nations University/Zed Books.

Dutt, R. and K. P. M. Sandaram (1991) *Indian Economy*, New Delhi: S. Chand and Co.

Dworkin, A. (2000) *The Jews, Israel and Women's Liberation*, London: Virago.

Earle, R. (2001) 'Creole patriotism and the myth of the loyal Indian', *Past & Present*, 172: 125–45.

Eckstein, S. (ed.) (1989) *Power and Popular Protest: Latin American Social Movements*, Berkeley: University of California Press.

ECOSOC (1999) 'Thematic issues before the Commission on the Status of Women, report of the Secretary-General' (E/CN6/1999/4), New York.

Ehrenreich, B. and F. F. Piven (1983) 'Women and the welfare state', in I. Howe (ed.), *Alternatives: Proposals for America from the Democratic Left*, New York: Pantheon.

Einhorn, B. (2000) 'Gender and citizenship in the context of democratisation and economic reform in East Central Europe', in S. Rai (ed.), *International Perspectives on Gender and Democratisation*, Basingstoke: Macmillan.

Eisenstein, Z. R. (ed.) (1979) *Capitalist Patriarchy and the Case for Socialist Feminism*, New York: Monthly Review Press.

Ekatra (2003) *Women and Governance: Reimagining the State*, New Delhi: Ekatra.

Elson, D. (1989) 'How is structural adjustment affecting women', *Development*, 1: 67–74.

— (1992) 'Gender analysis and development economics', Paper presented at the ESRC Development Economics Study Group Annual Conference, March.

Elster, J. (1998) 'Introduction', in J. Elster (ed.), *Deliberative Democracy*, Cambridge: Cambridge University Press.

Engels, D. (1989) 'The limits of gender ideology: Bengali women, the colonial state, and the private sphere 1890–1930', *Women's Studies International Forum*, 12(4).

Enloe, C. (1989) *Bananas, Beaches and Bases, Making Feminist Sense of International Politics*, London: Pandora Press.

Eschle, C. (2001) *Global Democracy, Social Movements and Feminism*, Boulder, CO: Westview Press.

Escobar, A. (1995) *Encountering Development: The Making and Unmaking of the Third World*, Princeton, NJ: Princeton University Press.

Evans, A. (1993) '"Contracted out": some reflections on gender, power and agrarian institutions', *IDS Bulletin*, 24(3).

Evans, H. (1992) 'Monogamy and female sexuality in the People's Republic of China', in S. Rai, H. Pilkington and A. Phizacklea (eds), *Women in the Face of Change: The Soviet Union, Eastern Europe and China*, London: Routledge.

— (1997) *Women and Sexuality in China*, Cambridge: Polity Press.

Falk, R. (1995) *On Humane Govern-*

ance: Toward a New Global Politics: The World Order Models Project Report of the Global Civilization Initiative, Cambridge: Polity Press.

Fanon, F. (1967) The Wretched of the Earth, Preface by J.-P. Sartre, Harmondsworth: Penguin.

Faundez, J. (ed.) (1997) Good Government and Law, Legal and Institutional Reform in Developing Counties, Basingstoke: Macmillan.

Fine, R. and S. M. Rai (1997) Civil Society, Democratic Perspectives, London: Frank Cass.

Fishlow, A. et al. (eds) (1994) Miracle or Design: Lessons from the East Asian Experience, Washington, DC: Overseas Development Council.

Foucault, M. (1991) Discipline and Punish: The Birth of the Prison, trans. Alan Sheridan, London: Penguin.

Frank, A. G. (1971) Capitalism and Underdevelopment in Latin America, Harmondsworth: Penguin.

Frankl, E. (2004) 'Quota as empowerment. The use of reserved seats in Union Parishad as an instrument for women's political empowerment in Bangladesh', Research Programme on Gender Quotas, Working Paper Series 2004:3, Stockholm: Department of Political Science, Stockholm University.

Franzway, S., D. Court and R. W. Connell (1989) Staking Claim: Feminism, Bureaucracy, and the State, Cambridge: Polity Press.

Fraser, N. (1997) 'From redistribution to recognition? Dilemmas of justice in a "poststructuralist" age', New Left Review, 212, July/August.

Fukayama, F. (1991) The End of History and the Last Man, New York: Free Press.

Fuller, E. (1955) Tinkers and Genius, New York: Hastings House.

Fuss, D. (1989) Essentially Speaking: Feminism, Nature, Difference, New York: Routledge.

Geiger, S. (1997) TANU Women: Gender and Culture in the Making of Tanganyikan Nationalism, 1955–1965, Oxford: James Currey.

Gellner, E. (1983) Nations and Nationalism, New Perspectives on the Past, Oxford: Blackwell.

— (1997) 'A reply to my critics', New Left Review, 221, January/February, pp. 81–118.

Ghosh, A. (2003) 'Women's reservation in urban local bodies: a perspective from Chennai Municipal Corporation Election 2001', Indian Journal of Gender Studies, 10(1): 117–41.

Giddens, A. (1987) Nation-State and Violence, Cambridge: Polity Press.

Gill, S. (1995) 'Globalisation, market civilisation, and disciplinary neoliberalism', Millennium, 23(3): 399–423.

Gilpin, R. (2002) The Challenge of Global Capitalism. The World Economy in the 21st Century, Princeton, NJ: Princeton University Press.

Goetz, A.-M. (1996) 'Dis/organising gender: women development agents in state and NGO poverty-reduction programmes in Bangladesh', in S. M. Rai and G. Lievesley (eds), Women and the State: International Perspectives, London: Taylor and Francis.

— (1997) Getting Institutions Right for Women in Development, London: Zed Books.

— (2003) 'National women's machinery: state-based institutions to advocate for gender equality', in S. M. Rai (ed.), Mainstreaming

Gender, Democratizing the State? Institutional Mechanisms for the Advancement of Women, Manchester: Manchester University Press.

Gopal Jayal, N. (2005) 'Development or empowerment? Women's participation in panchayati raj institutions', *Democratization*, 13(1): 15–35.

Graff, I. (2005) *Empowerment, Accountability and Equality, Quotas for Women in International Law and Pakistani Politics*, Oslo: Institutt for offentlig retts skriftserie.

GRAIn (GAIA and Genetic Resources Action International) (1998) *Global Trade and Biodiversity in Conflict*, London, 1 April.

Grieder, J. B. (1981) *Intellectuals and the State in Modern China, a Narrative History*, New York: Free Press.

Guarnizo, L. E. and M. P. Smith (1998) 'The location of transnationalism', in M. P. Smith and L. E. Guarnizo (eds), *Transnationalism from Below*, New Brunswick, NJ: Transaction Publishers, p. 21.

Guha, R. (ed.) (1982–87) *Subaltern Studies: Writings on South Asian History and Society*, Delhi/Oxford: Oxford University Press.

— (1997) *A Subaltern Studies Reader, 1986–1995*, Minneapolis/London: University of Minnesota Press.

Gunew, S. (ed.) (1990) *Feminist Knowledge: Critique and Construct*, London: Routledge.

Gupta, A. and J. Ferguson (1992) 'Beyond "culture": space, identity and the politics of difference', *Cultural Anthropology*, 7.

Hall, C. (1992) *White, Male and Middle-class: Explorations in Feminism and History*, Cambridge: Polity Press.

Hardt, M. and A. Negri (2000) *Empire*, Cambridge, MA: Harvard University Press.

Harriss-White, B. (1998) 'Female and male grain marketing systems, analytical and policy issues for West Africa and India', in C. Jackson and R. Pearson (eds), *Feminist Visions of Development*.

Hartsock, N. (1983/1997) 'The feminist standpoint: developing the ground for a specifically feminist historical materialism', in S. Harding and M. Hintikka (eds), *Discovering Reality*, Dordrecht: Reidel, pp. 283–305, reprinted in A. Jaggar, 'Love and knowledge: emotion in feminist epistemology', in S. Kemp and J. Squires (eds), *Feminisms*, Oxford Readers, Oxford: Oxford University Press.

Held, D. (1991) 'Democracy, the nation-state and the global system', *Economy and Society*, 20(2): 138–72.

Helie-Lucas, M. (1991) 'Women in the Algerian liberation struggle', in T. Wallace with C. March (eds), *Changing Perceptions, Writings on Gender and Development*, Oxford: Oxfam.

Heng, G. (1997) 'A great way to fly: nationalism, the state and the varieties of Third-World feminism', in J. M. Alexander and C. T. Mohanty (eds), *Genealogies, Colonial Legacies, Democratic Futures*, New York: Routledge.

Hernes, H. (1987) *Welfare State and Women Power. Essays in State Feminism*, Oslo: Norwegian University Press.

Hewson, M. and T. J. Sinclair (eds) (1999) *Approaches to Global Governance Theory*, New York: State University of New York Press.

Hobsbawm, E. (1990) *Nations and Nationalism Since 1780: Programme, Myth, Reality*, Cambridge: Cambridge University Press.

Hoggard, S. (1994) 'Politics and institutions in the World Bank's East Asia', in A. Fishlow et al. (eds), *Miracle or Design: Lessons from the East Asian Experience*, Washington, DC: Overseas Development Council.

Honculada, J. and R. Pineda Ofreneo (2003) 'The national commission on the role of Filipino women, the women's movement and gender mainstreaming in the Philippines', in S. M. Rai (ed.), *Mainstreaming Gender, Democratising the State.*

Hoogvelt, A. (1997) *Globalisation and the Postcolonial World*, Basingstoke: Macmillan.

Hopkins, P. D. (ed.) (1998) *Sex Machine, Readings in Culture, Gender and Technology*, Bloomington and Indianapolis: Indiana University Press.

Hoskyns, C. and M. Newman (eds) (2000) *Democratizing the European Union: Issues for the Twenty-first Century*, Manchester: Manchester University Press.

Hoskyns, C. and S. M. Rai (1998) 'Gender, class and representation: India and the European Union', *European Journal of Women's Studies*, 5(3–4): 345–65.

— (2005) 'Gendering international political economy', CSGR Working Paper no. 170/05.

— (2007) 'Recasting the global political economy: counting women's unpaid work', *New Political Economy*, 12(3), September.

Howe, I. (1983) *Alternatives: Proposals for America from the Democratic Left*, New York: Pantheon.

Humm, M. (1989) *The Dictionary of Feminist Theory*, London: Harvester-Wheatsheaf.

Hunt, A. and G. Wickham (1994) *Foucault and Law: Towards a*

Sociology of Law as Governance, London: Pluto Press.

Huntington, S. P. (1968) *Political Order in Changing Societies*, New Haven, CT/London: Yale University Press.

— (1996) *The Clash of Civilisations and the Remaking of World Order*, New York: Touchstone.

IDEA (1998) *Women in Parliament: Beyond Numbers*, Stockholm: International IDEA.

— (2005) *Women in Parliament: Beyond Numbers. A Revised Edition*, Stockholm: International IDEA.

Jacquette, J. and S. L. Wolchik (eds) (1998) *Women and Democracy: Latin America and Eastern Europe*, Baltimore, MD: Johns Hopkins University Press.

Jaggar, A. (1997) 'Love and knowledge: emotion in feminist epistemology', in S. Kemp and J. Squires (eds), *Feminisms*, Oxford Readers, Oxford: Oxford University Press, pp. 188–93.

Jayawardene, K. (1987) *Feminism and Nationalism in the Third World*, London: Zed Books.

Jezerska, Z. (2003) 'Gender awareness and the national machineries in the countries of Central and Eastern Europe', in S. M. Rai (ed.), *Mainstreaming Gender, Democratizing the State? Institutional Mechanisms for the Advancement of Women*, Manchester: Manchester University Press.

John, M. E. (2000) 'Alternate modernities? Reservations and women's movement in 20th century', *India Economic and Political Weekly*, 35(43/44): 3822.

Johnson, C. (1982) *MITI and the Japanese Miracle: The Growth of Industrial Policy*, Stanford, CA: Stanford University Press.

Joseph, S. (1993) 'Gender and civil society', *Middle East Report*, 183: 149–74.

Kabeer, N. (1988) 'Subordination and struggle: women in Bangladesh', *New Left Review*, 168: 95–121.

— (1994) *Reversed Realities: Gender Hierarchies in Development Thought*, London: Verso.

— (1995) 'Targeting women or transforming institutions? Policy lessons from NGO anti-poverty efforts', *Development and Practice*, 5(2): 108–16.

— (1999) 'Resources, agency, achievements: reflections on the measurement of women's empowerment', *Development and Change*, 30: 435–64.

Kamal Pasha, M. (1996) 'Globalisation and poverty in South Asia', *Millennium*, 25(3), Special issue on 'Poverty in world politics: whose global era?'

Kandiyoti, D. (1991a) 'Bargaining with patriarchy', *Gender and Society*, 2(3).

— (ed.) (1991b) *Women, Islam and the State*, Basingstoke: Macmillan.

Kapur, R. and B. Cossman (1993) 'On women, equality and the constitution: through the looking glass of feminism', *National Law School Journal*, 1, Special issue on 'Feminism and law'.

Karam, A. (1998) *Women in Parliament: Beyond Numbers*, Stockholm: International Institute for Democracy and Electoral Assistance.

— (2000) 'Democrats without democracy: challenges to women in politics in the Arab world', in S. M. Rai (ed.), *International Perspectives on Gender and Democratisation*, Basingstoke: Macmillan.

Kardam, N. and S. Acuner (2003) 'National women's machineries: structures and spaces', in S. M. Rai (ed.), *Mainstreaming Gender, Democratizing the State? Institutional Mechanisms for the Advancement of Women*, Manchester: Manchester University Press.

Kedourie, E. (ed.) (1970) *Nationalism in Asia and Africa*, London: Frank Cass.

Kemp, S. and J. Squires (eds) (1997), *Feminisms*, Oxford Readers, Oxford: Oxford University Press.

Keyala, B. K. (1998) *TRIPS Agreement on Patent Laws: Impact on Pharmaceuticals and Health for All*, New Delhi: Centre for the Study of Global Trade System and Development.

Khor, M. (2000) *Globalisation and the South: Some Critical Issues*, United Nations Conference on Trade and Development discussion paper no. 147, April, <www.unctad.org/en/docs/dp_147.en.pdf>.

Klein, N. (2001) *No Logo: No Space, No Choice, No Jobs*, New York: Picador.

Knight, J. and J. Johnson (1997) 'What sort of political equality does deliberative democracy require?', in J. Bohman and W. Rehg (eds), *Deliberative Democracy*, Cambridge, MA: MIT Press.

Kooiman, J. (2003) *Governing as Governance*, London: Sage.

Kumar, R. (1989) 'Contemporary Indian feminism', *Feminist Review*, 3, Autumn, pp. 20–29.

Kwesiga, J. (2003) 'The national machinery for gender equality in Uganda: institutionalised gesture politics?', in S. M. Rai (ed.), *Mainstreaming Gender, Democratizing the State? Institutional Mechanisms for the Advancement of Women*, Manchester: Manchester University Press.

Kymlicka, W. (ed.) (1995) *The Rights of*

Minority Cultures, Oxford: Oxford University Press.

Lemke, T. (2000) *Foucault, Governmentality, and Critique*, <www. thomaslemkeweb.de/ publikationen/Foucault,%20 Governmentality,%20and%20 Critique%20IV-2.pdf>.

Liddle, J. and R. Joshi (1985) 'Gender and imperialism in British India', *Economic and Political Weekly*, 26 October.

— (1986) *Daughters of Independence*, London: Zed Books.

Liddle, J. and S. M. Rai (1998) 'Feminism, imperialism and orientalism: the challenge of the "Indian Woman"', *Women's History Review*, 7(4): 495–520.

Lie, J. (1991) 'Embedding Polanyi's market society', *Sociological Perspectives*, 34(2).

Ling, L. H. M. (1997) 'The other side of globalization: hypermasculine developmentalism in East Asia', Paper presented at the International Studies Association Meeting, Toronto, 18–22 March.

Lister, R. (1997) *Citizenship: Feminist Perspectives*, Basingstoke: Macmillan.

London Edinburgh Weekend Return Group (1980) *In and Against the State*, London: Pluto.

Longrigg, C. (1991) 'Blood money', *Amnesty*, February/March.

Lovett, M. (1990) 'Gender relations, class formation, and the colonial state in Africa', in J. Parpart and K. Staudt (eds), *Women and the State in Africa*, 2nd edn, Boulder, CO: Lynne Rienner.

Luckham, R. and G. White (1996) 'Introduction: democratising the South', in *Democratisation in the South: The Jagged Wave*, Manchester: Manchester University Press.

Lynch, C. (1998) 'Social movements and the problem of globalization', *Alternatives: Social Transformation and Humane Governance*, 23(2).

McBride Stetson, D. and A. G. Mazur (1995) *Comparative State Feminism*, London: Sage.

McClintock, A. (1993) 'Family feuds: gender, nationalism, and the family', *Feminist Review*, 44, Summer.

McGrew, A. (2002) 'Liberal internationalism: between realism and cosmopolitanism', in D. Held and A. McGrew, *Governing Globalization, Power, Authority and Global Governance*, Cambridge: Polity Press.

Mackenzie, F. (1995) 'Selective silence: a feminist encounter with environmental discourse in colonial Africa', in J. Crush, *Power of Development*, London: Routledge.

McMichael, P. (2000) *Development and Social Change: A Global Perspective*, 2nd edn, Thousand Oaks, CA: Pine Force Press.

Mahtab, N. (2003) 'Women in urban local governance: a Bangladesh case study', Paper presented at the international conference on Women's Quotas in Urban Local Governance: A Cross-national Comparison, New Delhi, February.

Mani, L. (1993) 'Contentious traditions: the debate on sati in colonial India', in K. Sangari and S. Vaid, *Recasting Women, Essays in Colonial History*, New Delhi: Kali for Women.

Mann, M. (1984) 'The autonomous power of the state', *Archives Européennes de Sociologie*, XXV(2).

Mao Zedong (1941) 'On contradictions', in *Selected Works*, vol. 2, Beijing: People's Publishing House.

Marchand, M. and J. Parpart (eds) (1995) *Feminism/Postmodernism/Development*, London: Routledge.

Marchand, M. and A. S. Runyan (eds) (2000), *Gender and Global Restructuring, Sightings, Sites and Resistances*, London: Routledge.

Matthew, G. (2002) 'Ten years on', *The Hindu*, 27 December.

Maunaguru, M. (1995) 'Gendering Tamil nationalism: the construction of "woman" in projects of protest and control', in P. Jeganathan and Q. Ismail (eds), *Unmaking the Nation: The Politics of Identity and History in Modern Sri Lanka*, Colombo: Social Scientists Association.

Mazumdar, V. (1975) *Women's Participation in Politics*, Occasional Paper, New Delhi: Centre for Women's Development Studies.

Meehan, J. (ed.) (1995), *Feminists Read Habermas: Gendering the Subject of Discourse*, London: Routledge.

Mehdid, M. (1993) 'Feminist debate on women and the state in the Middle East', Paper presented at the Conference of Socialist Feminists, London, July 1992.

— (1996) 'En-gendering the nation-state: women, patriarchy and politics in Algeria', in S. M. Rai and G. Lievesley (eds), *Women and the State: International Perspectives*, London: Taylor and Francis.

Melotti, U. (1977) *Marx and the Third World*, Basingstoke: Macmillan.

Mernissi, F. (1988) 'Democracy as moral disintegration: the contradiction between religious belief and citizenship as a manifestation of the ahistoricity of the Arab identity', in N. Toubia (ed.), *Women in the Arab World: The Coming Challenge*, London: Zed Books.

— (1991) *Women and Islam*, Oxford: Blackwell.

Metcalf, T. R. (1995) *Ideologies of the Raj*, Cambridge: Cambridge University Press.

Meyer, M. K. and E. Prugl (eds) (1999) 'Gender politics in global governance', in *Gender Politics, Global Governance*, Maryland: Rowman and Littlefield.

Mies, M. and Shiva, V. (1993) *Ecofeminism*, London: Zed Books.

Miller, C. and S. Razavi (eds) (1998) *Missionaries and Mandarins: Feminist Engagements with Development Institutions*, London: IT Publishers.

Moghadam, V. (ed.) (1994) *Identity Politics and Women, Cultural Reassertions and Feminisms in International Perspective*, Boulder, CO: Westview Press.

Mohanty, B. (1999a) 'Panchayat raj institutions and women', in B. Ray and A. Basu (eds), *From Independence Towards Freedom, Indian Women Since 1947*, New Delhi: Oxford University Press.

Mohanty, B. and V. Mahajan (2003) 'Women's empowerment in the context of Seventy-third and Seventy-fourth Constitutional Amendment Acts', Paper presented at the conference 'A Decade of Women's Empowerment Through Local Government in India', New Delhi, October.

Mohanty, M. (1990) 'Duality of the state process in India', in *Capitalist Development: Critical Essays*, Bombay: Popular Prakashan.

Molyneux, M. (1998) 'Analysing women's movements', *Development and Change*, 29: 219–45.

Mouffe, C. (1992) *Dimensions of Radical Democracy: Pluralism, Citizenship, Community*, London: Verso.

Mukund, K. (1999) 'Women's property rights in South India', *Economic and Political Weekly*, Mumbai, 29 May–4 June.

Munachonga, M. L. (1999) 'Women and the state: Zambia's development policies and their impact on women', in J. Parpart and K. Staudt (eds), *Women and the State in Africa*, 2nd edn, Boulder, CO: Lynne Rienner.

Myrdal, G. (1968) *Asian Drama: An Enquiry into the Poverty of Nations*, New York: Pantheon.

Nairn, T. (1981) *The Break-up of Britain: Crisis and Neo-nationalism*, 2nd edn, London: Verso.

Nandy, A. (1983) *The Intimate Enemy: Loss and Recovery of Self Under Colonialism*, New Delhi: Oxford University Press.

Nanivadckar, M. (1997) *Electoral Process in Corporation Elections: A Gender Study*, Mumbai; Bharatiya Stree Shakti.

Nathan, I. (1998) *When Poor People Participate. A Case Study of a Local Government Election in a Locality of Rural Bangladesh*, Århus: Politica.

Navarro, M. (1989) 'The personal is political: las Madres de Plaza de Mayo', in S. Eckstein (ed.), *Power and Popular Protest: Latin American Social Movements*, Berkeley: University of California Press.

Nayyar, D. (ed.) (1997) *Trade and Industrialisation*, New Delhi: Oxford University Press.

Nayyar, D. and J. Court (2002) *Governing Globaliszation: Issues and Institutions*, Helsinki: UNU/WIDER.

Nehru, J. L. (1990) *The Discovery of India*, Oxford: Oxford University Press.

Nelson, C. and L. Grossberg (eds) *Marxism and the Interpretation of Culture*, Basingstoke: Macmillan.

NGO Coordinating Committee for Bejing + 5 (2000) 'Women 2000: gender equality, development and peace for the 21st century', *Pakistan NGO Review*, February, pp. 116–17.

Nussbaum, M. (2003) 'Gender and governance: an introduction', in M. Nussbaum, A. Basu, Y. Tambiah and N. Gopal Jayal, *Essays on Global Governance*, New Delhi: Human Development Resource Centre, UNDP.

Nyerere, J. K. (1973) *Freedom and Development, a Selection from Writings and Speeches*, Dar Es Salaam: Oxford University Press.

Oberoi, P. (ed.) (1996) *Sexuality and the State in India*, New Delhi: Sage.

O'Brien, R., J. A. Scholte, A. M. Goetz and M. Williams (2000) *Contesting Globalisation*, Cambridge: Cambridge University Press.

O'Hanlon, R. and D. Washbrook (1991) 'Histories in transition: approaches to the study of colonialism and culture in India', *History Workshop Journal*, 32: 110–27.

Oman, C. (1994) *Globalisation and Regionalisation: The Challenge for Developing Countries*, Paris: Development Centre Studies, OECD.

Onis, Z. (1991) 'The logic of the developmental state', *Comparative Politics*, 24(1).

Page, S., M. Davenport and A. Hewitt (1991) *The GATT Uruguay Round: Effects on Developing Countries*, London: Overseas Development Institute.

Palan, R. (1999) 'Global governance and social closure', in M. Hewson and T. J. Sinclair (eds), *Approaches to Global Governance Theory*, New York: State University of New York Press.

Palmer, I. (1992) 'Gender equity and economic efficiency in adjustment programmes', in H. Afshar and C. Dennis (eds), *Women and Adjustment Policies in the Third World*, New York: St Martin's Press.

Panchayati Raj Update (2003) 'Fact file Bihar Panchayat election 2001', New Delhi: Institute of Social Sciences.

Panich, L. and S. Gindin (2005) 'Superintending global capital', *New Left Review*, 35, September/ October.

Papanek, H. (1994) 'Ideal woman and ideal society: control and autonomy in the construction of identity', in V. Moghadem (ed.), *Identity Politics and Women, Cultural Reassertions and Feminisms in International Perspective*, Boulder, CO: Westview Press.

Parpart, J. and K. Staudt (1999) *Women and the State in Africa*, 2nd edn, Boulder, CO: Lynne Rienner.

Parpart, J. L., S. M. Rai and K. Staudt (2002) *Rethinking Empowerment, Gender and Development in a Local/ Global World*, London: Routledge.

Pateman, C. (1983) *The Sexual Contract*, Cambridge: Polity Press.

— (1989) 'Feminism and democracy', in *The Disorder of Women*, Cambridge: Polity Press.

Pathak, Z. and R. Suder Rajan (1992) 'Shahbano', in J. Butler and J. W. Scott (eds), *Feminists Theorize the Political*, London: Routledge.

Pattan Development Organization (2004) *Voices of Women Councillors*, Islamabad: Pattan Development Organization.

Pearson, R. (2004) 'The social is political', *International Feminist Journal of Politics*, 6(4): 603–22.

Peterson, V. S. and A. S. Runyan (1999) *Global Gender Issues*, Boulder, CO: Westview Press.

Pettman, J. J. (1996) *Worlding Women, a Feminist International Politics*, London: Routledge.

Phillips, A. (1991) *Engendering Democracy*, Cambridge: Polity Press.

— (1993) *Democracy and Difference*, Cambridge: Polity Press/ Blackwell.

— (1995) *The Politics of Presence*, Oxford: Oxford University Press.

Pieterse, J. N. (1997) 'Going global: futures of capitalism', *Development and Change*, 28: 367–82.

Pioneer (1992) 'Janpath hawker women win legal battle', 2 October.

Polanyi, K. (1980) *The Great Transformation: The Political and Economic Origins of Our Time*, Boston, MA: Beacon Press.

Pringle, R. and S. Watson (1992a) 'Fathers, brothers, mates: the fraternal state in Australia', in S. Watson (ed.), *Playing the State, Australian Feminist Interventions*, London: Verso.

— (1992b) 'Women's interests and the post-structuralist state', in M. Barrett and A. Phillips (eds), *Destabilizing Theory*, Cambridge: Polity Press.

Rai, S. (1994) 'Gender and democratisation or what does democracy mean for women in the Third World?', *Democratization*, 1(2).

— (1995) 'Women negotiating boundaries: gender, law, and the state', *Social and Legal Studies*, 4: 391–410.

— (1996) 'Women and the state: issues for debate', in S. Rai and G. Lievesley (eds), *Women and the State: International Perspectives*, London: Taylor and Francis.

— (1997) 'Crossing boundaries:

Women's North–South Cooperation Seminar – a report', *Journal of
Gender Studies*, 6(1): 63–70.

— (ed.) (2000) *International Perspectives on Gender and Democratisation*, Basingstoke: Macmillan.

— (2002) *Gender and the Political
Economy of Development: From
Nationalism to Globalisation*,
Cambridge: Polity Press.

— (2003) *National Machineries for
the Advancement of Women: Mainstreaming Gender, Democratising
the State?* (ed. for the UN Division
for the Advancement of Women),
Manchester: Manchester University Press.

— (2004) 'Gendering global governance', *International Feminist
Journal of Politics*, 6(4): 579–601.

— (2007) 'Deliberative democracy
and the politics of redistribution:
the case of the Indian Panchayats',
*Hypatia: A Journal of Feminist
Philosophy*, 22(4), Fall.

Rai, S. and G. Lievesley (eds) (1996)
*Women and the State: International
Perspectives*, London: Taylor and
Francis.

Rai, S. M. and K. Sharma (2000)
'Democratising the Indian
Parliament: the "Reservation for
Women" debate', in S. M. Rai
(ed.), *International Perspectives on
Gender and Democratisation*, Bas-
ingstoke: Macmillan, pp. 149–65.

Rai, S. M. and G. Waylen (2007) 'Feminist perspectives on analysing and
transforming global governance',
in S. M. Rai and G. Waylen (eds),
*Global Governance: Feminist
Perspectives*, Basingstoke: Palgrave
Macmillan.

Rai, S. M., N. Shah and A. Ayaz (2007)
*Achieving Gender Equality in Public
Offices in Pakistan*, Islamabad:
UNDP.

Ramachandra, A. (1977) 'Self-reliance
in technology and the patent system', in WIPO, *World Symposium
of the Patent System in Developing
Countries*, no. 638(E), Geneva.

Raman, V. (2003) 'The implementation of quotas for women: the
Indian experience', in 'The
implementation of quotas: Asian
experiences', in IDEA, *The Implementation of Quotas*, Asian Experiences Quota Workshops Report
Series, Stockholm: International
Institute for Democracy and Electoral Assistance, pp. 22–32.

— (2004) *Globalisation, Sustainable
Development and Local Self-
Government. Challenges of the 21st
Century: The India Experience*,
New Delhi: Centre for Women's
Development Studies.

Ramusack, B. (1990) 'Cultural missionaries, maternal imperialists,
feminist allies: British women
activists in India 1865–1945',
*Women's Studies International
Forum*, 13: 309–23.

Ramusack, B. N. and S. Sievers (1999)
*Women in Asia: Restoring Women
to History*, Bloomington: Indiana
University Press.

Randall, V. and G. Waylen (eds) (1997)
Gender, Politics and the State,
London: Routledge.

Reyes, S. L. (2003) 'Quotas in Paki-
stan: a case study', in IDEA, *The
Implementation of Quotas*, Asian
Experiences, Quota Workshops
Report Series, Stockholm: Interna-
tional Institute for Democracy and
Electoral Assistance, pp. 42–7.

Riles, A. (2000) *The Network Inside
Out*, Ann Arbor: University of
Michigan Press.

Risseeuw, C. (1991) 'Bourdieu,
power and resistance: gender
transformation in Sri Lanka',

in K. Davis et al., *The Gender of Power*, London: Sage.

Rosa, K. (1987) 'Organising women workers in the Free Trade Zone, Sri Lanka', in M. Davis (ed.), *Third World, Second Sex*, London: Zed Books.

Rosenau, J. N. and E.-O. Czempiel (eds) (1992) *Governance without Government: Order and Change in World Politics*, Cambridge: Cambridge University Press.

Rostow, W. W. (1979) *Getting from Here to There*, London: Macmillan.

Routledge Encyclopedia of Women's Studies (2000) New York: Routledge.

Rubery, J. (ed.) (1988) *Women and Recession*, London: Routledge & Kegan Paul.

Rueschemeyer, D. E. H. S. and J. D. Stephens (1992) *Capitalist Development and Democracy*, Cambridge: Polity Press.

Said, E. (1979) *Orientalism*, New York: Vintage.

Sangari, K. and S. Vaid (1989) *Recasting Women: Essays in Indian colonial history*, New Delhi: Kali for Women.

Sarkar, S. (1975) 'Rammohun Roy and the break with the past', in V. C. Joshi (ed.), *Rammohun Roy and the Process of Modernization in India*, Delhi: Vikas.

— (1983) *Modern India, 1885–1947*, Delhi: Macmillan.

SARN (South Asian Research Network) (2002), *Proceedings of the Inaugural Conference August 25–29, 2002*, <www.sarn-glg.net>.

Sawer, M. (2003) 'The life and times of women's policy machinery in Australia', in S. M. Rai (ed.), *Mainstreaming Gender, Democratizing the State? Institutional Mechanisms for the Advancement of Women*, Manchester: Manchester University Press.

Scholte, J. A. (2000) *Globalisation: A Critical Introduction*, Basingstoke: Macmillan.

Scott, J. W. (1992) 'Experience', in J. Butler and J. W. Scott (eds), *Feminists Theorize the Political*, London: Routledge.

Sell, S. K. (1998) *Power and Ideas: North–South Politics of Intellectual Property and Anti-Trust*, New York: State University of New York.

Sen, A. (1982) *The State, Industrialisation, and Class Formation in India, a Neo-Marxist Perspective*, London: Routledge & Kegan Paul.

Sharma, A. (2003) 'Women's political participation and leadership in the governance of municipal institutions in an Indian state', Paper presented at the International Conference on Women and Politics in Asia, Halmstad, June.

Sharma, K. (n.d.) 'From representation to presence: the paradox of power and powerlessness of women in PRIs', Occasional paper, CWDS.

Shiva, V. (1989) *Staying Alive: Women, Ecology and Development*, London: Zed Books.

— (2000) 'Poverty and globalisation', Reith Lectures, <www.news.bbc.co.uk/reith_2000>.

Shiva, V. and R. Holla-Bhar (1996) 'Piracy by patent: the case of the neem tree', in J. Mander and E. Goldsmith, *The Case Against Global Economy*, San Francisco, CA: Sierra Club Books.

Siddiqui, T. (2002) 'Effective participation of women and strengthening of local government in Bangladesh', Paper presented at the seminar 'Good Governance and Local Government:

Changes and Challenges', Dhaka, December.

Skjeie, H. (2006) '"Gender equality": on travel metaphors and duties to yield', in S. K. Hellsten, A. M. Holli and K. Daskalova (eds), *Women's Citizenship and Political Rights*, London: Palgrave Macmillan.

Smart, C. (1991) 'The woman of legal discourse', *Social Legal Studies*, 1(1).

Smyth, I. (2002) 'Slaying the serpent: knowledge management in development NGOs', in P. Newell, S. M. Rai and A. Scott (eds), *Development and the Challenge of Globalisation*, London: IT Publishers.

Sperling, V., M. Marx Ferree and B. Risman (2001) 'Constructing global feminism: transnational advocacy networks and Russian women's activism', *Signs: Journal of Women in Culture and Society*, 26(4): 1155–86.

Spivak, G. (1988) 'Can the subaltern speak?', in C. Nelson and L. Grossberg (eds), *Marxism and the Interpretation of Culture*, Basingstoke: Macmillan.

Spivak, G. C. (1987) '"Draupadi": Introduction to a Bengali short-story', *Critical Inquiry*, 8(2): 381–92.

Stacey, J. (1983) *Socialism and Patriarchy in Communist China*, Princeton, NJ: Princeton University Press.

Stallabrass, J. (2006) 'Spectacle and terror', *New Left Review*, 37, January/February.

Stanley, A. (1983) 'Women hold up two-thirds of the sky', in P. D. Hopkins (ed.), *Sex Machine, Readings in Culture, Gender and Technology*, Bloomington/Indianapolis: Indiana University Press.

— (2000) 'Invention', in *Routledge Encyclopedia of Women's Studies*, New York: Routledge.

Staudt, K. (2003) 'Gender mainstreaming: conceptual links to institutional machineries', in S. M. Rai (ed.), *Mainstreaming Gender, Democratizing the State? Institutional Mechanisms for the Advancement of Women*, Manchester: Manchester University Press.

Stewart, A. (1993) 'The dilemmas of law in women's development', in S. Adelman and A. Paliwala (eds), *Law and Crisis in the Third World*, London: Hans Zell Publishers.

Stewart, F. (1993) 'Biases in global markets: can the focus of inequity and marginalisation be modified', Paper submitted to the North–South Round Table Meeting, 1–13 September, Bretton Woods, NH.

Stienstra, D. (2000) 'Making global connections among women 1970–1999', in R. Cohen and S. M. Rai (eds), *Global Social Movements*, London: Athlone Press.

Stokes, W. (2003) 'The government of the United Kingdom: the Women's National Commission', in S. M. Rai (ed.), *Mainstreaming Gender, Democratizing the State? Institutional Mechanisms for the Advancement of Women*, Manchester: Manchester University Press.

Stolcke, V. (1994) 'Invaded women: sex, race and class in the formation of colonial society', *European Journal of Development Research*, Special issue on Ethnicity, Gender and the Subversion of Nationalism, 6(2): 7–21.

Stone, D. (2003) 'The "Knowledge Bank" and the Global Development Network', *Global Governance*, 9.

Strange, S. (1995) 'The defective state', *Daedalus, Journal of the American Academy of Arts and Sciences*, Spring.

Supreme Court of India (1989),

Judgment on Sodan Singh and etc. etc., Petitioners v. New Delhi Municipal Committee and another etc., Respondents.

— (1992) *Sodan Singh et al. v. New Delhi Municipal Committee et al.*, DN1250/88/Sec. X.

Swanson, T. (1997) *Global Action for Bio-Diversity – an International Framework for Implementing the Convention on Biological Diversity*, Cambridge: Earthscan.

Sylvester, C. (1999) '"Progress" in Zimbabwe: is "it" a woman?', *International Feminist Journal of Politics*, 1(1): 89–118.

Talwar, V. B. (1993) 'Feminist consciousness in women's journals in Hindi: 1910–1920', in K. Sangari and S. Vaid (eds), *Recasting Women: Essays in Indian Colonial History*, New Delhi: Kali for Women.

Tambiah, Y. (ed.) (2002) *Women and Governance in South Asia: Re-imagining the State*, Colombo: International Centre for Ethnic Studies.

Taylor, V. (2000) *Marketisation of Governance: Critical Feminist Perspectives from the South*, DAWN, <www.DAWN.org/publications>.

Teske, R. L. and M. A. Tetreault (eds) (2000) *Conscious Acts and the Politics of Social Change, Feminist Approaches to Social Movements, Community and Power*, vol. 1, Columbia: University of South Carolina Press.

Thörlind, R. (2003) *Development, Decentralization and Democracy. Exploring Social Capital and Politicization in the Bengal Region*, Dhaka: Pathak Shamabesh Books.

UN (United Nations) (1996) *The Beijing Declaration and the Platform for Action*, Fourth World Conference on Women, Beijing, 14–15 September 1995, New York: Department of Public Information.

— (1998) 'Recommendations to the Expert Group Meeting on National Machineries for Gender Equality by NGO Committee on the Status of Women Task Force on Institutional Mechanisms for the Advancement of Women', EGM/NM/1988/0P.1, August.

— (1999) *World Survey on the Role of Women in Development: Globalization, Gender and Work*, New York: United Nations.

— (2000) *Further Actions and Initiatives to Implement the Beijing Declaration and Platform for Action*, Resolution adopted by the General Assembly, 16 November, <www.un.org/womenwatch/daw/followup/ress233e.pdf>.

UN Commission on Global Governance (1995) *Our Global Neighborhood*, New York: United Nations.

UNCTAD (United Nations Conference on Trade and Development) (1996) *Globalisation and Liberalisation: Effects of International Economic Relations on Poverty*, Geneva: United Nations.

UN/DAW (1998) 'Recommendations to the Expert Group Meeting on National Machineries for Gender Equality by NGO Committee on the Status of Women Task Force on Institutional Mechanisms for the Advancement of Women', EGM/NM/1988/0P.1, August

UNDP (United Nations Development Programme) (2000) *Human Development Report*, Oxford: Oxford University Press.

UNHCR (United Nations High Commissioner for Human Rights) (2000) *Building on Achievements:*

Women's Human Rights Five Years After Beijing, May, <www.unhchr.ch/html/menu2/contribeijing.htm>.

UNIFEM (1999) *Women Making a Difference in Science and Technology – Case Studies*, UNESCO World Conference, Budapest, 26 June–1 July.

Vaistos, C. (1972) 'Patents revisited: their function in developing countries', *Journal of Development Studies*, 9, October.

Van Staveren, I. (2001) 'Global finance and gender', in J. A. Scholte and A. Schnabel (eds), *Civil Society and Global Finance*, London: Routledge.

Vega Ugalde, S. (2003) 'The role of the women's movement in institutionalizing a gender focus in public policy: the Ecuadorian experience', in S. M. Rai (ed.), *Mainstreaming Gender, Democratizing the State? Institutional Mechanisms for the Advancement of Women*, Manchester: Manchester University Press.

Vidal, J. (1999) 'The seeds of wrath', *Guardian Weekend*, 19 June.

Walby, S. (1997) *Gender Transformations*, London. Routledge.

Wallace, T. with C. March (eds), *Changing Perceptions, Writings on Gender and Development*, Oxford: Oxfam.

Walzer, M. (1992) 'The civil society argument', in C. Mouffe (ed.), *Dimensions of Radical Democracy: Pluralism, Citizenship, Community*, London: Verso.

Ware, V. (1992) *Beyond the Pale, White Women, Racism and History*, London: Verso.

Watson, S. (ed.) (1990) *Playing the State*, London: Verso.

Waylen, G. (1994) 'Women and democratization: conceptualizing gender relations in transition politics', *World Politics*, 46(3): 327–54.

— (2007) *Engendering Transitions: Women's Mobilization, Institutions, and Gender Outcomes*, Oxford: Oxford University Press.

Waylen, G. and S. M. Rai (2004) 'Introduction', *International Feminist Journal of Politics*, 6(4): 553–5.

Weedon, C. (1993) 'Feminism and postmodernism', Paper presented at the Women's Studies Network (UK) Conference.

White, G. (1993) 'Towards a political analysis of markets', *IDS Bulletin*, 24(3).

Williams, P. J. (1991) *The Alchemy of Race and Rights*, London: Harvard University Press.

Wilson, E. (1977) *Women and the Welfare State*, London: Tavistock.

WIPO (1998) *World Symposium of the Patent System in Developing Countries*, no. 638(E), Geneva, <www.undp.org/unifem/ec_tech.htm>.

Woel, S. (2007) 'Global governance as neo liberal governmentality: gender mainstreaming in the European employment strategy', in S. M. Rai and G. Waylen (eds), *Global Governance: Feminist Perspectives*, Basingstoke: Palgrave Macmillan.

Woods, N. (2002) 'Global governance and the role of institutions', in D. Held and A. McGrew, *Governing Globalization: Power, Authority and Global Governance*, Cambridge: Polity Press.

World Bank (1992) *Governance and Development*, Washington, DC: World Bank.

— (2002) *Building Institutions for Markets*, <http://econ.worldbank.org/wdr/WDR2002>.

World Food Programme (1999) *Elected Woman Members of UP; a Socio-Economic Study*, Dhaka: World Food Programme.

WRPE (Women's Role in the Planned Economy) (1947), Subcommittee on Women's Role in the Planned Ecnomy, Bombay: Vora.

Young, I. M. (1990) *Justice and the Politics of Difference*, Princeton, NJ: Princeton University Press.

— (1995) 'Together in difference: transforming the logic of group political conflict', in W. Kymlicka (ed.), *The Right of Minority Cultures*, Oxford: Oxford University Press.

— (1997) 'Unruly categories: a critique of Nancy Fraser's dual systems theory', *New Left Review*, 222, March/April, pp. 147–60.

Yuval-Davis, N. (1997) 'Women, citizenship and difference', *Feminist Review*, 57, Special issue on 'Citizenship', pp. 4–27.

Yuval-Davis, N. and W. Pnina (1999) *Women, Citizenship and Difference*, London: Zed Books.

Zulu, L. (2000) 'Institutionalising changes: South African women's participation in the transition to democracy', in S. M. Rai (ed.), *International Perspectives on Gender and Democratisation*, Basingstoke: Macmillan.

Index

11 September attacks, 127

abortion, 2
Abu Ghraib prison, mistreatment in, 132
accountability, 68, 71, 125, 172, 180
Aganice, 138
agriculture: changing patterns of, 20; women's work in, 1–2, 29
AIDS, drugs for, 150
Algeria, 80; women's position in, 36
All-India Medical Institute, 151
All-India Women's Committee, 34
All-India Women's Congress, 95
Alvarez, Sonia, 2
Ambedkar, B.R., 93, 94
Amma, a street trader, 44–5
Arab culture, restrictions on women, 63–4
Arcona, Jane, 144
Association of Local Authorities (Sweden), 81
Australia, 83, 87
authenticity, inscribed in women's bodies, 63
autonomy of the political, 52, 53
Azad, Gulam Navi, 45

Bandaranaike, Sirimavo, 90
bandini, 40
Banerjea, Surendranath, 14
Bangladesh, 90–112
banjara community, 40–4, 48
Beijing Platform for Action (1995), 6, 72, 75, 84–5
Bentz, Malita, 143
Bhagwat, Kamala, 138–9
Bhagwati, Judge, 52
Bhutto, Benazir, 90, 101

biopiracy, 149–50
boundaries, negotiation of, 50–8
British Empire, 16
Bull, Hedley, 122
Butler, Judith, Gender Trouble, 131–2

Canada, 87
caste, discrimination by, 106
Central American Common Market, 163
Chandra, Ramesh, 45
chastity, 26
child-bearing, duty of, 36
Chile, 63, 80
China, 36; 'woman question' in, 26
Chipko movement, 21
citizenship, 36; of women, 7, 11, 13, 17, 29, 31, 35, 65, 67, 69, 110
civil society, 4, 6, 56, 59, 64, 66, 71, 76, 87, 116; global, 136; links with national machineries, 83–5; mobilization of, 87–8
colonial subject, 159
colonialism, 16, 94; discourse on gender, 18–19; ideologies of, 17–22; resistance to, 25
Commission on Global Governance, 129
Commission on the Status of Women in India, 96
commons, sequestration of, 20
Connelly, Ann, 143
conscientization, 3, 178
Contagious Disease Acts, 19
context, importance of, 61
Convention for the Elimination of All Forms of Discrimination Against Women (CEDAW), 1, 75, 84, 102
Convention on Biodiversity (1992), 147

copyright, 141
corruption, 44, 46, 49, 54; in police *see* police, corruption in
Cosbey, A., 145–6
cosmopolitical democracy, 173
Cox, Robert, 123
credit: women's access to, 154 (limited, 176)
'crimes of honour', 134
culture, fixed as law, 23
Curie, Marie, 156
customary Law, 25

Das, Arjan, 46
Debord, Guy: *Comments on the Society of the Spectacle*, 130; *The Society of the Spectacle*, 130
decentralization, 86
decolonization, 13
demilitarization, 116
democracy, 128; cosmopolitical, 173; deliberative, 171; norms of, 160–3
democratic deficit, 122; of global institutions, 126
democratic structures, establishment of, 164–7
democratization, 4, 6–7, 59–70, 71–89, 124–5, 175; and entitlements, 66–7; and globalization, 67–8; emergence of, as discourse, 128; in Eastern Europe, 65–6; of the state, 85–9
Department for International Development (DfID) (UK), 161
depletion, in economic discourse, 177–8
development, and globalization, 113–36
development agendas, women and, 37
Devi, Bhanwari, rape of, 178
devolution, political, 85–6, 101
diasporic communities, 134
division of labour, 11; gendered, 67
dress of women, 26

e-mail, used in building networks, 163
Eastern Europe, democratization in, 65–6
ecological struggles, 68
ECOSOC Agreed Conclusions (1997), 72
education: of women and girls, 66, 108, 151–2; primary, 2
Eglui, Ellen, 138
Ekatra organization (India), 107
embeddedness, 124; of networks, 162; of the state, 53, 56
empowerment, 23, 173; as struggle for survival, 178–9; definitions of, 104; of women, 3, 93, 97, 102, 110, 163 (measurement of, 111); structural barriers to, 179
Enlightenment, 18, 25
entitlements, 66–7
epistemic communities, 115, 129
epistemologies, subaltern, 158–60
equality, 96, 120; barriers to, 176; in science, 140; language of, 72; political, 88
exclusion, 179, 180; of women, 7, 137, 142, 143, 151 (from scientific discovery, 140)
exclusive marketing rights, 149, 150
exoticism, and profit, 40–1

Fanon, Frantz, *Wretched of the Earth*, 22
feminism, 3, 5, 27, 30, 135, 140, 171; and democracy, 136; and global governance, 118; and globalization, 167; and the state, 50, 71, 136; challenges of, 132–6; democratization debate within, 59; engagement of, 60–2; incompatible with nationalism, 37–8; methodologies of, 61–2; patriarchal, 33; scholarship of, 8, 12, 59, 77, 120, 125, 126, 129–30, 158–60; state feminism, 98; tropes of, 15–17; Western, 34

Ford Foundation, 161
Foro de Mujeres para la Integración (Central America), 163
Foucault, Michel, 140, 180; *Discipline and Punish*, 131
Fraser, Nancy, 2, 176–7
Fukuyama, Francis, 127

Gandhi, Indira, 88, 90
Gandhi, Mahatma, 92
Gandhi, Rajiv, 96
Gellner, Ernest, 14, 19
gender, 61, 62, 120, 136, 137; and democratization, 6, 62–3; and nationalism, 11–13; constructions of, 17–22; de-politicization of, 2; fixing of identities, 37; mainstreaming of, 6, 71–89, 125 (definition of, 72–3); nation-building and, 10–38; theorization of, 59–70
gender blindness, 126; of governance literature, 117–18; of TRIPS, 154
gender budgets, 87
gender issues, of knowledge production, 150–5
gender policy agencies, 5
global governance, 8, 113–36; definition of, 115–32; literature of, 113–15
globalization, 113–36, 175; a contested concept, 172; contradictions in, 123; democratization and, 67–8; of the false, 130; unevenness, 137
Gokalp, Ziya, 24
governance, 120; as ideology, 127–30; as spectacle, 130–2; emergence of, as concept, 127–8; institutions of, as failed state, 121–7; of markets, 118–21; of polities, 133; theory of, 117–18; transnational, 116 *see also* global governance
Government of India Act (1935), 92
governmentality, 117
Guatemala, democratization movement in, 64

handicrafts, in India, 40–1
ul-Haq, Zia, 63, 96
hawking *see* street trading
health care: of women, 150; privatization of, 67, 86; spending cuts, 66
Helle-Lucas, M., 31–2
Herschel, Caroline, 138
Hildegard of Bingen, 138
Hobsbawm, Eric, 23
home, relation to nationalism, 25
'honour crimes', 2, 19
household and social reproduction, 177
Hudood Ordinances (1979) (Pakistan), 63, 96; resistance to, 102
Huntington, Samuel, 127
Hypatia of Alexandria, 138

ideology: governance as, 127–30; importance of, 114–15
illiteracy, among women, 2, 57, 94, 151
India, 81, 86, 88, 90–112; British presence in, 33; Constitutional Amendment Acts, 99; Government of India Act (1935), 34; modernization in, 29; partition of, 93; Supreme Court, 40–58; 'Woman's Role in the Planned Economy', 28; women in, 28–9, 39–58
indigenous peoples, 19; movements of, 68
infrastructural power, 53–5
innovation, definition of, 141
intellectual property rights (IPR), 137–8, 152; and WTO, 141–6 *see also* TRIPS
Inter-Parliamentary Union (IPU), 75
International Labour Organization (ILO), 1
International Monetary Fund (IMF), 120
inventions, women and, 143–6
invisibility of women, 13, 20, 153

Islam, 93, 95; discrimination against, 35; fundamentalism, 128; *umma*, 33

Jacob, M.M., 45
Jahan, Rounaq, 171
Janpath Lane, New Delhi, 40-2
Jayal, Gopal, 96

Kemal, Mustafa, 33
Khor, Martin, 156
Kidd, Benjamin, 16
knowledge: agents of, 158-62; as learned discourse, 140; as power, 158-62, 180; definition of, 155; relation to power, 137-56; social, 147-9
knowledge networks, 157, 160-3; politics of, 170-4
knowledge production: privatizing of, 150-5; theorization of, 130; women's contribution to, 137
Krishna, a street trader, 45, 46, 47
Kuman, Saajan, 45
Kuru Development Trust, 139

labour movement, 116
land, improvement of, 21
land tenure, in Africa, 21
law, and institutionalization of market liberalism, 120
legalism, soft, 52-3
liberal internationalism, 126
liberalism, 59; embedded, 129
liberalization, 66, 83, 97
local government, women's representation in, 103, 105
Local Government Commission Report (Bangladesh), 100
London Edinburgh Weekend Return Group, *In and Against the State*, 58

marginalization of women, 94
market: embeddedness of, 145; gendered critiques of, 136; politics of, 144-5

market nature of Western civilization, 128
marketized institutions, 120
markets, governance of, 114, 118-21
Marrakesh Agreement, 149
marriage: laws, 21; under colonialism, 20
Marxism, 23, 26, 29, 36, 117, 122-3, 125, 126
memory, relation to nationalism, 15
micro-credit, 97, 109, 152
migration: of labour, 126; of women, 21
Mill, J.S, *History of India*, 18
mirror work, 40
Mistry, Rohinton, *A Fine Balance*, 179
modernity, 29, 32; and the 'woman question', 26
modernization strategies, 151
Molyneux, Maxine, 77
motherhood, construction of, 32
Mothers of the Plaza de Mayo (Chile), 63

Nandy, Ashis, *The Intimate Enemy*, 22
nation, imaging of, 13-30
nation-building: and gender, 4-5, 10-38; project of, 16-17
nation-state, 11-12, 35; as focus of women's movement, 73; creation of, 10; hollowing-out of, 172; leap-frogging of, 167; of the Third World, 16; retreat of, 68
National Council of Women in India, 34
national machineries, 73, 75-6, 78-85, 90; links with civil society, 83-5; location of, 78-81; mandates and functions, 81-3; resources of, 83; varieties of, 78
National Plan for Action (1998) (Pakistan), 97
National Policy for Development and Empowerment of Women (2002) (Pakistan), 97

National Policy for the Advancement
of Women (Bangladesh), 98
nationalism, 4; akin to kinship and
religion, 25; as development,
29–30; codifying of, 34–7;
gendered nature of, 13–14; project,
incompatible with feminism, 3,
37; tropes of, 15–17; types of, 24
nationalist movements: and self-
determination of 30–4; and
women, 35
nature: definition of, 142; exploitation
of, 21
neem tree, patenting of, 148–9
Negri, Antonio, and Michael Hardt,
Empire, 117
Nehru, Jawaharlal, 28, 29
neoliberalism, 129, 135
networking, across borders, 157–74
networks: heterogeneity of, 174;
sustainability of, 168–70
new constitutionalism, 119
New Delhi Municipal Corporation
(NDMC), 40, 42, 43, 44, 45, 46, 49,
51; corruption in, 54, 55
Nigeria, women's position in, 36
non-governmental organizations
(NGOs), 83–5, 87, 97, 102, 108–9
Norwegian Agency for Development
Cooperation (NORAD), 162,
169–70
Ntcoxo, Cgose, 139–40

Orientalism, 63
othering, central to nationalist
discourse, 24
Overseas Development Institute
(ODI), 161

Pakistan, 81, 84, 90–112; Devolution
of Power Plan, 101
panchayat system, 99–100, 106, 107,
109; all-women, 96
parliament, women in, 1, 94, 97, 98
(in Pakistan, 96)
Paro, a street trader, 47

participation, 7, 175, challenges to,
104–9, in institutional politics,
65–6, in knowledge production,
152, in local government, 103,
political, 37, 64–5, 125 (costs of,
62; payment for, 107)
patenting, 141–2, 156; as property,
146; effectiveness of law, 148; of
neem tree, 148–9; of seed, 142;
origins of patents in developed
world, 148–50; patents granted to
India, 153; social, 155
patents, and the global market, 144–6
patriarchy, 26, 33, 57, 106; and
democratic politics, 62–3;
structural power of, 175
Pattan Development Organization,
108
pavement traders, in New Delhi,
39–58
*People's Union for Democratic Rights v.
Union of India* case, 52
Permanent Settlement Act (1793)
(India), 20
Philippines, 80, 87
Plant Variety ProtectionAct (1970)
(USA), 146
Polanyi, Karl, 53, 124
police: brutality of, 54, 55; corruption
of, 44, 46
political institutions, women in, 74–5,
88
political man / economic man, 10
political parties, role of, 86–7
politics of recognition, 176, 179
popular, appropriation of, 23
post-colonial state, 5, 7, 94; women
and, 39–58
post-colonialism, 52
poverty, 1, 67; feminization of, 129
prime ministers, women as, 90
private-public boundaries, 60–1
privatization, 85–6
process, politics of, 170–4
prostitution, 19
Public Interest Litigation, 52

public sphere, inclusion in, 61

quotas: for women, 86, 88–9, 125, 168; in context, 90–112; in practice, 102–9; in South Asia, 7

Radha, a street trader, 42
Rai, Shirin, *Gender and the Political Economy of Development*, 113
Rai, Usha, 46
Raman, Sir C.V., 138–9
rape, 54, 178
Ratan, a street trader, 41, 44, 45
regional networks, importance of, 163
regionalization, from below, 163–4
religion, 34, 62
Report of the Commission of Inquiry for Women (Pakistan), 97
Resist Globalization and Assert Our Rights movement, 67
rights: common, 116; of women, 162 (to vote, 1, 28); universal, 72
rule of law, 22

Said, Edward, 179–80
San people, 139–40
Sartre, Jean-Paul, 22
Scheduled Castes and Scheduled Tribes (India), 108
seclusion of women, 106
secularism, 34
self-determination, 23
Self-Employed Women's Association (SEWA), 48
Sen, Amartya, 67
Sen, Anupam, 51
Senghor, Léopold, 26
sexual orientation, 2
Sharif, Nawaz, 101
Sharma, Livleen, 40, 41, 44, 45, 48–9, 55, 104
Sheikh, Begum, 90
Sherman, Patsy, 144
Shiva, Vandana, 142, 155–6; and Maria Mies, *Ecofeminism*, 140

Sixty-second Amendment Act (1989) (India), 95
Sodan Singh and others vs. New Delhi Municipal Corporation case, 42–3, 53
son preference, 2
South Africa, 65, 86, 87; AIDS drugs issue, 150
South Asia Research Network (SARN) on Gender, Law and Governance, 9, 157–74 *passim*; Coordinating Group, 165, 166, 168; networking in, 168; Panel of Advisers, 165; setting up of, 164; structures of, 164–7; terms of reference, 161; website, 166
South Asian Regional Cooperation (SARC), 164
sovereignty: leaking, 121; loss of, 121, 122
spectacle: and production of meanings, 115; governance as, 130–2
Spivak, Gayatri, 179
squatting, 43
Sri Lanka, 32
standpoint theory, 158
state, 51; as network of power relations, 50–1; autonomy of, 123; delegitimization of, 124; democratization of, 71–89; embeddedness of, 53; gendered constitution of, 124; in and against, 56–8, 74; incapacity of, 121; interdependence of, 126; possible promotion of women's interests, 73–7; post-colonial, 39–58; regulation role of, 114; role of, 128; weak, 122; women's engagement with, 71, 176
street traders, women, in Delhi, 5, 41–2; strike of, 44–7
structural adjustment, 86
Study on the Institutional Review of the WID Capability of the Government of Bangladesh, 100
subaltern epistemologies, 158–60

subaltern voice, 179; resistance by,
    157
substantive representation, 90
substate, 116
suprastate, 116

Tanganyika: Matengo system in, 21;
    'women problem' in, 21
Tanzania, women's movement in, 32
Thareja, G.P., 43, 44, 48, 49, 54, 55
Thareja Committee, 42, 46–7, 51, 52,
    55
Thatcher, Margaret, 88
time-use surveys, 177
Trade Related Intellectual Property
    regimes (TRIPS), 7, 8–9, 130, 137,
    141, 142–3, 145, 146–55; effects
    on developing countries, 153;
    safeguards for "underclass", 155–6
transnational corporations, 114;
    boycotts of, 68; regulation of, 126
transversal politics, 171
travel metaphor, 176
Turkey, 80; 'new woman', 33
Turkish Women's Federation, 33
Tytler, Jagdish, 45

Uganda, 83, 88
Union for the Protection of New
    Varieties of Plant, 142
Union of Soviet Socialist Republics
    (USSR), 130; collapse of, 128
Union Parishad, 100, 109
United Kingdom (UK), 88
United Nations (UN), 6, 65, 71, 72,
    74, 75, 96, 118; General Assembly
    on Gender Equality, Development
    and Peace for the Twenty-first
    Century, 75; study of national
    machineries in Africa, 80; Women
    in Development framework, 97
UN Children's Fund (UNICEF), 178
UN Commission on Global
    Governance, 115; Report of, 116
UN Commission on the Status of
    Women, 102, 146

UN Expert Group Meeting on
    National Machineries, 82, 85
UN World Conferences on Women:
    Mexico (1975), 73, 95; Beijing
    (1995), 73, 98, 145, 163 *see also*
    Beijing Platform for Action
UN Committee on Trade and
    Development (UNCTAD), report on
    TRIPS, 153
United States of America (USA), 130;
    hegemonic position of, 117
unity of women, demands for, 31–2
Universal Declaration of Human
    Rights, 72–3
universalism, 72

vernacular press, delineation of
    women, 27
violence, 84; against women, 2, 28,
    96, 129, 134, 168, 175, 178; of the
    state, 57
vote, women's right to, 1, 28

wage differentials, 1
war on terror, 97, 127–8
Warangal farmers, India, suicides of,
    151
welfare state, erosion of, 97, 135
Whitney's cotton gin, 143
witchcraft, 147
women: access to health care, 86;
    advancement of, 154, 168; altered
    position in agrarian societies,
    22; and nationalist movements,
    30–4; and the post-colonial state,
    39–58; as innovators, 153; as
    inventors, 137–41, 143–6, 155
    (stereotyped, 154); as members
    of parliament, 75; as subjects
    of rights, 64; as waged workers,
    30; authenticity inscribed in, 63;
    central to nationalist discourse,
    11, 12; control over, 25; dependent
    on private sector health, 57;
    engagement with policy-making
    institutions, 171–2; exclusion of,

60; ideal view of, 24; in the home, 26; operations for, 151; portrayal of, in vernacular press, 27; veiled, 128; ways of doing politics, 171, work of, 11, 20, 126 (domestic, 177; in knowledge production, 147; waged, 66, 124, 176)
Women's Action Forum (Pakistan), 63
Women's Indian Association, 34
women's interests, representation of, 76–7
women's movements, 3, 4, 6, 10, 70, 71, 110; and democratization, 62–4; in India, 54, 93; in Pakistan, 96
Women's National Coalition (WNC) (South Africa), 65

Women's People's Party (Turkey), 33
World Bank, 120, 175–6; Global Development Network (GDN), 160; World Development Reports, 121–2
World Intellectual Property Organization, 148
World Trade Organization (WTO), 9, 120, 130, 150, 147; and intellectual property rights, 141–6

Yalow, Rosalyn Sussman, 154
Yuval-Davis, Nira, 23–4

zamindar, property rights of, 20
Zia, Begum, 90